STUDIES
IN THE RELIGION
OF ANCIENT ISRAEL

SUPPLEMENTS

TO

VETUS TESTAMENTUM

EDITED BY
THE BOARD OF THE QUARTERLY

G. W. ANDERSON - P. A. H. DE BOER - G. R. CASTELLINO
HENRY CAZELLES - J. A. EMERTON - E. NIELSEN
H. G. MAY - W. ZIMMERLI

VOLUME XXIII

LEIDEN
E. J. BRILL
1972

STUDIES
IN THE RELIGION
OF ANCIENT ISRAEL

LEIDEN
E. J. BRILL
1972

ISBN 90 04 03525 7

CONTENTS

ISRAEL'S PLACE AMONG THE RELIGIONS OF THE ANCIENT NEAR EAST

BY

H. RINGGREN
Uppsala

The main problem alluded to by the above heading is one of similarity and difference. Since the discovery and decipherment of the hieroglyphic and cuneiform documents, it has been known that there are many points of close similarity between Biblical religion and the religions of the ancient Near East. On the other hand, Biblical religion claims to be unique, and it is obvious that the religion of Israel as a totality is different from each of those religions. The main difficulty is to find a method to evaluate the various points of similarity and at the same time do justice to the specific character of each religion.

Comparative research in the Biblical field has often become a kind of "parallel hunting." Once it has been established that a certain Biblical expression or custom has a parallel outside the Bible, the whole problem is regarded as solved. It is not asked, whether or not the extra-Biblical element has the same place in life, the same function in the context of its own culture.

The first question that should be asked in comparative research is that of the *Sitz im Leben* and the meaning of the extra-Biblical parallel adduced. It is not until this has been established that the parallel can be utilized to elucidate a Biblical fact. This general principle was stressed by E. R. DALGLISH in his book on *Psalm Fifty-One* [1] where he points out that any comparison between Biblical and Sumero-Accadian psalms is unsatisfactory unless it takes into account the various genres of Sumero-Accadian literature. An example can be drawn from Ps. lxxiv. This is a psalm of lament which describes the destruction of the temple and asks for Yahweh's interference. F. WILLESEN has called our attention to a parallel in a Babylonian psalm which describes the destruction of a temple in much the same words as the Hebrew psalm. [2] The conclusion is that both psalms deal with

---

[1] Leiden 1962, Preface pp. XI f.
[2] *VT* 2, 1952, pp. 289 ff.

"a cultic destruction of the temple." But WILLESEN has not asked the
question of the *Sitz im Leben* of the Babylonian psalm. It turns out
that such laments were recited by the *kalû* priests at the rededication
of a temple after its restauration or after it had been polluted in some
way. Very interestingly, both Ps. lxxiv and some Babylonian texts of
this category have recourse to the creation myth in this connection.
This means that the rededication of a temple marks a new beginning,
which is given its mythological motivation by quoting the myth of
creation. In a similar way Deutero-Isaiah has recourse to the creation
myth in lix 9-11 as a background to the new-beginning marked by the
expected new Exodus.[1] Thus a correct understanding of the *Sitz im
Leben* of the Babylonian parallel throws light on Biblical ideas.

It is a well known fact that the annunciation formula in the Imma-
nuel oracle in Is. vii הנה העלמה הרה וילדת בן has an almost literal
counterpart in the Ugaritic Nikkal text: *hl ǵlmt tld bn*. But what does
this mean? Is the Nikkal text a ritual text and is the phrase consequently to be considered a cultic formula? Or does the formula reflect
an everyday custom, a common way of announcing the expected birth
of a child? Unless we find an answer to these questions, the utilization
of the parallel remains dubious.

In a difficult passage in Ps. lxxiii we are told that the wicked "put
their mouth in heaven, while their tongue walks on the earth." There
is a similar passage in a Ugaritic text, in which certain mythological
beings are described thus: "One lip to earth, one lip to heaven—and
the birds of heaven and the fishes from the sea enter their mouths." [2]
What use can be made of this parallel? No doubt, the Ugaritic text is
mythological and probably ritual. The context in Ps. lxxiii, however,
is of a different kind. It seems probable that the author has used a
mythological motif to indicate the demoniac character of the wicked
and their behaviour. They belong to the world of evil and behave
accordingly.[3] This example illustrates the necessity of defining the
function of the element under consideration both in the extra-Biblical
and the Biblical context.

In the last two cases there can be no doubt concerning the age of
the two texts involved: the Ugaritic texts are older than the Biblical

---

[1] H. RINGGREN, "Die Funktion des Schöpfungsmythus in Jes 51," *Schalom*,
Festschrift A. Jepsen, Berlin 1971, pp. 38-40.

[2] H. RINGGREN, "Einige Bemerkungen zum lxxiii. Psalm," *VT* 3, 1953, pp.
265 ff.

[3] Cf. H. RINGGREN, *Faith of the Psalmists*, Philadelphia 1963, pp. 44 f.

ones. In other cases, there is at least the possibility of doubt. No one can deny that there is similarity between the Egyptian teaching of Amen-em-ōpe and Prov. xxii 17-xxiii 14. But which of the two is older? Has the author of Proverbs utilized Amen-em-ōpe or vice versa? It has been argued that the language of Amen-em-ōpe is strange and contains semitisms which indicate a translation from some Semitic idiom. Since the date of Amen-em-ōpe is uncertain, it is possible therefore, that he has borrowed from Proverbs and not the reverse. It would seem however, that it is easier to understand the text of Proverbs as an abridgement of Amen-em-ōpe than the latter as an expansion of Proverbs. This would speak in favour of an earlier date for the Egyptian collection.[1]

There are other cases when there is no discussion of the chronological priority but the historical connection is not easily explained. There is an obvious similarity in wording and in contents between Ps. civ and the famous sunhymn of Echnaton. However, history teaches us that Echnaton's capital was destroyed and his religion forgotten shortly after his death. If there is a connection between his hymn and the psalm, how is the transmission of the material to be explained? No satisfactory answer has been found so far—most scholars have not even asked the question. But assuming that there is a connection we should like to emphasize the fundamental difference in outlook that characterizes the two hymns. Since the Egyptian hymn is directed to the sun, the night is regarded as an evil time, while the Israelite psalm, being a psalm in the honour of the Creator of all things, underlines the positive role of the night in the general order of the world.[2]

It goes without saying that the sources of a parallel should be checked, but there are cases when this has not been done. Much has been said on the symbolism of the tree of life in ancient Near Eastern religion. But it has remained unnoticed that the term itself is not found in Accadian literature. There is a "plant of life" *(šam balāṭi)*, there is "water of life" *(mē balāṭi)* and "food of life" *(akal balāṭi)* but no *iṣ balāṭi*. The pictures of a tree, on which certain (ritual?) acts are performed, may or may not represent a "tree of life," but there is no evidence to prove that it was actually so called. SIDNEY SMITH's allegation that there was a tree of life in the temple garden rests on a series of hypothetical assumptions, of which the basic one is certainly

---

[1] See the discussion in H. RINGGREN, *Sprüche, ATD* 16:1, pp. 90 ff.
[2] H. RINGGREN, *Faith of the Psalmists*, pp. 119 f.

wrong.[1] As a matter of fact, the tree of life is known by name only in the Old Testament. Any investigation of the tree-of-life motif would have to build not on the word but on the concept of life. This concept is bound up with certain objects, such as a plant, food, or water, and the possession or loss of such an object forms an essential element in certain myths. The problem is how to isolate this motif and to follow its combination with other mythological elements into coherent structures. I have dealt with this problem in another context,[2] but I should like to summarize my main ideas here. Each mythological composition consists of a number of elements of various kind: episodes, motifs, symbols. The same elements can be found in the mythologies of different peoples, in most cases combined in a different way. The comparative study of Near Eastern mythology offers some very instructive examples.

There are certain details in the Gilgamesh epic which are reminiscent of the story of the Fall in Gen. iii. It is a woman (a courtesan, Eve) who "seduces the type-figure of a primitive man (Enkidu, Adam) from his original innocence... on the course that leads inevitably to death." The seduction involves the giving of sexual knowledge or experience, and this knowledge makes man "like God" (Gilg. IV 34 "You are wise, Enkidu, you have become like a god," Gen. iii 5 "You shall become like God, knowing good and evil"). The acquisition of a certain amount of civilization is involved in both cases: Enkidu learns civilized life and loses his contact with the animals; Adam and Eve discover their nakedness and God makes clothes for them. Finally, it is a serpent who is the real culprit of the drama: in the Gilgamesh epic by snatching away the plant of life, in Genesis by setting the whole course of events in movement.[3] The Gilgamesh epic knows a *plant* of life, Genesis a *tree* of life. "Thus there are a number of details, all connected with one specific problem of human life, which are the same in both stories but have been fitted into a context that is different in each instance based on different presuppositions." [4] It seems to me that both the details and each of the two compositions are important if we want to make a comparative study.

The interesting point is that all these parallels are found in those

---

[1] See my review of E. O. JAMES, "The Tree of Life" in *JSS* 13, 1968, pp. 298 f.

[2] *Near Eastern Studies in honor of W. F. Albright*, Baltimore 1971, pp. 407-411.

[3] S. G. F. BRANDON, *Creation Legends of the Ancient Near East*, London 1963, pp. 131 ff.

[4] *Studies Albright*, p. 408.

parts of the Gilgamesh Epic that have no Sumerian counterpart. They obviously belong to a stratum of the Gilgamesh tradition which is definitely Semitic. It is not at all certain that the Bible has borrowed these elements from Mesopotamia; they could just as well be of West Semitic origin.

The problem of man's mortality has occupied mythopoeic though in other connections, too. In Mesopotamia there is also the Adapa myth which tells the story of a man's prideful rebellion against the gods and his consequent missing the food of life and water of life offered to him. Except for the fact that all three stories deal with man's mortality, this story has little in common with the Gilgamesh story or the story of the Fall. It is interesting, however, that the idea of life in all three cases is bound up with an object (tree, plant, food, and water).

In other cases two myths have so to speak the same structure but contain different elements. The Aqhat Epic, for instance, exhibits a striking similarity with the Baal cycle. Aqhat dies a violent death just as Baal. The consequence in both cases is that vegetation withers and life declines on earth. Finally, just as Baal's sister Anat sets out to rescue her brother and restore him to life, Aqhat's sister *Pġt* makes arrangement to recover her brother and bring him back to life. Because of the damaged condition of the Aqhat text we do not know whether or not she was successful, but it is quite probable that Aqhat returned to life (in spite of the fact that the motif of man's mortality occurs earlier in the epic).

This parallelism between two myths can be explained in various ways. They might reflect the same ritual background, i.e., the death and resurrection of the fertility god. Or they might be literary variations of a basic motif, the origin of which we cannot trace. But the fact remains that the Baal cycle and the Aqhat Epic are to some extent parallel in that they contain three identical mythological elements, and in the same order. But these elements are combined with other elements so as to form two entirely different bodies of mythology.

A third example can be drawn from the cosmogonic myths. In Accadian, Ugaritic, and Israelite texts, the conflict motif, involving the slaying of a dragon, plays a decisive role.

But this element is used in a different way in each of the religions in question. In the Enuma Elish, Marduk fights and kills Tiāmat and creates the universe out of her body. In Ugaritic mythology, Baal fights Yam, the Sea, and defeats him, thus putting an end to his reign and acquiring kingship for himself. There is no express reference to creation, even if the acquisition of kingship may be regarded as a creation in the sence of organizing the universe and establishing its order. Incidentally, Yam is also referred to as the River *(nhr)*, the dragon *(tnn)*, the slippery serpent *(bṯn ʿqltn)*, or Lotan *(ltn)*.

In Israel we find many of the same elements, but in a different combination. There is a very strong emphasis on Yahweh's kingship in connection with creation, and the defeat of the dragon (called Rahab, *tannīn* or Leviathan) is referred to from time to time. This is obviously part of Israel's Canaanite heritage. On the other hand, there are several allusions to *tehōm* (i.e., Tiāmat) as the entity defeated by Yahweh in the beginning. In Gen. i this motif has been "demythologized": *tehōm* is more or less a lifeless matter, but enough has been preserved to show the mythological origin of the concept.[1]

It is interesting to notice that the conflict motif occurs in West Semitic and Accadian myths but is absent from Sumerian cosmogony. Does this mean that it is a specific Semitic, perhaps even West Semitic, feature?

The above observations illustrate the way myths are formed and transformed. A certain element can be combined with one set of elements in one religion and with other sets of elements in another religion. It may be assumed that each element conveys a certain idea, but it can be modified through its combination with other elements. In a limited geographical area such as the Near East, it is probable that the presence of a certain mythical element in two or more religions is due to some kind of historical connection. It follows from this that in order to analyse a myth it is necessary to break it down into small units and to find out where these units occur and what combinations they build up.

S. H. HOOKE created the term "pattern" for those mythical and ritual elements which the various civilizations of the ancient Near East had in common. He was criticized because each people in the area was supposed to have a cultural pattern of its own.[2] Obviously, his critics were not aware of the problem of definition involved. When HOOKE used the word "pattern" he meant a sum of mythical and ritual

---

[1] *Ib.* p. 411.
[2] H. FRANKFORT, *The Problem of Similarity in Ancient Near Eastern Religion*, London 1951, H. BIRKELAND, *The Evildoers in the Book of Psalms*, Oslo 1955, pp. 17 ff. See HOOKE's comments in *Myth, Ritual and Kingship*, ed. by S. H. HOOKE, Oxford 1958, pp. 1 ff.

elements which are found more or less in all the countries of the ancient Near East. His opponents defined "pattern" in a different way, namely as a term for the entire configuration of elements forming a specific civilization. On that understanding of the term, both parties are right. If "pattern" means what HOOKE takes it to mean, there is admittedly a common stock of mythical and ritual elements shared by all the Near Eastern cultures, just as Europe and America today share the same Western civilization without being identical. On the other hand, if "pattern" is taken as an organic totality of culture elements characteristic of one specific civilization, it is only self-evident that there can be no common pattern, but only a Babylonian, an Egyptian, and an Israelite pattern. From this point of view it must be admitted that the elements which constitute the "myth and ritual pattern" form a much more coherent pattern in Assyro-Babylonian religion than anywhere else. The agreement is more apparent among the Western Semites who lived in a closer cultural contact with Mesopotamia. In Egypt the elements of the pattern are scattered and occur in entirely different contexts; in other words they form a different pattern.

The religions which have "influenced" the religion of Israel fall into two main categories according to the nature of the contact which has taken place between them. To the first category belong Mesopotamian and Egyptian religion.

The patriarchal narratives insist on the Mesopotamian origin of the Hebrew people. It is only natural, then, that some part of their religious heritage should derive from the same source, though it is difficult to define it in detail. The tradition of the Flood obviously belong to this category, since it is found also among the Sumerians. Other Sumerian elements, such as the idea of the sacred marriage [1] or the Klage-Er-hörung pattern,[2] are somewhat doubtful because of the distance in time between the Sumerian texts and the possible examples in the Old Testament. Certain cosmological ideas are common to Accadian texts and the Old Testament and obviously belong to a common stock. The cosmogonical elements, on the other hand, are found also among the western Semites, and at least the possibility of a western origin should be left open. The structure of hymns and psalms of lament is so similar in Babylon and in the Old Testament that some kind of historical

---

[1] S. N. KRAMER in: *Proceedings of the American Philosophical Society*, 107, 1963, pp. 485 ff.

[2] H. GESE, *Lehre und Wirklichkeit in der alten Weisheit*, Tübingen 1958, pp. 63 ff., 74 ff.

connection must be assumed.[1] The nature of this connection, however, remains obscure.

With Egypt several points of contact exist. The sojourn of the Israelites in Egypt may account for the genuine Egyptian colouring of the Joseph stories (though the Egyptian model for the story of Potiphar's wife is neglected by some recent commentators of Genesis.[2] The time of Solomon provides another possibility for the influx of Egyptian ideas. The general pattern of the wisdom literature may have been introduced in this period, as perhaps also some features of the sacral kingship ideology (e.g. the throne names of Is. ix).[3] Certain literary patterns, such as the Königsnovelle,[4] may also belong to this period or even be later. Generally speaking, however, the Egyptian influence is less spectacular than the Mesopotamian.

The second category is formed by Canaanite religion. Though the Biblical texts are unanimous in rejecting it, it is obvious that the long period of coexistence must have left more traces that the Biblical sources are willing to admit. The discovery of the Ugaritic documents has taught us that the elements common to Israel and the Canaanites are more numerous than was expected. But so far no consensus has been reached in this question. Some scholars insist on the syncretistic character of Israelite religion,[5] others take a more cautious position. It should be kept in mind, however, that a religion can influence another in different ways, even so to speak negatively. When Hosea insists on Yahweh as the giver of fertility, he does so in obvious polemic against Canaanite ideas and is thus negatively influenced by the religion he fights. Perhaps also his use of marriage symbolism should be understood in this way. Obviously we are not yet at the end of this discussion. This is a field for further research.

We have only been able to deal with a few selected questions in this article. They are meant as examples to illustrate a difficult problem that will have to remain controversial for a long period of time. It is necessary that it be dealt without preconceptions and in a way that is methodologically sound.

---

[1] G. WIDENGREN, *The Accadian and Hebrew Psalms of Lamentation as Religious Documents*, Uppsala 1936, E. R. DALGLISH, *Psalm Fifty-One*, Leiden 1962.

[2] G. VON RAD, *Das erste Buch Mose*, *ATD* 2-4, pp. 320 f. mentions it briefly, A. J. BJØRNDALEN et al., *Første Mosebok*, Oslo 1970, does not.

[3] G. VON RAD, "Das judäische Königsritual," *ThLZ* 72, 1947, cols. 211 ff. = *Ges. Studien*, pp. 205 ff.

[4] S. HERRMANN, "Die Königsnovelle in Ägypten und Israel," *WZ* Leipzig 3, 1953-54, pp. 51-62.

[5] E.g. G. AHLSTRÖM, *Aspects of Syncretism in Israelite Religion*, Lund 1963.

DER BEITRAG DES KÖNIGTUMS ZUR ISRAELITISCHEN RELIGION [*]

VON

J. ALBERTO SOGGIN
Roma

1. *Einleitung.* a) In seiner alttestamentlichen Theologie hat GERHARD VON RAD [1] eindrücklich dargestellt, was die Einführung des Königtums für Israel theologisch bedeutet hat; in seiner vor Kurzem erschienenen Geschichte der alttestamentlichen Religion hat GEORG FOHRER [2] diese als das Produkt verschiedener „Impulse" beschrieben, deren zweiter das Königtum bildet. Aber, möchte ich hinzufügen, während alle anderen Impulse eine gewisse, je nach ihrem jeweiligen Inhalt bedingte, mehr oder weniger lange und verwickelte Vorgeschichte haben (vgl. die „mosaische Jahwereligion," die Prophetie, die deuteronomische Theologie usw.), wird das Königtum in einer verhältnismässig kurzen Zeit, während der letzten Jahrzehnte des 2. Jtds., eingeführt. Die durch den Druck der Philister geschaffene Notlage hat dabei den Prozess beschleunigt, aber man darf wohl behaupten, dass das Königtum in Israel eingeführt wurde einfach weil die Zeit für eine neue, zentralisierte Staatsordnung reif war.[3] Örtlich gebundene und deswegen bedingte Versuche, die Monarchie in gewissen Gegenden oder Stadtstaaten einzuführen, brauchen uns hier nicht zu interessieren, denn sie zeugen gerade deswegen, weder von einer allgemeinen Gesinnung, noch von einem Bewusstsein der Notwendigkeit eines neuen, derartigen Gebildes.

---

[*] Der vorliegende Aufsatz möchte u.A. einige Teile meines Buches: *Das Königtum in Israel. Ursprünge, Spannungen, Entwicklungen* (BZAW Nr. 104), Berlin 1967, auf den heutigen Stand der Forschung bringen und, wo vonnöten, verbessern. Auf die dort enthaltene Bibliographie bis 1966-67 möchte ich ausdrücklich hinweisen.

[1] G. VON RAD, *Theologie des Alten Testaments*, Bd. I, München 1957, S. 317 ff.; ⁴1962, S. 331 ff.

[2] G. FOHRER, *Geschichte der israelitischen Religion*, Berlin 1969, § 11-12.

[3] Dies wurde mit Recht hervorgehoben von G. BUCCELLATI, „Da Saul a Davide," *Bibbia e Oriente* 1 (1959), S. 99-128, bes. S. 101 ff. und *Cities and Nations of ancient Syria* (Studi Semitici, Nr. 26), Roma 1967, S. 99 ff.; vgl. noch *Das Königtum...*, S. 7 (mit Literatur).

Solche beschleunigte, besonders wenn durch einen Notstand bedingte Entwicklungen auf politischem und religiösem Gebiet (und
man wird in der alten Welt sowohl im Osten als im Westen beide
nicht leicht, wenn überhaupt, von einander trennen können), verlaufen
in einer stark traditionsgebundenen und deshalb konservativ einge-
stellten Gesellschaft fast nie ohne starke Reibungen. In Israel dürfte
man, wenn man es wagt, eine derartig moderne Terminologie in diesem Zusammenhang zu brauchen, geradezu von einer traumatischen
Wirkung reden, die breite Schichten der Bevölkerung erfasste: bevor
die Notwendigkeit der Sache eingesehen werden konnte, wurde sie
einem geradezu aufgedrängt und zwar von äusseren Faktoren! Man
wuchs also nicht in diesen neuen Sachverhalt hinein, indem man entweder den früheren ablehnte oder sonstwie (wie z.B. die Römer erst
im Übergang vom Königtum zur Republik, dann von dieser zum
Kaiserreich), sondern man fand sich auf einmal in ihn hineingeworfen,
als einzige Alternative zum totalen Untergang.

Das Trauma des zwar der politischen Reife des Volkes entsprechenden, doch durch Not aufgedrungenen Königtums taucht hie und
da unter der israelitischen Bevölkerung in der ambivalenten Stellung,
die es dem Königtum während seiner ganzen Existenz von ungefähr
einem halben Jahrtausend entgegenbrachte, immer wieder auf. Die
allgemeine Skepsis der Institution und seinen Vertretern gegenüber,
wenn sie sich auch niemals in einer grundsätzlichen Ablehnung des
Königtums kund tut, weht uns aus den prophetischen Büchern, aus
dem Deuteronomium und dem deuteronomistischen Geschichtswerk
entgegen und es bleiben sehr wenige unter den Königen übrig, die
nach ihren strengen Kriterien als Gott wohlgefällig gelten dürfen.

b) Es ist allerdings nicht leicht, den Umfang und den Inhalt der
durch das Königtum verursachten politischen und religiösen Änderungen mit einiger Genauigkeit festzustellen. Dies weil wir über die
vorstaatlichen Verhältnisse in Israel nur durch stark vom Dtr. G.
überarbeitete oder sogar neugeformte Quellen unterrichtet sind. Wie
die Lage in diesen beschrieben wird ist bekannt und wurde vor über
40 Jahren durch MARTIN NOTH [1] in einem seither klassisch gewordenen Werk dargestellt. Ein Zwölf-Stämme-Bund, aus unabhängigen
Einheiten bestehend, politisch ganz lose, religiös aber durch ein gemeinsames Zentralheiligtum um so stärker verbunden, bildete die

---

[1] M. NOTH, *Das System der Zwölf Stämme Israels* (BWANT IV, 1), Stuttgart 1930
(= Darmstadt ²1966); es hat über 30 Jahre das Bild der Forschung beherrscht.

Grundlage dessen, was sich „Israel" nannte. In Notfällen konnte u.U.
dieser hauptsächlich auf religiösen Grundlagen ruhende Bund, auch
auf politischem Gebiet tätig werden: Bedrohungen durch Feinde von
Aussen, aber auch innenpolitische Angelegenheiten brachten die
Stämme zusammen. Als einleuchtendes Beispiel für die zweite Möglichkeit wurde auf die „Schandtat" von Gibea und ihre Bestrafung,
Jdc xix-xxi, verwiesen. Dieses Gebilde, das aber der Bedrohung durch
die Philister nicht gewachsen war, wurde von Noth „Amphiktyonie"
genannt, wegen der immer wiederkehrenden Zwölfzahl der Stämme
und seiner angeblichen Analogien mit ähnlichen Einrichtungen im
alten Griechenland und im vorrömischen Italien.[1] Das Wort ist aber
unglücklich, wie wir schon seit über einem Jahrzehnt wissen: es setzt
für Israel Verhältnisse voraus, die sich nicht belegen lassen; es ruft
Analogien hervor, die unhaltbar sind; sogar ein *terminus technicus*, mit
dem der Begriff bezeichnet würde, fehlt im Hebräischen vollkommen,[2]
es sei denn, das Wort „Israel" habe diese Bedeutung gehabt. Das lässt
allerdings die Frage offen, ob und inwiefern die von M. Noth so
plastisch dargestellte Rekonstruktion der vorstaatlichen Zeit durch
das Dtr. G. nicht doch faktuell im grossen Ganzen glaubwürdig ist,
sowohl auf religiösem als auch auf politischem Gebiet; und, wenn
man auch zugeben mag, dass dieses Bild stark idealisiert sei und mehr
den Wünschen des Dtr. G.s als einem historisch verifizierbaren Tatbestand entspreche,[3] so hiesse dies noch nicht, dass die *Gesamt*dar-
stellung nicht zutrifft. Gegen die Existenz des „Bundes" sprächen an
sich einige gute Gründe: ein gemeinsames Heiligtum treffen wir nirgends, es sei denn, man betrachte die Lade als solches, was aber keines-

---

[1] Man hat sogar versucht, durch das Buch Noths angeregt, Amphiktyonien in
Sumer und unter den Philistern zu finden, vgl. W. W. Hallo, „A Sumerian
Amphiktyiony," *JCS* 14 (1960), S. 88-114 und B. D. Rahtjen, „Philistine and
Hebrew Amphiktyonies," *JNES* 24 (1965), S. 100-104; letzterer lehnt den Begriff
für Israel ab, beide sind ein eindrückliches Beispiel für den Erfolg dieses Ge-
dankens.

[2] So H. H. Rowley, *IDB* II (1962), S. 753 f.; zu derselben Zeit begann man auch
an dem Stämmebund als solchem zu zweifeln, vgl. *Das Königtum...*, S. 12, Anm. 1.

[3] Vgl. hierzu zuletzt S. Herrmann, „Autonome Entwicklungen in den König-
reichen Israel und Juda," *Suppl. VT* 17 (1969), S. 139-158; meinen Bericht „L'ipo-
tesi anfizionica negli studi più recenti ed il problema del Canone," in *Atti della XX
Settimana biblica*, Brescia 1970, S. 191-202; G. W. Anderson, „Israel: Amphic-
tyony: ᶜAm; Kāhāl; ᶜÉdāh," in *Translating and Understanding the Old Testament, Essays
... H. G. May*, Nashville 1970, S. 135-151 und R. de Vaux, „La thèse de l'amphic-
tyonie israélite," *HThR* 64 (1971), S. 415-436. Anderseits bejaht G. Buccellati,
Cities and Nations ..., S. 114-116 den Begriff, wenn er auch das Wort Amphiktyonie ablehnt, als Übergangsinstitution vom halbnomadischen zum sesshaften
Leben.

wegs unanfechtbar ist,[1] und man bekenne sich zweitens zur Theorie
der periodischen Ladewanderung von einem heiligen Ort zum ande-
ren, wie sie von JAN DUS, aber von niemand sonst, anfangs der '60-er
Jahre vertreten wurde.[2] Denn nur so liesse sich die Tatsache einer
Mehrzahl israelitischer Heiligtümer mit der Einzahl der Lade, also des
Zentralheiligtumes, vereinigen. Ähnlich verhält es sich auf politischem
Gebiet, sei es gegen den gemeinsamen Feind von Aussen, sei es in
gemeinsamen, inneren Angelegenheiten: wenn wir den ältesten Text,
Jdc v, betrachten, so ist es leicht zu beobachten, dass aus ihm eher
das Gegenteil eines Stämmebundes hervortritt: jede Einheit handelt
nach eigenem Gutdünken, sodass letzten Endes die Schlacht nur von
den unmittelbar interessierten, nicht von den anderen Verbänden geschlagen wird,[3] was selbstverständlich ein *gemeinsames* Handeln gegen
den Feind von Aussen ausschliesst. Und dennoch: wer dieses Stück
mehrmals untersucht kann sich des Eindruckes nicht erwehren, dass
seine Voraussetzung dennoch ein Aufgebot an *alle* Stämme ist und
zwar im Namen des gemeinsamen Gottes Jahwe. Allerdings, wie
R. SMEND mit Recht bemerkt und von FOHRER angenommen wird,
erweist sich dabei die Zwölfzahl unhaltbar, was abermals die Legitimität des Gebrauches eines Wortes wie Amphiktyonie, nicht aber die
Existenz des Stämmebundes in Frage stellt. Also: Aus diesem alten,
nicht dtr. überarbeiteten Text geht hervor, dass es doch etwas gemeinsames, verbindendes zwischen den Stämmen gegeben hat, wodurch
sie zich sowohl von den Kanaanäern als auch von den Nachbar-
völkern aus dem Süden (Philister) und aus dem Osten (Ammon, Edom
und Moab, mit denen Israel sich sonst ethnisch verwandt wusste)
unterschieden. Und alles zeugt dafür, dass es die gemeinsame Jahwereligion gewesen ist, die dieses verbindende Element bildete. Auf dieser Grundlage war es also möglich, dass Israel, und vielleicht auch
Juda,[4] sich unter Saul völlig freiwillig zusammenschlossen und der

---

[1] Das gilt auch, wenn wir die von J. MAIER, *Das altisraelitische Ladeheiligtum*
(BZAW Nr. 93), Berlin 1965 vorgeschlagene These, die Lade sei während der
Philisterzeit angefertigt worden, nicht annehmen.

[2] J. DUS, „Der Brauch der Ladewanderung im Alten Testament," *ThZ* 17
(1961), S. 1-16 und „Noch zum Brauch der ‚Ladewanderung'," *VT* 13 (1963),
S. 126-132.

[3] Hierzu R. SMEND, *Jahwekrieg und Stämmebund* (FRLANT Nr. 84), Göttingen
1963, S. 12 und G. FOHRER, „Altes Testament—‚Amphiktyonie' und ‚Bund',"
ThLZ 91 (1966), Sp. 801-816. 893-904 (= *Studien zur alttestamentlichen Theologie und
Geschichte*, [BZAW Nr. 115], Berlin 1969, S. 84-119), bes. Sp. 811-S. 98 f.

[4] R. SMEND, „Gehörte Juda zum vorstaatlichen Israel?", in *Fourth Congress of
Jewish Studies*, Papers, Bd. I, Jerusalem 1967, S. 57-62.

letzte Richter zum ersten König wurde,[1] im streng politischen Sinn des Titels. Wie wir noch sehen werden, entstanden diesem neuen Gebilde viel weniger Schwierigkeiten auf der rein politischen als auf der religiösen Ebene.

David erging es ähnlich: nach den Unruhen, die auf den Tod Sauls folgten, während derer er zum König über Juda in Hebron ernannt wurde, 2 Sam. ii-v, traten Israel und Benjamin freiwillig dem neuen Gebilde bei und nur von Seiten Nathans erfolgte eine hauptsächlich religiöse Opposition gegen die Handlungen des Königs im Kultus. Die späteren Aufstände, 2 Sam. xv ff. und xx, beruhten nicht so sehr auf einer grundsätzlichen Ablehnung des monarchischen Prinzips (Absalom plante ja selbst König zu werden und es wäre ihm beinahe gelungen), sondern auf der Nichtbeachtung der Rechte der Stämme durch den König. Und dies war später der Grund, dass nach Salomos Tod das Grossreich zwar sich auflöste, 1 Reg. xii, ohne dass das monarchische Prinzip an sich in Frage gestellt wurde.

c) Anders verhält es sich freilich mit der Episode, über die Jdc xix-xxi berichtet und die bis in die jüngste Zeit als Beweis für ein innenamphiktyonisches Ethos, das unter Umständen auch mit Gewalt durchgesetzt werden konnte, gebraucht wurde. Wie seinerzeit von O. Eissfeldt dargestellt und vor kurzem von K.-D. Schunck bestätigt, handelt es sich um territoriale Schwierigkeiten, in denen der unter Landmangel leidende, weil zwischen Juda und Ephraim eingepresste Benjamin mit seinem nördlichen Nachbarn, der viel günstiger gelegen war, geriet. Der darauffolgende Krieg endete mit einer schweren Niederlage Benjamins.[2] Ob bei dieser Episode die Erzählungslust die Oberhand gewinnt, oder ob eine tatsächlich verübte „Schandtat" von Seiten einer benjaminitischen Stadt den öffentlichen,

---

[1] Hier sollte man die m.E. zu wenig beachtete, doch mit einigen Korrekturen durchaus wahrscheinliche These von G. Wallis, „Die Anfänge des Königtums in Israel," *Wiss. Zeits. Halle* 12 (1962-63), S. 239-247 (= *Geschichte und Überlieferung*, Berlin 1968, S. 45-66) einschalten. Die Korrekturen müssten hauptsächlich die Beziehungen zwischen Gilead und Benjamin klären, zwei Gruppen welche nach Jdc xxi und 2 Sam ii eng miteinander verbunden waren. Vielleicht dürfen wir sagen, dass Saul über Gilead-Benjamin, über Ephraim und über weitere Nordstämme zum *nāgîd* bzw. zum König ausgerufen wurde; diesem Gebilde hätte sich dann auch Juda angeschlossen, vgl. R. Smend in der vorigen Anmerkung.

[2] O. Eissfeldt, „Der geschichtliche Hintergrund der Erzählung von Gibeas Schandtat," *Festschrift* G. Beer..., Stuttgart 1935, S. 19-40 (= *Kleine Schriften* Bd. II, Tübingen 1963, S. 64-80); K.-D. Schunck, *Benjamin* (BZAW Nr. 86), Berlin 1963, S. 57 ff.; vgl. noch A. Besters, „Le sanctuaire central dans Jud. XIX-XXI," *Ephem. Theol. Lovan.* 41 (1965), S. 20-41 und G. Fohrer a.a.O. Sp. 812-S. 99 f.

willkommenen Vorwand für den Krieg lieferte, kann freilich nicht mehr ausgemacht werden. Wir wissen allerdings, dass dies nicht die einzige kriegerische Auseinandersetzung zwischen Einzelstämmen gewesen ist, vgl. Jdc xii (und es dürfte kein Zufall sein, dass gerade Gilead, ein Benjamin verwandter Stamm, es war, der Ephraim geschlagen hatte). Auch die Kämpfe zwischen David in Hebron und ʾEšbaʿal mit Abner gehören wohl zu dieser Kategorie, vgl. 2 Sam. ii-v.

Die These eines gemeinsamen, innerhalb des Verbandes herrschenden, und falls vonnöten, mit Waffengewalt von den anderen Mitgliedern durchgesetzten gemeinsamen Ethos erweist sich damit als hinfällig; ja, sogar der vorher aufgestellten These, dass es ein gemeinsames Band gab, welches „Israel" von den anderen Völkern unterschied und später seinen Zusammenschluss ermöglichte, wird somit eine Grenze gesetzt.

d) Endlich entwirft die Rekonstruktion dieser Epoche durch das Dtr. G. ein religiöses Bild, dass man wohl mit Recht als Theokratie bezeichnet hat. Im Unterschied zu den benachbarten Völkern, war es Jahwe, und nicht der irdische König, der über sein Volk herrschte, wie sich dies konkret auch gestaltet haben mag.[1] Ob das Wort Theokratie die Absicht des Dtr. G. richtig wiedergibt, sei dahingestellt.

Nun ist es m.E. besonders wichtig festzustellen, dass vom Gedanken eines Königtums Jahwes in vorköniglicher Zeit keineswegs nur im Dtr. G. die Rede ist: die gewöhnlich nicht nach dem Ende des 2. Jtds. angesetzten Stellen Ex. xv 18, Num xxiii 21 und Dtn xxxiii 5 bezeugen ihn ausdrücklich; ja, noch in der zweiten Hälfte des 8. Jhdts. soll er nach Jes. vi 5 weiterbestanden haben. Für ein altes, doch leider nicht genau feststellbares Datum zeugt ferner Jdc viii 22 f., eine Stelle die von W. RICHTER [2] einer zwar verhältnismässig jungen, doch vorprophetischen Schicht des „Retterbuches," und nicht zur dtr. Überarbeitung desselben, zugerechnet wird. Es darf also ruhig behauptet werden, dass die Richtigkeit der vom Dtr. G. vorausgesetzten theo-

---

[1] Vgl. *Das Königtum...*, S. 18 f. und meinen Artikel מלך, *ThHAT* Bd. I, München 1971, Sp. 908-920, bes. Sp. 914 f. (mit Lit.). Archäologisches Material zur Theokratie bietet A. E. GLOCK, „Early Israel as the Kingdom of Yahweh," *Concordia Theological Monthly* 41 (1970), S. 558-605: sie soll sich als Vassallentum des Volkes gegenüber Jahwe geäussert haben. Es ist hier nicht der Ort, die These zu überprüfen.

[2] W. RICHTER, *Traditionsgeschichtliche Untersuchungen zum Richterbuch* (BBB Nr. 18), Bonn 1963, S. 235 f. und zuletzt *Die sogenannten vorprophetischen Berufungsberichte* (FRLANT Nr. 101), Göttingen 1970, S. 47.

kratischen Ordnung für die vorkönigliche Zeit, sich auch aus anderen, unabhängigen Quellen verifizieren lässt und sie somit zum Hauptbestand der israelitischen Religion gehörte. Es verwundert darum kaum, dass mit der Einführung des Königtums als politische Institution eine Spannung zwischen diesen beiden Begriffen entstehen musste und dass das erstere mit dem zweiten einen Ausgleich, ja seine Legitimation finden musste.[1] Eine allerdings schwierige Aufgabe, wenigstens während der ersten Jahrzehnte.

e) Ich fasse zusammen. Für die vorkönigliche Zeit weiss das Dtr G. von einem Stämmebund zu berichten, dessen Mitglieder das Königtum des Gottes Jahwe anerkannten. Einzelheiten, besonders Exemplifizierungen und Deutungen dieses Tatbestandes, sind oft anfechtbar; im grossen Ganzen gesehen aber, gibt es keine triftigen Gründe, das Bild als solches grundsätzlich abzulehnen, umsomehr als das Dtr. G. (im Gegensatz zu einigen Propheten, welche die Rückkehr zum Nomadentum predigten und seine Institutionen als vorbildlich betrachteten), nicht nur keine Alternative zum politischen Königtum kennt (was freilich eine scharfe Kritik an Personen und Handlungen alles andere als ausschliesst), sondern ausdrücklich dem König eine Art *jus reformandi* zubilligt und bekanntlich die jeweiligen Monarchen nach der Ausübung desselben beurteilt.

2. Die Zeit Sauls und Davids. a) Die ersten Schwierigkeiten, so wird uns berichtet, die zwischen der Theokratie und dem politischen Königtum ausbrachen, spielen sich schon bei der Erwählung des ersten Königs ab, also, genau gesehen, zu einer Zeit, da es eigentlich noch kein politisches Königtum gab. Es ist bekannt, dass einer der drei Berichte von der Erhebung Sauls zum Thron, sowohl im Munde

---

[1] Theokratie heisst hier freilich nicht, dass es in vorköniglicher Zeit keine Art Synkretismus gegeben habe: er erwuchs aber natürlicherweise, aus dem Zusammenleben verschiedener Völker, und darin unterscheidet er sich vom Staatssynkretismus der königlichen Zeit (vgl. unten, Anm. 2, S. 20). H. Ringgren, *Israelitische Religion* (Die Religionen der Menschheit, Nr. 26), Stuttgart 1963, S. 39 ff. zeigt z.B., an Hand der Namengebung, dass Baal und Jahwe nicht immer scharf von einander getrennt wurden.
Ich möchte ferner noch kurz auf die Tatsache aufmerksam machen, dass man den Dtr. G. als Geschichtssammler meistens günstig beurteilt, abgesehen von seinen theologischen Tendenzen, vgl. M. Noth, *Überlieferungsgeschichtliche Studien* I, Halle 1943 (= Darmstadt ²1957 ff.), S. 95 ff. und „Zur Geschichtsauffassung des Deuteronomisten," in *Proceedings of the XXII Congress of Orientalists, Istanbul 1951*, Leiden, 1957 Bd. II, S. 558-566, und vom Verfasser, *Le Livre de Josué* (CAT Va), Neuchâtel 1970, S. 12 f. Noth beschreibt diese Einstellung als „grundsätzlich zunächst die *positive Haltung* des ehrlichen Maklers. . ." (von ihm gesperrt).

Samuels als auch in einem überlieferten Orakel, eine stark negative
Beurteilung der Monarchie enthält: 1 Sam. viii und x 17 ff., bes. viii
6, 11 ff., x 19 f. für Samuel; viii 7 ff. für das Orakel. Nun wäre es
bestimmt verlockend, diese negative Bewertung des Königtums (die
u.A., was viii 11 ff. betrifft, auf Situationen Bezug nimmt, die im
durchschnittlichen kanaanäischen Stadtstaat üblich gewesen sein mö-
gen, es in Israel aber nur äusserst selten, und dann nur als Missbrauch
der Institution von Einzelpersonen, gegeben hat, und die man deswegen kaum als typisch bezeichnen darf) als Produkt einer späteren
königsfeindlichen Überarbeitung eines ursprünglich nicht königsfeindlichen Berichtes zu betrachten [1]; die Sache ist aber verwickelter, ja
geradezu gefährlich, da die Hand des dtr. Überarbeiters mit Sicherheit
wahrnehmbar ist.[2] Beide müssen aber scharf von einander getrennt
bleiben, nicht nur wegen des rein hypothetischen Charakters des ersten
Vorschlags, sondern besonders weil das Dtr. G., wie gesehen, ja nicht
grundsätzlich königsfeindlich ist.[3] Ich glaube immer noch, dass der
Bericht, mit all seinen Unzulänglichkeiten auf historischem Gebiet,
uns dennoch ein fernes Echo von jenen Spannungen wiedergibt, die
durch die Einführung der neuen Regierungsform ausgelöst wurden.
Und einen der Gründe dieser Spannungen hat jüngstens H. J.
BOECKER,[4] m.E. richtig erkannt: der politische König tritt in der
Kriegsführung an die Stelle des von Jahwe erwählten charismatischen
Führers, vgl. 1 Sam. viii 20b; man bemerke ferner, dass auch im V. 20a
ein ähnlicher Gedanke vorliegt: wenn wir, wie höchst wahrscheinlich
ist, die dort vorkommende Wurzel *špṭ* mit „regieren" übersetzen, so
war die ganze Theokratie durch das „Volksbegehren" (BUBER) in
Frage gestellt, während die Kriegsführung nur die zeitbedingte Phi-
listernot betraf. Dies wird von den gut bezeugten, dynastischen Be-
strebungen Sauls nur bestätigt.

b) Ferner, nach den beiden uns erhaltenen Berichten, stellte sich

---

[1] Vgl. *Das Königtum...* S. 32 und die dort Anm. 8 und 9 genannte Literatur.

[2] So M. NOTH, *Überlieferungsgeschichtliche Studien...* S. 61 f. ohne eingehende Be-
handlung des Textes, dem sich H. J. BOECKER, *Die Beurteilung der Anfänge des
Königtums in den deuteronomistischen Abschnitten des Samuelbuches* (WMANT Nr. 31),
Neukirchen 1969, S. 10-12 und 16-19 anschliesst.

[3] Überhaupt ist die exilische und nachexilische Zeit nicht königfeindlich, wie
K.-H. BERNHARD, *Das Problem der altorientalischen Königsideologie im Alten Testament*
(Suppl. VT Nr. 8), Leiden 1961, S. 114 ff. zeigt. Dasselbe haben wir schon für das
Dtn. und das Dtr. G. feststellen können, vgl. noch unten, § 3a.

[4] H. J. BOECKER, a.a.O. S. 32 ff.; vgl. hierzu neuerdings W. H. SCHMIDT,
„Kritik am Königtum," in *Probleme biblischer Theologie, Fests.* G. VON RAD, München 1971, S. 440-461.

die Frage, ob und eventuell wie der König im Kultus tätig sein sollte. Im ersteren wird Saul bekanntlich getadelt, weil er Jahwe ein Opfer dargebracht hatte, eine Handlung zu der er sich geradezu genötigt sah wegen des verspäteten Eintreffens Samuels, der dadurch verursachten Einstellung jeglicher kriegerischen Handlung und der Auflösung seines Heeres, 1 Sam. xiii 5-14; es handelt sich um eine nicht dtr. Stelle, die von der zweiten, nicht königsfeindlichen Traditionsschicht von der Königswahl abhängig ist: ix 1-x 16. Der zweite Bericht findet sich 1 Sam. xv 12-15; dort, in einer allgemein (sogar von konservativen Autoren) anerkannten späteren Schicht, die sich eng verbunden mit dem Dtr. G. erweist, stossen wir auf eine in der LXX bezeugte Variante, in der Saul abermals für die Darbringung eines Opfers getadelt wird. Die Variante muss in den Text aufgenommen werden, denn nur so wird der folgende Spruch, Jahwe habe grösseren Gefallen an Gehorsam als an Opfern, sinnvoll, es sei denn, man entferne diesen Spruch aus dem Text.[1] Wenn es uns erlaubt ist, auch dieses letzte, äusserst problematische Material als Quelle zu verwerten, so kann man aus beiden Texten nur den Widerstand gegen jeglichen Eingriff des Königs im Kultus ablesen, was hier durch die Darbringung eines Opfers veranschaulicht wird. Ja, nicht einmal das anerkannte Vorhandensein eines offensichtlichen *status necessitatis* wie 1 Sam. xiii rechtfertigt noch entschuldigt so einen Eingriff: politisches Königtum und Theokratie konnten zwar nebeneinander existieren, unter der Bedingung aber, dass der König sich der Theokratie und seinen Organen unterwarf und nicht in den Kultus eingriff. Diese Lage sollte sich aber bald zu Gunsten der Monarchie ändern.

c) Unter David fand sich die Religion Israels einer viel stärkeren Persönlichkeit und besonders einer vollkommen zu ihren Ungunsten umgestalteten politischen und ethnischen Lage gegenübergestellt. Die Einverleibung grosser kanaanäischer Gebiete im West- und Ostjordanland, die Errichtung der Reichshauptstadt im kanaanäischen Stadtstaat Jerusalem hatten aus einer lose zusammengeschmiegten Gruppe rein israelitischer Stämme einen gemischten Territorialstaat geschaffen, in dem die Ureinwohner nicht nur zahlenmässig, sondern auch kulturell und wirtschaftlich überlegen waren. Was die Lage innerhalb des von Israel kontrollierten Gebietes betrifft, hatte das eigenmächtige Einholen und Aufstellen der Lade im Bezirk der neuen Hauptstadt, ein kultischer Akt von grundlegender Bedeutung, eine vollkommen

---

[1] Vgl. *Das Königtum...* S. 53-57.

neue Lage geschaffen, durch welche die neue Hauptstadt auf einmal
auch zum israelitischen Heiligtum geworden war. Dies war geschehen
unter einer Reihe von kultischen Handlungen, bei denen der König
die Hauptrolle gespielt hatte. Es fehlte nur noch, dass David in Jerusalem für die Lade ein Heiligtum baute, damit das Gebilde des unter
königlichem Patronat stehenden Tempels mit einem neuen Staatskultus nach altorientalischem Muster vollständig gewesen wäre (der
Chronist weiss mit Stolz davon zu berichten, dass David schon alle
Materialien zu diesem Zweck vorbereitet hatte!). Ja, wir wissen von
einer Strömung innerhalb der Religion Israels, die mit dem Zustandekommen des Grossreichs Davids die Verwirklichung der an den Erz-
vätern ergangenen Landes- und Nachkommenschaftsverheissungen zu
verbinden wusste; sie fand ein wenig später ihren Niederschlag in der
Theologie des „Jahwisten".[1] Das geht schon aus dem Anfang der
Erzvätergeschichten hervor. Gen. xii 1-3 (4a), eine Stelle die nicht aus
altem Traditionsgut, sondern aus der Theologie des „J" selbst stammt,
verheisst Abraham u.A., Jahwe werde ihn zum „grossen *gôj*" machen,
V. 2; nun hat aber das für Israel sehr selten gebrauchte Wort *gôj* zwei
Hauptbedeutungen: eine negative, die hier durch den Zusammenhang
ausgeschlossen wird, und eine positive, im Sinn von „Nation" als
politisch-räumlichem Gebilde[2]; ein solcher Gedanke aber hat sich nur
zur Zeit Davids und Salomos im Grossreich verwirklicht. Ferner entspricht eine in der Verheissung für Abraham gebrauchte Formel Gen.
xii 2: *waᵃgaddᵉlāh šᵉmékā* fast wörtlich der aus 2 Sam. vii 9b für David
überlieferten: *wᵉcāśîtî lᵉkā šēm gādôl*, was kaum zufällig sein kann. Zeigt
es sich also, dass eine Strömung innerhalb der israelitischen Religion
bestrebt war, das Königtum nicht nur als von Gott geradezu gewollt,
sondern als schon zur Zeit Abrahams verheissen darzustellen und so
zu legitimieren, so konnten die Stimmen, die sich bereits zur Zeit
Samuels und Sauls gegen das Königtum erhoben hatten, und jede

---

[1] Hierzu H.-W. WOLFF, „Das Kerygma des Jahwisten," *Ev. Theol.* 24 (1964),
S. 73-98 (= *Gesammelte Studien*, München 1964, S. 345-373), bes. S. 83-356 ff. und
E. BRUEGGEMAN, „David and his Theologian," *CBQ* 30 (1968), S. 156-181; ferner
S. HERRMANN, *Die prophetischen Heilserwartungen im Alten Testament* (BWANT V, 5),
Stuttgart 1965, S. 76 f. und R. E. CLEMENTS, *Abraham and David* (SBTh II, 5),
London 1967, S. 16 ff., 35 ff., 57 und *passim*.

[2] Hierzu E. A. SPEISER, „ ‚People' and ‚Nation' in Ancient Israel," *JBL* 79
(1960), S. 157-163 (= *Oriental and Biblical Studies*, Philadelphia 1967, S. 160-170)
und A. CODY, „When is the Chosen People called a *Gôy*?" *VT* 14 (1964), S. 1-6.
Wenn eine ältere Schicht des „J" zur Zeit des Königtums Davids in Hebron ange-
setzt werden könnte, so G. WALLIS, „Die Tradition von den Ahnvätern," *ZAW*
81 (1969), S. 18-40, dann hätten wir ein Zeugnis, dass dieser Prozess schon einige
Jahre früher angefangen hatte.

Sonderstellung des Königs im Kultus prinzipiell ablehnten, nicht ausgeschaltet werden; denn die Monarchie besass noch nicht genügend Festigkeit, um ohne sie auszukommen.

d) Nach diesen Voraussetzungen habe ich versucht, das Zustandekommen der Verheissung Nathans an das „Haus" Davids zu erklären.[1] Der politische Hintergrund der Handlung ist jetzt von religiös-theologischen Elementen verdunkelt, aber er tritt leicht hervor, wenn wir annehmen, es handle sich um das Ergebnis eines Kompromisses zwischen David und den religiös-königsfeindlichen Gruppen; bei dieser Handlung trat Nathan, so dürfen wir wohl sagen, als Vermittler auf, und das Ergebnis war, dass nach der Überführung der Lade nach Jerusalem, David sich jeglicher kultischen Handlung enthielt; dafür bekam er die Verheissung an sein Haus, wodurch das Südreich bis zum endgültigen Untergang 587 ein politisch stabiles Gebilde wurde.[2]

3. *Das Reiche Salomos.* a) Die Handlungen Salomos auf religiösem Gebiet sind beträchtlich und leiten einen grossen Umschwung ein. Durch den Tempelbau erhielt der König die Rolle des Patronats, wie sonst im alten Orient üblich; bei der Einweihung des Tempels unternahm ferner der König eine Reihe von Handlungen, die ausgesprochen priesterlich sind: er bot eine Menge von Opfern dar, er sprach ein öffentliches Fürbittegebet im Namen des Volkes, er segnete es, vgl. 1 Reg. viii 5 ff., 12 ff., und 54 ff.[3] Die starke dtr. Überarbeitung des Berichts lässt den ursprünglichen Tatbestand trotzdem erkennen. Gegen diese neuen Befugnisse des Königs hat das Dtr. G. nichts einzuwenden gehabt, da es, wie gesehen, solche Rechte nicht nur dem König zubilligte, sondern entsprechende Handlungen sogar von ihm verlangte, man vgl. nur die Fälle Hiskias' und Josias', die sich von denen Salomos einzig darin unterscheiden, dass sie die von ihm begründete Einverleibung des Königs in den Kultus einfach fortgesetzt haben.

---

[1] *Das Königtum...*, S. 72, bes. Anm. 32. Für eine andere Erklärung, die aus Nathan einen Feind des jebusitischen Heiligtums macht, vgl. H. RINGGREN a.a.O. S. 52 ff. (mit Literatur).

[2] Wiesehr der König von der Unterstützung von Seiten der israelitischen Religion abhängig war, ist richtig dargestellt worden von R. HALLEVY, „The place of the Monarchy in Israelite Religion," *Tarbiz* 32 (1962-63), S. 215-224 (Hebr., Engl. summ.), der diesen Gedanken bis zur Exilszeit verfolgt.

[3] Hierzu richtig G. WIDENGREN, *Sakrales Königtum im Alten Testament und im Judentum*, Stuttgart 1955, S. 14-16. Für den Ausdruck, vgl. unten das Ende der Anm. 2, S. 24; ferner R. DE VAUX, *Les Institutions de l'Ancient Testament*, Bd. I, Paris 1958, S. 174-176.

Wenn also unter David die Gruppen, die dem König keine Ein-
griffe in den Kultus zubilligten, im grossen Ganzen sich hatte behaupten können, auch wenn sie sich bei dem Fall der Einholung der Lade
mit der vollendeten Tatsache hatten abfinden müssen, so gelang es
Salomo, das ganze Problem nach seinen eigenen Absichten zu lösen.
Dies geschah allerdings unter starker Anlehnung an die Bräuche des
kanaanäischen Stadtstaates, die einfach auf den neuen Territorialstaat
übertragen wurden.[1] Wir hören von keinem Widerstand von Seiten
der früher so starken und aktiven Gruppen; anderseits wurde Salomo
zu diesen Massnahmen bis zu einem gewissen Grad auch von der ziemlich bunt gestalteten, nicht nur ethnischen, sondern auch religiösen
Zusammensetzung des Grossreiches veranlasst. Es entstand so das,
was ich früher eine Art Staatssynkretismus genannt habe,[2] in dem der
König die in der Umwelt üblichen Funktionen im Staatskultus über-
nahm und der Tempel zum Staatsheiligtum, also zum Heiligtum für
alle Völker des Reiches und nicht nur für Israel, wurde.

Auf diesem Gebiet erfuhr die israelitische Religion also die erste,
ihre Grundsätze betreffende Änderung: seit Salomo steht der König
fest verankert im Kultus; er ist zwar, technisch gesprochen, nicht
Priester, doch es obliegen ihm priesterliche Funktionen: zu gewissen
Anlässen opfert er, segnet er, übt er Fürbitte. Der Tempel ist, wie
gesehen, nicht nur für Israel bestimmt, doch formell wenigstens hat
Israel in ihm den Ehrenplatz: im Allerheiligsten steht die Lade Jahwes,
nicht irgend ein Gottesbild, der Name des angebeteten Gottes ist
Jahwe, und nicht Baʿal oder der einer sonstigen kanaanäischen Gottheit; doch wenn wir dem dtr. Bericht 2 Reg. xxiii 4 ff. Glauben schenken dürfen (und angesichts der Hochschätzung und der Exklusivität,
die der Tempel sowohl im Dtn. als auch im Dtr. G. einnimmt, sollte
der Bericht glaubwürdig sein), so ersehen wir aus der Aufzählung der

---

[1] Für die Begriffe Stadtstaat, Territorialstaat usw. vgl. G. BUCCELLATI, *Cities
and Nations*... S. 19 ff.

[2] „Der offiziell geförderte Synkretismus im 10. Jahrhundert," *ZAW* 78 (1966),
S. 179-204 (mit Literatur). Weiteres zum Gegenstand bei N. POULSSEN, *König und
Tempel im Glaubenszeugnis des Alten Testaments* (Stuttgarter Bibl. Mon. Nr. 3), Stuttgart 1967 S. 72 ff. Ein viel optimistischeres Bild der religiösen Lage in Israel seit
der Einrichtung des Königtums bietet in einem bibliographisch ziemlich unvoll-
ständigem Artikel H. D. HUMMEL, „The influence of Archaeological evidence on
the reconstruction of Religion in Monarchical Israel," *Concordia Theological Monthly*
41 (1970), S. 542-557: nach ihm soll es keine grundsätzlichen Änderungen, abgesehen vom Eindringen einiger geringerer heidnischer Elemente, gegeben haben.
Ob sich diese These nach dem hier und weiter unten, § 4, gesagtem halten lässt,
darf der Leser selbst beurteilen.

entfernten Personen, Tiere und Gegenstände was für eine Art Kult dort stattfand; Ezc. viii berichtet uns ferner, dass im Tempelareal der Tammuzkult betrieben wurde und vielleicht dürfen wir auch annehmen, dass der Jer. vii 18 und xliv 17 bezeugte Kultus an die Himmelskönigin (Astarte) dort seinen Hauptsitz hatte.

b) Die vorher gestreifte Frage nach dem Modell des von David versuchten, von Salomo verwirklichten Staatssynkretismus ist für unser Thema äusserst wichtig. Ein geradezu als klassisch betrachteter Lösungsversuch ist der von H. S. NYBERG 1938 unternommene,[1] weil er von den Meisten heute ausdrücklich oder stillschweigend angenommen wird: das Modell sei der Kultus des von David eroberten und einverleibten Stadtstaates Jerusalem gewesen. Aus ihm stammt wohl der auf einmal nach der Eroberung der Stadt aus dem Nichts auftauchende Priester Ṣādôq 2 Sam. viii 17; Namen mit der Wurzel ṣdq sind im Alten Testament belegt und zwar immer in Verbindung mit Jerusalem: Malkî-ṣédeq Gen. xiv 18-20, ʾAdônî-ṣédeq Jos. x 1 (wo aber die LXX, wie der M.T. Jdc i 5 ff., ʾAdônî-bézeq gelesen hat); allerdings ist der Ertrag der ᶜAmarna-Briefe bekanntlich ganz verschieden, da in ihnen nur der hurritische Name ᶜAbdu-Ḫepa vorkommt.[2] Und die erwähnte Malkî-ṣédeq-Stelle Gen. xiv 18-20 (der ich hier mit O. PROCKSCH [3] einen hohen, ja, ich würde hinzufügen, einen traditionsgestaltenden Wert zuschreiben möchte, denn es ist doch wohl offensichtlich so, dass das ganze Kapitel als Rahmen für dieses Stück zusammengesetzt wurde, auch wenn es, rein literarisch gesehen, den jetzigen Zusammenhang unterbricht) wäre dann das Beweisstück für das Alter und die Legitimität der Beziehungen zwischen Abraham-David und dem Jerusalemer Heiligtum gewesen. Es ist hier freilich nicht der Ort, sich mit Einzelheiten zu befassen; es genüge die Feststellung, dass diese Hypothese, wenn auch neuerdings

---

[1] H. S. NYBERG, „Studien zum Religionskampf im Alten Testament," *ARW* 35 (1938), S. 329-387, bes. S. 351 ff.; vgl. noch die Aussagen des immer sehr vorsichtigen H. H. ROWLEY, „Melchizedek and Zadok (Gen. 14 and Psalm 110)," *Festschrift für* A. BERTHOLET, Tübingen 1950, S. 461-472; ferner G. VON RAD, *Das erste Buch Mose* (ATD 2-4), Göttingen 1949 ff., zu Gen. xiv; H. RINGGREN a.a.O. S. 54 und G. FOHRER a.a.O. S. 118. Dagegen K.-H. BERNHARDT, *Das Problem...* S. 92 ff. und 304. Eine Sonderstellung finden wir bei B. MAISLER (MAZAR), „Das vordavidische Jerusalem," *JPOS* 10 (1930), S. 181-191, der eine „amorrhäische" bis zum 12. Jhdt. dauernde, gefolgt von einer jebusitischen Epoche für Jerusalem annimmt; David besetzte die jebusitische Stadt, soll aber den amorrhäischen Gott ʾEl ᶜEljôn wieder zu Ehren gezogen haben.

[2] Die Schwierigkeit liesse sich ohne Weiteres lösen, wenn wir den eben erwähnten Vorschlag von B. MAISLER (MAZAR) annähmen.

[3] O. PROCKSCH, *Die Genesis* (KAT I), Leipzig ²⁻³1924, S. 510 f.

mit guten Gründen angegriffen,[1] immer noch den besten Versuch darstellt, das Eindringen kanaanäischer religiöser Elemente und Begriffe
durch den vom Königtum geförderten Staatssynkretismus zu erklären.

*4. Durch das Königtum bedingte, synkretistische Elemente in der israeliti-
schen Religion.* a) Eine vollständige Behandlung dieses Gegenstandes
würde eine eigens zu diesem Zweck verfasste Monographie benöti-
gen; wir werden uns also hier auf einige Hauptelemente beschränken
müssen.

Wir haben gesehen, dass wir das von Dtr. G. entworfene theo-
kratische Bild der vorköniglichen israelitischen Verfassung im grossen
Ganzen als glaubwürdig betrachten können; wir haben weiter festgestellt, dass Salomo sich einen Platz im Kultus sicherte durch den
Tempelbau und die Übernahme gewisser bestimmten priesterlicher
Befugnisse, wenn auch nur zu Anlässen; wir dürfen vielleicht noch
sagen, dass das königliche Patronat über den Tempel ihm nicht nur
eine Rolle, sondern die Hauptrolle im Kultus sicherte, weswegen auch
in vorexilischer Zeit kaum die Rede von einem Hohepriester ist. Diese
Entwicklung vollzog sich, wie gesehen, innerhalb weniger Jahrzehnte,
wenn auch nicht ohne grossen Widerstand, und erklärt das gebrochene
Verhältnis der isrealitischen Religion gegenüber der Monarchie. Die
Behauptung G. FOHRERS, die am Anfang dieses Aufsatzes zitiert wurde,
dass das Königtum einen der Hauptimpulse der israelitischen Religion
gebildet hat, hat sich also historisch bewährt. Wir dürfen allerdings
noch hinzufügen, dass dieser Impuls stark in die Richtung einer An-
gleichung Israels an die herrschenden Begriffe und Bräuche Südsyriens
gedrängt hat, wenigstens was die erste Hälfte des 1. Jtds. v. C. betrifft.
Hierzu gibt es viele konkrete Beispiele.

b) Das Verhältnis des Königs zum Gotte Israels, also zu Jahwe,
wurde nach kanaanäischem Muster durch ein Adoptions- bzw. Legiti-
mationsverfahren begründet, der vermutlich zur Zeit und im Ritual
der Thronbesteigung, wie dies eindrücklich in Ps. ii 7, vgl. noch 2
Sam. vii 14 und Jes. ix 5, dargestellt ist,[2] stattfand. Für die Legitima-

---

[1] K.-H. BERNHARDT, *Das Problem*..., S. 92 ff.; B. LACK, „Les origines d'ᶜElyôn,
le Très-Haut, dans la tradition cultuelle d'Israel," *CBQ* 24 (1962), S. 44-64, der
auf die Verbreitung des ᶜEljôn-Kultus aufmerksam macht, weswegen Israel gar
nicht erst auf die Eroberung Jerusalems zu warten brauchte, um ihn sich anzu-
eignen; und ferner J. C. GREENFIELD, Rezension in *JAOS* 87 (1967), S. 631-633,
welcher sich fragt, ob man so nicht zuviel in Gen xiv 18-20 hineinliest.

[2] Für den ersten Begriff vgl. meinen Aufsatz „Zum zweiten Psalm," in *Wort-
Gebot-Glaube*, W. EICHRODT *zum* 80. *Geburtstag* (ATANT Nr. 59), Zürich 1970,

tion spricht, wenn auch nur mittelbar, zweifelsohne die Tatsache, dass ein Adoptionsverfahren im Alten Testament nicht oder kaum bezeugt ist und es deswegen nicht leicht ist, sich einen solchen Begriff für den König zu Jerusalem vorzustellen, wie H. DONNER gezeigt hat; auch diese Frage kann hier natürlich nicht ausführlicher untersucht werden. Wichtig ist aber die Feststellung, dass auch in Ugarit ähnliche Begriffe für die Beziehungen zwischen der Gottheit und dem König, wenn auch mit viel stärkenen, mythischen Zügen, belegt sind: König *Krt* ist zwar im Text (Gordon) Nr. 125, 10-11 körperlich nur der Sohn seiner Eltern, und nicht auch des 'El und der *Qdš*, aber sein langersehnter Nachfolger, *Jṣb*, wird an der Brust der ^cAnat gesäugt, vgl. Text Nr. 128, II, 125; es handelt sich also eher um ein Pflegeverhältnis als um eines der Adoption bzw. Legitimation. Auf diese Art konnte nunmehr die Dialektik Theokratie—Monarchie insofern überwunden werden, als der König während des Rituals seiner Thronbesteigung und vielleicht auch in den Zeremonien, mit denen dieser jährlich gedacht wurde, durch dies besondere, ihm eigene Verhältnis zu Jahwe, der das „wirkliche" Königtum ausübte, durch die Sohnschaft zum irdischen Vertreter ernannt wurde, wodurch gleichzeitig jeglicher Zeugungsgedanke nach ägyptischem Muster ausgeschlossen war.

c) Als „Gottessohn," wenn auch nach der beschriebenen, beschränkten Art, verwundert es nicht, dass der König Ps. xlv 7 als *'elōhîm* angeredet wird,[1] oder dass 2 Sam. xxi 17 die Männer Davids ihn beschwören, nicht mehr mit ihnen in die Schlacht zu ziehen, „Damit du den Leuchter Israels nicht auslöschest," vgl. ferner den Satz Lam. iv 20: „Der Odem unserer Nase, der Gesalbte Jahwes, wurde in ihrer Grube gefangen; derjenige von dem wir sagten: ,In seinem Schatten können wir unter den Völkern am Leben bleiben!' " [2] An letzterer Stelle scheint mir besonders wichtig die Tatsache, dass der Sänger anscheinend glaubte, ohne König nicht leben zu können, ohne Land in der Verbannung aber wohl, ein theologisch gewagter Satz, gehört doch die Landesverheissung zu den ursprünglichen Elementen der Religion Israels, das Königtum aber offensichtlich nicht. Auch die von falschen Zeugen erhobene Anklage gegen Naboth 1 Reg. xxi 10,

---

S. 191-207, bes. S. 194 f. (mit Literatur); für den zweiten H. DONNER, „Adoption oder Legitimation?" *Or. Ant.* 8 (1969), S. 87-119 (auf S. 113 Anm. 138 die Literatur zum Adoptionsgedanken), einen Artikel den ich für den letztgenannten nicht mehr gründlich verwenden konnte.

[1] Der Psalm ist vorexilisch.

[2] Für die beiden letzten Stellen vgl. A. R. JOHNSON, *Sacral Kingship in ancient Israel*, Cardiff ²1967, S. 1 ff.

13, er habe „Gott und König" verflucht, zeugt von dieser Wertung
der Monarchie, umsomehr als wir kein Gesetz kennen, das Gott und
König auf diese Art in einem Zug erwähnt und verbietet, den letzteren
zu verfluchen. So ein Gesetz hätte manchen Propheten in eine schwierige Lage bringen können! Die Paarung erscheint noch Ps. ii 2c.[1] Ja,
falls es zum Kriege kommt, gürtet Jahwe ihn selbst, Ps. xviii 40; sonst
erhebt ihn ᶜEljôn hoch über die anderen Menschen empor, 2 Sam.
xxiii 1.[2]

d) Sogar die Fruchtbarkeitsideologie Kanaans, der Gegenstand der
erbittersten Worte der Propheten und des Dtn., wird im Alten Testa-

---

[1] Dass dieser Satz nicht gestrichen werden darf, hoffe ich im oben Anm. 2,
S. 22 f. erwähnten Aufsatz, S. 193, bewiesen zu haben. Das Gegenteil bei S. HERR-
MANN, *Die prophetischen Heilserwartungen*. . ., S. 101 Anm. 45, doch ohne Begründ-
ung. Bei den jüngeren Kommentaren geschieht das nur bei H. J. KRAUS, (BK XV,
1), Neukirchen ²1962; G. R. CASTELLINO, Torino 1955, strukturieren den ganzen
Satz anders.

[2] Lies הֻקָּם anstatt von *ḥuqqām* (= M.T.), sodass עַל, wie manchmal im Alten
Testament, eine abgekürzte Form von ᶜEljôn ist, mit É. DHORME, *Les livres de
Samuel*, Paris 1910; H. S. NYBERG, *art. cit.* S. 378; H. CAZELLES, „La titulature du
Roi David," in *Mélanges bibliques*. . A. ROBERT, Paris [1957], S. 131-153, bes. S. 133
und jüngstens H. N. RICHARDSON, „The last words of David: some notes on II
Sam. 23, 1-7," *JBL* 90 (1971), p. 257-266. A. R. JOHNSON, a.a.O. S. 18 Anm. 1
scheint mir hier zu vorsichtig. Der Tatbestand ist ziemlich eindeutig: der M.T.:
„Orakel des Menschen, der hoch emporgehoben wurde" passt nicht zum Parallelismus mit dem im folgenden Vers bezeugten „Gott Jakobs" und wirkt im Zusammenhang banal, vgl. die Einzelheiten bei G. BRESSAN, *Samuele*, Torino 1954
(= ²1963). Die Seltenheit von ᶜāl als Substantiv wird von allen Wörterbüchern
vermerkt, vgl. ferner schon S. R. DRIVER, *The Books of Samuel*, Oxford ²1913,
S. 356. Unser Fall ist endlich einzigartig: das Wort steht alleine, ohne Präposition,
als Objekt eines Verbes, sodass es als *hápax legómenon* zu klassifizieren wäre. Über
2 Sam xxiii 1-7 teilen sich die Ansichten über das Alter: für RICHARDSON ist das
Stück sehr alt, für S. HERRMANN a.a.O. S. 100, bes. Anm. 41 und L. PERLITT,
Bundestheologie im Alten Testament (WMANT Nr. 36), Neukirchen 1969 ist das
Stück jung. Der 2. Teil von Ps. xviii ist vorexilisch. Alle hier vermerkten Datie-
rungen stammen hauptsächlich aus (E. SELLIN-) G. FOHRER, *Einleitung in das Alte
Testament*, Wiesbaden ¹⁰1965 (= ¹¹1969), S. 308 ff.

Die Frage, ob es berechtigt ist, von einem „Sacralen Königtum," u.A. mit
G. WIDENGREN und A. R. JOHNSON zu reden, muss hier unbeantwortet bleiben;
manche werden auch hier eine Auseinandersetzung mit der skandinavischen
Forschung und der *Myth and Ritual School* vermissen. Mir scheint, vorläufig, dass
die Bezeichnung und was sie einschliesst höchstens übertrieben, nicht aber falsch
ist, auch wenn man kein allgemeines, einigermassen homogenes kultisches Schema
(pattern) für den alten Orient annehmen kann, weil es jede Nuance zu bedecken
droht. Man darf aber wohl fragen, ob die oft lautgewordene Kritik nicht eher
einzelne Übertreibungen als die Hauptsache selbst trifft. Für diese Kritik vgl.
M. NOTH, „Gott, König, Volk im Alten Testament," *ZThK* 47 (1950), S. 157-191
(= *Gesammelte Studien*, Bd. I, München ³1966, S. 188-229); J. DE FRAINE, *L'aspect
religieux de la royauté israélite* (Analecta Biblica Nr. 3), Roma 1954, *passim* und
K.-H. BERNHARDT, a.a.O. Kap. 7.

ment irgendwie mit dem Königtum verbunden, genau wie dies in den Texten Ugarits belegt ist: wenn dort der König erkrankt, erkrankt auch die Natur, vgl. Text Nr. 125, 10-23 und das 'Aqht-Epos. Im Alten Testament sind uns allerdings nur wenige, zerstreute Reste dieser Gedanken bekannt: Ps. xxi 5: „Du (der König) hast ihn (Jahwe) um Leben gebeten, und du (Jahwe) hast es ihm gewährt, eine ewige, nie aufhörende Langlebigkeit!"; Ps. lxxii 6: „Steige er (der König) hinab, wie Tau auf das gemähte Gras, wie der Regen auf die Erde fällt (?)"; oder dortselbst, V. 16: weil der König lebt, „Wird es einen Überfluss an Getreide im Land geben, auf den Höhen der Hügel; die Ähren werden wogen wie die Bäume auf dem Libanon und die Bewohner der Städte werden erblühen wie das Gras der Erde." Beide Psalmen sind vorexilisch. Auch Israel also, oder wenigstens gewisse Hofkreise, scheinen eine Art von Lebens- und Fruchtbarkeitsideologie mit der Person des Königs als solcher, und nicht nur im Zusammenhang mit seiner Gerechtigkeit, verbunden zu haben,[1] ein Gedanke der aber entweder nicht lebensfähig, weil er Israels Religion zu fremd war, oder aber später fleissig aus den zu überliefernden Texten entfernt wurde, sodass nur ganz geringe Reste von ihm übrig geblieben sind. Solches Gut war sowieso mit dem Untergang des Königtums 587 zum Aussterben verurteilt.

5. Ausblick. Das Königtum ist bekanntlich mit der zweiten Deportation untergegangen und nie mehr aufgerichtet worden in Israel, von der kurzen, makkabäischen Zwischenzeit abgesehen, deren Könige jedoch nie als legitim betrachtet wurden. Doch der Königsgedanke lebte in nachexilischer Zeit weiter, wenn auch der grösste Teil seines synkretistischen Zubehörs entweder unterging oder in grundsätzlich umgearbeiteter Form, praktisch unkenntlich gemacht, erhalten blieb. Das wird ersichtlich aus den Königspsalmen lxxxix und cxxxii, in denen in nachexilischer Zeit vorexilisches Gut verarbeitet wird [2] und

---

[1] Angesichts dieser letzten, aber z.T. auch der vorher erwähnten Stellen, bin ich nicht sicher, ob der von R. HENTSCHKE, „Die sakrale Stellung des Königs in Israel," *Evang.-Luth. Kirchenzeitung* 9 (1955), S. 69-74 herausgearbeitete Unterschied zwischen Israel und Kanaan auf diesem Gebiet, folgens dem sich der erstere auf die Geschichte, der zweite sich auf die Natur stütze, konsequent haltbar ist. Er hat natürlich Recht, wenn er behauptet, das Problem sei eines der meistumstrittenen.

[2] Ps. lxxxix 39.52 und cxxxii 10 brauchen beide den Titel *māšîaḥ* nicht, wie HERRMANN und PERLITT, a.a.O. es behaupten, „für einen *erwarteten* Herrscher aus davidischen Stamm" (Sperrung von mir), sondern einfach für den herrschenden oder höchstens für den abgesetzten König; er kann also für Datierungzwecke

die alte, israelitische Theologie erhalten bleibt und sich entwickelt. Dabei ergibt sich das Paradox, dass, um das Königtum erst recht in eine Institution der israelitischen Religion zu verwandeln, zu der es kein gebrochenes Verhältnis, sondern eine klare Hoffnung gab, es seiner Zerstörung auf politischem Gebiet bedurfte. Denn nun vermochte sich erst recht der Gedanke vom Königtum, von politischen und religiös-synkretistischen Kompromissen befreit, zu entfalten, indem es sich zur messianischen Hoffnung bildete, was allerdings erst einige Jahrhunderte später geschehen konnte.

nicht gebraucht werden. Für das Wort selbst vgl. E. KUTSCH, *Salbung als Rechtsakt* (BZAW Nr. 87), Berlin 1963, S. 53. Auf die Einzelprobleme dieser beiden Psalmen kann hier nicht eingegangen werden. Folgende Werke und Abhandlungen konnte ich nicht mehr benützen: L. SCHMIDT, *Menschlicher Erfolg und Jahwes Intiative* (WMANT Nr. 38), Neukirchen 1970; F. STOLZ, *Strukturen und Figuren im Kult von Jerusalem* (BZAW Nr. 118), Berlin 1970; R. SMEND, ,,Zur Frage nach der israelitischen Amphiktyonie", *Ev. Theol.* 31 (1971), S. 623-630, sowie einige Aufsätze aus den *Near Eastern Studies in Honor of* WILLIAM FOXWELL ALBRIGHT, Baltimore 1971. (Korrekturnachtrag).

AN ASPECT OF SACRIFICE

BY

P. A. H. DE BOER

Leiden

I. Divine Bread

Some remarks on the meaning of לחם הפנים

In the rabbinic discussions about *leḥem (ha)pānîm* the difficulty of reconciling Lev. xxiv 8 with the daily necessity of preparing essential food is reflected. The regulation, described as a perpetual obligation of the Israelites, reads: "every sabbath day he shall set it (the bread) in order before Yhwh continually." [1] Although the text does not mention baking, but prescribes the table arrangement in the temple before Yhwh, the inference of baking once a week just before each new sabbath is obvious.[2] GALLING mentions at least the possibility of a daily renewal of the loaves [3] and NOTH remarks in connection with Ex. xxv 23-30, "The table is chiefly for the "bread of the Presence" (v. 30), i.e. for the cakes of bread which are to be set down—and renewed daily—as gifts before the "Presence" of Yahweh." [4] However, they deviate from the text of Leviticus.

The bread set down before Yhwh is to be eaten by Aaron and his sons, that is by the priests, "and they shall eat it in a holy place." [5] The bread would have been moulded and stone-hard on the "ninth

---

[1] Lev. xxiv 8. The subject, 3rd pers., does not correspond to the second person in the verses 5f, where Moses is meant. *RSV* adds Aaron, an interpretative rendering. Cf. too M. HARAN, "The complex of ritual acts performed inside the Tabernacle", *Scripta Hierosolymitana*, Vol. VIII Jerusalem 1961, p. 278f. M. NOTH, commentary *ATD*, 1962, p. 155, supposes "eine spätere Regelung", because of Ex. xxv 30.

[2] Comp. Josephus, Ant. III, x, 7: "bread without leaven... baked the day before the sabbath... they remained till another sabbath, and then other loaves were brought in their stead; the loaves were given to the priests for food, the frankincense was sacrificially burnt..."

[3] K. GALLING, *RGG*, 3rd ed., *sub voce* Tempelgeräte in Israel (1962), "die täglich oder wöchentlich erneuert wurden."

[4] M. NOTH, commentary *ATD*, Exodus, 1959, p. 167, "wohl täglich erneut." In the English translation, 1962, p. 206, "and renewed daily."

[5] Lev. xxiv 9.

day," [1] and the question which is asked in the midrashic explanation of this requirement, "It is usual for a king to eat fresh bread. Would he eat stale bread?" is as understandable as the comment of Joshua ben Levi, "A great miracle occurred with *leḥem hapānîm:* at its removal it was similar to its piling up." [2] It is not surprising that ways have been sought to curtail this great miracle which so clearly contradicts the daily experience with the bread as food. In connection with the text of Leviticus, which speaks of two rows, rather piles, of six (flat) cakes to which pure frankincense must be added, and concerning the service of the sons of Qohat in the tent of meeting, who must keep the table in the sanctuary in order (Numb. iv 4ff.), an explanation is given to the articles required on the table, *hamm^enaqqijjôt*, which must keep the bread acceptably fresh.[3] "By *m^enaqqijjôt*—as we read in Midrash rabbah to Numbers [4]—the tubes are meant. There were twenty-eight hollow tubes of gold, susceptible to defilement... fourteen for one pile and fourteen for the other pile. ... Why were tubes inserted between them (i.e. the cakes)? So that the air might have free access to them and prevent the bread from becoming mouldy." The libation jars (Ex. xxv 29) also are interpreted as hollow canes,[5] which ought to have had the same function. It is stated in the Mishnah that the loaves of the so-called Shewbread were prepared in a mould.[6] Rabbi Meir says, "... a space of two handbreadths was left in the midst (of two rows), so that the wind could blow between them.[7]

The rabbinic discussions pertain to texts from writings which they believed to be holy and in large measure to those which contain the laws for the temple. Thus they do not deal with actual practice. But the difficulty, which led to artificial explanation in the rabbinic literature, must have also existed before the temple was destroyed. The image on the arch of Titus shows that a table was among the precious

---

[1] Midrash rabba on Leviticus: "The shewbread was not eaten less than nine days after baking, and not more than eleven days after. How is this to be understood? It was baked on the Sabbath eve, and eaten on the Sabbath after nine days; if a festival happened to fall on the Sabbath eve it was eaten after ten days; if the two festival-days of New Year (preceded the Sabbath) it was eaten after eleven days, as mentioned in Tanhuma." Translation of J. J. SLOTKI, The Soncino Press, London, 1961, p. 411.

[2] נס גדול נעשה בלחם הפבים סילוקו כסידורו bMenahot 96b.

[3] מנקיות אלה קנים bMenahot 97a. The passage continues a discussion on the form of the standards which must support the cakes on a pile.

[4] IV 14. SLOTKI's translation, op. cit., p. 114.

[5] bMenahot 96a. See too Rashi ad Ex. xxv 29.

[6] Menahot XI 1 טפוס.

[7] Menahot XI 5 כדי שתהא הרוח מנשבת ביניהם.

things of the temple of Herod. Vessels can be seen on this represen-
tation of a table, but it remains uncertain whether it represents the
table of the so-called Shewbread. Even if we suppose it to be this
table, no information is given us about the rite. The Gospels know
the story of David in Nob, 1 Sam. xxi. In a discussion of what is
forbidden on the sabbath, Mark. ii 25f., Jesus said, "Have you never
read what David did when he and his men were hungry and had
nothing to eat? He went into the House of God, in the time of
Abiathar the high priest, and ate the sacred bread, though no one but
a priest is allowed to eat it, and even gave it to his men." [1] We remain,
however, with the uncertainty whether the rite of the bread existed
in Jesus' time. According to 1 Macc. i 22 the table of the bread of
Presence was taken from the temple together with other things by
Antiochus Epiphanes, but it was replaced by another under Judas
Maccabeus, 1 Macc. iv 49 Whether these events mean an interruption
and a restoration of the rite is not mentioned.

Both the story about David in Nob and the stipulation in Lev.
xxiv 9 leave no doubt that the bread in the sanctuary was also eaten.
The baking of bread and the consumption of it is not an affair in
Palestine which takes more than one day, let alone more than seven
days. Bread is often baked more than once a day. Though not explicitly stated to be so, the cakes were most probably unleavened. Unleavened bread is even more inedible after seven or more days. All in
all one is forced to suppose that the connection between the rite of
the loaves in the sanctuary and the rite of the sabbath every seven days
from the Priestly Code is not original.[2] To what extent the regulations

---

[1] Parallels in Matth. xii 4 and Luke vi 4.

[2] The institution of a sabbath every seven days seems to be later than the
sabbath as a special day devoted to religious duties. The bringing in of systems
with preference for numbers—seven, twelve, forty etc.—belongs to the means
with which the priestly circles after the exile regulated the faith and the community of the Judean people in order to establish and to preserve the people in a
period without national independence. Systematizing is a human attempt to master
a complicated reality. It does often clarify, but the tendency is to simplify the real
problems. If the introduction of the system is successful it in turn becomes a
reality, which reveals much about those who made the system but less about the
complicated reality which it seeks to order. NOTH's theory about the six and
twelve tribes seems to me to suffer from a neglect of this point (*Das System der
zwölf Stämme Israels*, Stuttgart, 1930; *Geschichte Israels*, 6th ed. 1966). Not the
number but other factors have caused the events, both Deborah's coalition and
David's monarchy, and Samaria's policy and so on. Common interests, common
experiences, common faith, threats from within and outside, geographic and cli-
matic conditions, dominant personalities, vigorous counties and towns—there are
so many factors which can determine situations and periods. During the rise of

about the baking, the placing of the dozen cakes in two piles or rows, and the information about the construction of the table, or tables,[1] about the sons of Qohat,[2] and about the consumption of the bread in a holy place by the priests—"since it is for him (Aaron and his sons) a most holy portion out of the offerings [3] to Yhwh, a perpetual due," Lev. xxiv 9—contain data derived from the practice of believers will never be known with certainty. Should the connection of the rite, setting down before the deity a table spread with food and drink, with the sabbath every seven days be secondary, and should the regulations contain still more artificial traits whose origins are to be found in the closed circles of priests, writers and scholars of the law,[4] the rite itself is in all probability old.[5] In order to come more closely to the meaning, which the believers of ancient Israel themselves attached to the rite, we must answer the following questions: What is the connection between the placing of the bread before Yhwh and the consumption of the bread by the priests? *(a)*. Does the name offer any indication of the significance of this special food? *(b)*.

a

That a connection existed between the placing of the bread before Yhwh and its consumption by the priests can be deduced from the story about David in Nob. Ahimelek answers David's demand for bread with the statement that there is no ordinary, only the sacred bread. This bread, however, may only be eaten by the ritually pure, that is by those who "have kept themselves from women," 1 Sam. xxi 4. The consumption is therefore no problem, only the ritual purity or uncleanness of the consumers. When David says that his expedition is a holy campaign—the story is one of the examples of David's

---

the Republic of the Netherlands, a confederation of seven provinces, not the number seven, but several other factors were determinative.

[1] Singular in 1 Kings vii 48, plural in 2 Chron. iv 19.

[2] Numb. iv 7; 1 Chron. ix 32.

[3] See J. Hoftijzer on *'ishshè* in *Baumgartner Festschrift*, *SVT* XVI, 1967, pp. 114ff.

[4] Even though historical interest was not the reason why they were occupied with ancient Israel, but rather the craving to acquire and to preserve some measure of independence in their own time and for their future, we are thankful to them that some information about ancient Israel has been preserved.

[5] Although the form in which the story of David in Nob has been preserved betrays a later revision, 1 Sam. xxi is a clear indication that the rite was known in the temples of ancient Israel. For comparable rites in neighbouring cultures see F. Blome, *Die Opfermaterie in Babylonien und Israel*, I, Rome 1934; H. Kees, *Aegypten*, 1933; W. Herrmann, "Götterspeise und Göttertrank in Ugarit und Israel," *ZAW* 1960, p. 205ff.

shrewdness—does the priest give him the sacred bread, "removed from before Yhwh, to place hot bread there, the day it was taken away," v. 7.[1] Likewise Lev. xxiv 5-9 leaves little doubt that the bread was eaten by the priests. The wording of Lev. xxiv 9 is not free from obscurity. The usual translation takes the bread as subject of the first verb and as the object of the second verb, "And it shall be for Aaron and his sons, and they shall eat it." But the first verb has a feminine subject, and the suffix of the second indicates a masculine object. We can consider *halla* and *lehem*, but we must agree with NOTH who calls it a badly constructed sentence.[2]

If we conclude from the scanty attention given by expositors to the consumption of the bread that the meaning of the rite of setting down bread before Yhwh was assumed not to lie in the eating, but in serving the bread before the deity during a specific time, several questions arise. The priestly regulations make the bread a sacrifice. BLOME points to the burning of incense and calls "das Liegenbleiben vor der Gottheit" a sacrifice, "wenn auch in eigenartiger Äusserung und Ausgestaltung." [3] DE VAUX considers *lehem hapānîm* as belonging to "offrandes végétables." [4] Likewise the burning of frankincense indicates a sacrificial character. A sacrificial character, however, does not exclude the consumption by the servants of the deity as an essential part of the rite. Neither the story in 1 Sam. xxi, nor the priestly regulation about the consumption by priests in a holy place, nor the name "divine bread" (Lev. xxi 6, 8, 17, 21f.; xxii 25), give reason to view the rite as closed when the bread is changed. On the contrary the re-

---

[1] "removed," read probably הַמּוּסָר instead of the plural, J. WELLHAUSEN, *Der Text der Bücher Samuelis*, Göttingen 1871 and many others. 4Qb supports this reading. DHORME, commentary 1910, p. 195, following WELLHAUSEN's suggestion, points to the secondary character of the expressions מִלִּפְנֵי יְהוָה and לָשׂוּם, showing P's influence, cf. Lev. xxix 6.7.8 and Ex. xl 23. Cf. H. GRESSMANN, *Die älteste Geschichtsschreibung* etc., 1910, and A. SCHULZ, commentary 1919. SCHULZ, p. 318ff., on verse 7b: a copyist displaying his knowledge of the law. H. W. HERTZBERG, commentary *ATD*, 1965, translates verse 7b in agreement with P as follows: "Die werden (sonst) vom Angesicht des Herrn (nur) entfernt, wenn man an dem Tag, da man's wegnimmt, frisches Brot hinlegt."

[2] Commentary Leviticus, *ATD*, p. 155: "dieser schlecht formulierte Satz." The *NEB* solves the difficulty by a paraphrastic rendering: "(8) ...This is a covenant for ever; (9) it is the privilege of Aaron and his sons, and they shall eat the bread...."

[3] BLOME, op. cit., par. 234.

[4] R. DE VAUX, *Les Institutions de l'Ancien Testament*, Vol. II, 1960, pp. 301f. In his *Les Sacrifices de l'Ancien Testament*, 1964, p. 38, he writes: "on traduirait mieux: les "pains personel" de Yahvé," a rendering borrowed from A. R. JOHNSON, "Aspects of the use of the Term *pānîm* in the Old Testament," in *Festschrift Eissfeldt*, Halle 1947, pp. 155-159.

moval of the bread in order to eat it seems to be the high point of the
rite. By consuming the sacred cakes the servants belong to the House
of their deity and are able to perform the divine service in the sanctuary. By eating the sacred cakes David received the strength to escape
Saul's threat of death and so Yhwh's purpose for David was realized.
The necessity of divine bread to the fulfillment of god's purpose by
his servants found expression in the addition *tamîd*, continually.[1] The
idea of bringing food to the deity is not contrary to the idea of re-
ceiving strength from that deity and might have been expressed in
one and the same rite.

b

The name of the cakes put before Yhwh is *leḥem hapānîm*. In addition to this name there is a series of other names, all derived from the
description of the rite. Except in 2 Chron. iv 19, a text parallel to
1 Kings vii 48, the Chronicler avoids the term *hapānîm*. He stresses
the setting in rows, using forms derived from the stem *ʿrk*, see the
summary of the terms used on page 33. This term, setting in rows,
also describes the table, and occurs as a substantive with *tamîd*. Ex.
xl 23 uses the same term: to set the row of breads in order on the table.

It seems evident that the ancient name is *leḥem hapānîm*, literally
translated, "facial bread." Once *hapānîm* also occurs as a description
of the table, Numb. iv 7, after which a list is given of what must be
placed on the table: the dishes, saucers, flagons, bowls and the *leḥem
tamîd*, "the continual bread," according to the Revised Version; "the
Bread regularly presented" according to the New English Bible. The
ancient versions excepting the Vulgate use next to renderings derived
from the description of the rite a literal translation, "bread of the
face." A survey of the texts with their rendering in the ancient versions
is given on page 33.

The rendering "Schaubrot" (Luther), "showbread", or "shewbread"
(Tyndale) [2] loses ground. Also *panes propositionis* (Vulgate), adopted
by many translators, is not adequate. It tells what should be done with
the cakes but does not translate *hapānîm*. The rendering, "les pains
d'obligation," [3] which coincides with the Greek translation of 1 Kings

---

[1] HARAN, art. cit., brings forth arguments for the translation "regularly", but
they are not wholly convincing.

[2] See P. R. ACKROYD, in *Hasting's Dictionary of the Bible*, 2nd ed. 1963, *sub voce*
Showbread.

[3] Thus a. o. DE VAUX, *Institutions; Les Sacrifices; Bible de Jérusalem.* No full
survey of the translations is given here. Next to them mentioned in the text I

לחם הפנים	1 Sam. xxi 7 Ex. xxxv 13; xxxix 36 1 Kings vii 48 2 Chron. iv 19	ἄρτοι τοῦ προσώπου	1 Sam. xxi 7 Ex. xxxv 13 Neh. x 34 Ex. xxv 30
לחם פנים	Ex. xxv 30	ἄρτοι ἐνώπιοι	Ex. xxxix 36 xl 23
שלחן הפנים	Numb. iv 7	ἄρτοι τῆς προθέσεως	2 Chron. iv 19
לחם התמיד	Numb. iv 7		1 Chron. ix 32 xxiii 29
חלות — החלה	Levit. xxiv 5		
ערך לחם	Ex. xl 23	ἄρτοι προκείμενοι	Ex. xxxix 36
לחם המערכת	Neh. x 34 1 Chron. ix 32 xxiii 29	ἄρτοι ἄρτοι διὰ παντός	Levit. xxiv 5 Numb. iv 7
מערכת לחם	2 Chron. xiii 11	ἄρτοι τῆς προσφορᾶς	1 Kings vii 48
מערכת תמיד	2 Chron. ii 3	προθέσεις ἄρτων	2 Chron. xiii 11
שלחן המערכת	2 Chron. xxix 18	προθέσις διὰ παντός	2 Chron. ii 3
שלחנות המערכת	1 Chron. xxviii 16	τράπεζα προκειμένα	Numb. iv 7
		τράπεζα τῆς προθέσεως	2 Chron. xxix 18
		τράπεζαι τῆς προθέσεως	1 Chron. xxviii 16

ܠܚܡܐ ܕܐ̈ܦܐ	1 Sam. xxi 7 Ex. xxxv 13 xxxix 36 1 Kings vii 48 2 Chron. iv 19	לח(י)ם אפיא	1 Sam. xxi 7 Ex. xxv 30 xxxv 13 xxxix 36 1 Kings vii 48 2 Chron. iv 19
ܐ̈ܦܐ ܠܚܡܐ	Ex. xxv 30	פתורא דלחים אפיא	Numb. iv 7
ܦܬܘܪܐ ܕܐ̈ܦܐ	Numb. iv 7	לחמא תדירא	Numb. iv 7
ܠܚܡܐ ܐܡܝܢܐܝܬ	Numb. iv 7	גריצן — גריצתא	Levit. xxiv 5
ܚ̈ܝܘܬܐ — ܚܕܐ	Levit. xxiv 5	סדרין דלחים	Ex. xl 23
ܕܠܚܡܐ ܣܕܪ̈ܐ	Ex. xl 23 2 Chron. xiii 11	לחם סדורא	1 Chron. ix 32 xxiii 29
ܠܚܡܐ ܕܣܕܪ̈ܐ	1 Chron. ix 32 xxiii 29	סדור לחמא	2 Chron. xiii 11
		לחם תדירא	2 Chron. ii 3
ܠܚܡܐ ܕܦܪܝܫܘܬܐ	Neh. x 34	פתורא דסדורא	2 Chron. xxix 18
ܦܬܘܪ̈ܐ ܕܐ̈ܦܐ	1 Chron. xxviii 16	פתוריא דסדוריא	1 Chron. xxviii 16

panes propositionis	1 Sam. xxi 7 Ex. xxv 30 xxxv 13 xxxix 36 xl 23 1 Kings vii 48 2 Chron. iv 19 Neh. x 34 1 Chron. ix 32 xxiii 29
panes	Levit. xxiv 5
mensa propositionis	Numb. iv 7 2 Chron. xxix 18
panes semper	Numb. iv 7
propositio panum	2 Chron. ii 3
proponere panes	2 Chron. xiii 11
mensae propositionis	1 Chron. xxviii 16

vii 48, indicates the sacrificial character but is similarly not a translation of *hapānîm*. A new translation of the Torah, published by the Jewish Publication Society of America [1], reads, "the bread of display." This is more or less in the line of the rabbinic tradition but is still no real translation of the term.[2] The translation of BUDDE, "Brot der persönlichen Gegenwart, ..." [3] we find in the commentaries of SMITH,[4] CASPARI [5] and others and has become acceptable in the English speaking world through the Revised Standard Version and the New English Bible. This rendering derives the meaning "Presence" for *hapānîm* from the statement which follows, "put, or, set down in order, before me, before Yhwh, *lᵉp̄anaj, lip̄ne Yhwh*. If we accept that "Presence" is a genuin translation of *hapānîm*, the sequence, *lᵉp̄anaj*, or, *lip̄ne Yhwh*, is almost a tautology.[6] This seems to me a valid objection. Moreover "Presence" is an interpretative rendering and not a real translation of *hapānîm*. This term means *face* and as far as I see nothing else. In his explanation of the translation "Les pains de proposition" DHORME rightly observes: "littéralement 'pains de la face'," but when he continues: "ainsi nommés parce qu'ils sont placés 'en face de Iahvé'," he too is close to a tautology.[7] The literal translation we find in the commentaries of SCHULZ,[8] NOTH [9] and HERTZBERG.[10]

In a well documented article, "Aspects of the use of the Term *pânîm* in the Old Testament," A. R. JOHNSON has proposed to translate "Yahweh's 'personel' bread." [11] The idea seems to me correct that the term indicates the divine character of the bread. These special cakes belong to the deity, a fact which is expressed by putting them before him. They are the food of the deity like *leḥem 'ᵉlohîm*,[12] and

---

quote here Rashi's "bread with faces," commenting, "because it had faces (surfaces) looking in both directions towards the sides of the House (the Sanctuary)." A. M. SILBERMANN's edition and translation, London 1946, p. 136a. Cf. Th. ERPENIUS' rendering *panis facierum*, in *Samuelis libri duo Ebraice et Latine*, Leiden 1621.

[1] Philadelphia, 1967, 2nd ed.
[2] Cf. Rashi and his predecessors.
[3] K. BUDDE, commentary, 1902, p. 148.
[4] H. P. SMITH, commentary *ICC*, p. 198.
[5] W. CASPARI, commentary, 1926.
[6] See CASPARI, op. cit., p. 268: "לפני, neben פנים fast tautologisch, ..."
[7] DHORME, commentary, p. 195. Cf. too his translation with notes in *La Bible*, Pléiade, 1956, Vol. I, p. 889.
[8] SCHULZ, commentary, p. 318ff.
[9] NOTH, commentary *ATD*, Exodus, 1959, p. 167 (E.T. "bread of the Presence").
[10] HERTZBERG, commentary *ATD*.
[11] JOHNSON, art. cit., p. 155. He refers to 2 Sam. xvii 11 where פנים = נשׂפ.
[12] Lev. xxi 6.8.17; xxii 25.

simultaneously at god's disposal. The construct of the term shows a genitive used as explicative of the preceding noun, indicating its quality or the genitive of specification.[1] A literal rendering of the term is "facial bread."

The visibility of the deity has been suppressed in the Jewish circles which have handed down to us the Israelite tradition. But there are enough traces in the texts of the ancient belief in god's face, traditions about his ability to see as well traditions about his being seen by his believers. Both in agreement with its construct and with the idea of god's visibility, I think that *hapānîm* indicates Yhwh's face which might have been portrayed on the loaves by a bread stamp.

If this suggestion is right, the rite of the "facial cakes" would date from the period of ancient Israel, in which Yhwh's worshippers, his special servants and his believers who had "hallowed" themselves, ate the holy bread. Yhwh himself is the host who presents himself to his believers, giving divine strength, divine life.[2] The rite of the "facial bread" has rightly been classified with the sacrifices, the vegetable sacrifices. It demonstrates that a sacrifice is simultaneously a gift to the deity as well as a gift presented by the deity. The idea of divine bread, god's food as well as man's, dates from times in which no distinction was made between natural and spiritual life.

Cakes stamped with an image of the deity, baked for sacrifice, are also mentioned in Jeremiah, vii 18 and xliv 19. The Prose Tradition in the Book of Jeremiah [3] makes mention of burning incense, pouring out libations and baking cakes marked with the image of a female deity. This cult was practised in Jerusalem and Judah, and among the exiles in Egypt. The literary form of the stories, and closely related herewith the repulsion of this cult may be much later but the worship of the goddess is pre-exilic. Her name is Queen of Heaven. It seems likely that she is worshipped in Mesopotamia as Ishtar. In Palestine she might have been identical with ᶜAnat.[4]

---

[1] Examples of the construct e.g. in A.B. DAVIDSON's *Hebrew Syntax*, 3rd ed. 1902, par. 24.

[2] CASPARI, commentary, p. 268, quotes WÜNSCH, Archiv für Religionswissenschaft, 1904, p. 115f.: "der Gläubige stifted das Brot, der Priester weiht es zur Speise Gottes; dann verteilt er es; die Essenden treten in heilvolle Gemeinschaft mit der Gottheit."

[3] Carefully treated by E. W. NICHOLSON in his recent monograph, *Preaching to the Exiles*, Oxford (Blackwell), 1970.

[4] Many commentators identify the Queen of Heaven with the goddess Ishtar from Mesopotamia. G. WIDENGREN, in his *Sakrales Königtum im Alten Testament und im Judentum*, Stuttgart 1955, p. 12, thinks it probable that the goddess ᶜAnat

These remarks on the expression *leḥem hapānîm*, "facial bread," do not cover every aspect of the subject. I will not give in to the temptation to allude to the idea of "bread from heaven," "bread of life," occurring in poetical texts of the Old Testament and in Christian rites, about which Lady DROWER wrote such a charming book.[1] My purpose is to draw attention to a somewhat neglected aspect of sacrifice — that is its gift character as presented by the deity. The believers offer the cakes but they are marked as divine, bearing the image of the deity. By setting them before Yhwh they acknowledge that the cakes belong to god. And god himself allows his believers to eat them. The sacrificial meal is in my opinion the climax of the rite, symbolizing god's favour, granting strength and salvation to his believers.

I conclude with a passage from W. ROBERTSON SMITH's *Lectures on the Religion of the Semites*,[2] "According to antique ideas, those who eat and drink together are by this very act tied to one another by a bond of friendship and mutual obligation. Hence we find that in ancient religions all the ordinary functions of worship are summed up in the sacrificial meal, and that the ordinary intercourse between gods and men has no other form, we are to remember that the act of eating and drinking together is the solemn and stated expression of the fact that all who share the meal are brethren, and that the duties of friendship and brotherhood are implicitly acknowledged in their common act. By admitting man to his table the god admits him to his friendship; but this favour is extended to no man in his private capacity; he is received as one of a community, to eat and drink along with his fellows, and in the same measure as the act of worship cements the bond between him and his god, it cements also the bond between him and his brethren in the common faith."

---

is meant. I follow his suggestion and refer to his arguments. In my opinion Gen. i 26 preserves another allusion to this goddess, see my "Genesis 1, een uiteenzetting" (an exposition about three strata in Gen. i) in *Theologie en Praktijk*, XXX 4, 1971, pp. 162f. The idea of a consort of god has become unacceptable for the priestly writers. Dr. H. J. FRANKEN draws my attention to "model bread offerings" found in Beth-shan, cf. A. ROWE, *The Four Canaanite Temples of Beth-shan*, 1939 and F. W. JAMES, *The Iron Age at Beth-shan*, Philadelphia 1966. Some of them have stamp impressions, probably comparable to unpublished seal found at Tell Deir ᶜAllā.

[1] E. S. DROWER, *Water into Wine* London 1956, especially chapter III, pp. 41-60.

[2] 3rd ed. London 1927, p. 265.

II. GOD'S FRAGRANCE

> . . . . *Let the fragrance linger!*
> *Let it bring here the great gods!*

from an Old Babylonian Prayer
translated by A. GOETZE, *JCS* 22

It is clear from various Old Testament texts that believers conceived of their god in an anthropomorphic form. The psalmist says contemptuously of strange gods: "they have mouths, but do not speak; they have eyes, but do not see; they have ears, but hear not; they have noses, but do not smell; their hands—they do not feel; their feet—they do not walk; and there comes no sound out of their throats." [1] And concerning the gods which are worshipped during the Exile, the faithful follower of Yhwh says: "the work of men's hands, from wood and stone, that does not see, does not hear, does not eat, does not smell." [2]

If we may conclude from this how the faithful imagined their own god, the following characteristics emerge: he speaks; he sees; he listens; he smells; he feels; he eats; he walks. That, according to them, their god speaks is clear in almost every story handed down to us. It is basic to the premises of the editions of the historical material. The cultic and social laws are taken to have been uttered by their god and the prophets repeat god's words. That he listens, may be spoken to, is also assumed by the believer; this he experiences in the hearing of his prayers. When his prayer is not answered, he is either disappointed or rebels; in both cases the assumption is that his god can both hear and speak. God's eye is also a frequently occurring image. So too god's hand with which he can lift up or cast down. Yet more often god's sensitivity is revealed, when believers describe him as being filled with care, even pain, about his creation and his people. Less frequent is the evidence for god walking and eating. He walks in the garden of Eden [3] and when he visits the pastures, his footprints drop fatness.[4] He eats the sacrifices, which in certain passages are called "the bread of

---

[1] Ps. cxv 4-7. See the instructive discussion with the emperor in Midrash rabba, Lament. I. 16, par. 50.

[2] Deut. iv 28.

[3] Gen. iii 8.

[4] Ps. lxv 10 ff. Comp. too "And his feet shall stand in that day upon the Mount of Olives," Zech. xiv 4.

god." [1] Furthermore the usual translation of הריח (ב)ריח ניחח in Gen. viii 21 and Lev. xxvi 31 is that god smells the reassuring odour of the sacrifice. These and similar passages ask for our attention. I will only remark here that it is supposed that the ancient concept was that god fed on the rising savour, but that the following is hastly added: "Allerdings wird dieser naturhafte Gottesbegriff bereits im Alten Testament überwunden: einerseits bekommt הריח Lev. xxvi 31; Am. v 21 die ganz allgemeine Bedeutung (Opfer) annehmen, andererseits wird an diesen Stellen deutlich, dass Jahve auf die Darbringung der ὀσμή nicht angewiesen ist." [2] VON RAD considers ריח ניחח to be an antiquated phrase.[3] His note [4] is also illuminating where he remarks that there can be no question that those who have handed down these texts took this concept (of a god who eats) seriously. "Anders mag es sich verhalten," he continues, "wenn wir an die Darbringer selbst sonderlich in der frühen Kultusgeschichte denken." But my concern is for the faithful of ancient Israel and their concepts, not what writers living centuries later have made of them.

A god who speaks and who can be spoken to; who sees and—at least according to some texts [5]—is also visible; who feels and is tangible in earthquake, fire, hunger, the sword (warfare) and probably also in and on those objects which are filled with his holiness and strength, his representatives; a god who eats and who in the closed circle of his servants is also eaten [6]—but a god who can smell and is also smelt? Are Angelus Silesius' words, with which LOHMEYER closes his study *Vom göttlichen Wohlgeruch*,[7]

Die Sinne sind in Gott all ein Sinn und Gebrauch

Wer Gott beschaut, der schmeckt, fühlt, riecht und hört ihn auch also applicable to the experience of god reflected in the Old Testament?

The term "god's fragrance" is not foreign to the history of religions. "According to ancient beliefs, the divine presence made itself known by scent, the perceptible form of the invisible spirit. In particular Egyptian evidence dating from the oldest period (the pyramid texts)

---

[1] Lev. xxi; xxii.

[2] DELLING, referring to WÜRTHWEIN, in *ThWzNT*, Vol. V, 1951.

[3] VON RAD, *Theologie des Alten Testaments*, I, 1957, p. 253.

[4] *Ibidem*.

[5] Isa. i 12; Pss. xi 7; xxvii 4; lxiii 3; Gen. xxxiii 10.

[6] See my treatment of the expression לחם פנים in this Volume, pp. 27-36.

[7] Sitzungsberichte der Heidelberger Akademie der Wissenschaften, 1919; Heidelberg 1919, p. 52.

is straightforward and conclusive about this; but the concept is spread all over the ancient world. Narcissus (the flower) entices Kore with his delicious fragrance to where Hades, the god of death, takes her to himself... Scent was the etheric robe of divinity." Thus KRISTENSEN in his Introduction to the history of religion.[1] LOHMEYER draws his arguments also from the Greek and Egyptian religious texts.[2] Aelianus, in his *De natura animalium* 12, 30, tells of a spring between the Euphrates and the Tigris, in which Hera has bathed after her marriage with Zeus and that to this day the Syrians say that the place gives off a sweet scent. When Apollo and Iris were sent by Hera to Zeus,[3] they find him sitting on the top of Gargarus, "and about him a fragrant cloud was wreathed," ἥμενον, ἀμφὶ δέ μιν Θυόεν νέφος ἐστεφάνωτο. In connection with Isis and Osiris Plutarch tells how Isis came to Byblos in search of Osiris, and used her divine odour to penetrate the court where the coffin of Osiris was.[4] In his commentary HOPFNER points out, en passant, that the oldest known form of kissing was the so-called nose kiss.

HORNING, in his recent book *Der Eine und die Vielen*,[5] makes reference to the fact that queen Hatschepsut was called divine after she had fulfilled her vow to Amon to make his temple into a land of incense in the heart of Egypt once the trade mission to Punt, the far-off African land of incense, had returned. Her aura and her fragrance, the divine fragrance from Punt, revealed her divinity. BRUNNER deals extensively with the texts concerning the divine origin of the Pharaohs.[6] Amon-Re takes the form of the Pharaoh and finds the queen asleep in her palace. She awakened by the divine fragrance and smiles at him. Amon-Re burns with love and "gives his heart," an expression which BRUNNER explains as follows: he showed her who he was, not her husband, but the god. The queen sings the praises of the perfect glory of the god. "Thou hast overshadowed my majesty with the aura, thy fragrance is in all my limbs." BRUNNER comments: the queen knows, when Amon-Re reveals who he is, that her moment has come. At her marriage she knew that the god himself would beget the successor to the throne.

---

[1] W. B. KRISTENSEN, *Inleiding tot de godsdienstgeschiedenis*, Arnhem 1955, p. 150 f.
[2] *Op. cit.* p. 8 ff. I draw several examples from LOHMEYER's well-documented paper.
[3] Homer, Ilias xv, 152 ff. Translation of A. T. MURRAY, The Loeb ed. 1947.
[4] See TH. HOPFNER, edition, translation and commentary, Darmstadt 1967.
[5] Darmstadt 1971, p. 54.
[6] H. BRUNNER, *Die Geburt des Gottkönigs*, Studien zur Überlieferung eines altägyptischen Mythos, Wiesbaden 1964.

Fragrance belongs to the essential being of gods.[1] The scent is not only a sign of recognition, revelation of the god, but also vitality from which gods and men profit. Flowers are laid before the image of the god, and the believer recognizes that their fragrance is divine. He inhales the scent and knows himself to be blessed. He takes with him into battle a fragrant flower belonging to his god, for the scent imparts vital strength.

LOHMEYER also dedicates a short paragraph to the Persian religion.[2] Ormuzd was shining light, pure, fragrant, surrounded by the good, and capable of all good deeds. Ahriman was black, impure, smelly, ill-tempered... Fragrant scent is mentioned as a moral quality in Persian texts. In Jewish texts from the post-Old Testament period the idea of a sweet-smelling garden, the garden of Eden, is linked to the sacrifice. Ben Sira praises wisdom by comparing it, among other things, to the scent of the cassia or camel-thorn, myrrh, galban, aromatic shell, gum resin—the incense in the sacred tent.[3] A paraphrase of "the smell of thy nose like apples," Song of Songs vii 9, runs, the name (fame) of Daniel, Hananiah, Mishael and Azariah, their scent shall spread all over the earth like the smell of the apples in the garden of Eden. The usual translation of Gen. viii 21a runs: "When Yhwh smelled a sweet savour." The Midrash [4] explains the savour by: "He smelled the savour of the patriarch Abraham ascending from the fiery furnace; he smelled the savour of Hananiah, Mishael and Azariah ascending from the fiery furnace.—He smelled the savour of the generation of destruction" (the martyrs after Bar Kochba's revolt). Josephus also sees a connection between fragrance and the temple.[5] And Philo makes use of the literal as well as the figurative meaning: "The wise man (wisdom) emanates a beneficial odour." [6] In the Book of Jubilees [7] Noah's offering after the Flood is enlarged with oil, wine and incense, so as to make an acceptable fragrance rise to god.

This evidence recognizes a "sweet smelling fragrance," a scent that can influence the mood of the deity in a satisfactory way, but it does not do so concerning god's odour, his revelation through fragrance,

---

[1] See also H. BONNET, *Reallexikon der Ägyptischen Religionsgeschichte*, Berlin 1952, *s.v.* Wohlgeruch; Räucherung; Salben; Blumen.

[2] *Op. cit.* p. 22 f.

[3] xxiv 15. Comp. LOHMEYER, *op. cit.* p. 26, 28, 30.

[4] Gen rabba 34.

[5] Antiq. VIII 101 f. Comp. LOHMEYER, *op. cit.* p. 29.

[6] Reference in STUMPFF, *ThWzNT* II, 1935, *s.v.* εὐωδία.

[7] vi 3 f.

his vital strength given to his worshippers. The change from ריח ניחח to נחת רוח, complacency, in the Midrash [1] indicates that the rabbis were trying to avoid the anthropomorphic concept. The Septuagint translates the term with εὐωδία, ὀσμὴ εὐωδίας, sweet-smelling fragrance, without further thought about the meaning of ניחח.

The early Christian texts date from the period when foreigners had made an end to the Jewish temple. In the Jewish world opinions concerning the Law filled the vacuum of the vanished cult in their temple. Thus we find the old cultic terms used for putting the Law into practice. "He who employs himself in the study of the Law, for the sake of the Law, for him it is a balsam of life", but it is a balsam of death for those who do so but not for its sake.[2] "Thy name is as oil poured forth," Song of Songs i 3b, has been explained in the Midrash [3] with a comparison. "All the precepts which the patriarchs performed before thee were mere fragrance, but for us 'Thy name is an ointment poured forth'—two hundred and forty-eight positive commandments and three hundred and sixty-five negative commandments." Another explanation is using the phrase: the oil of the Torah. The fragrance of the temple became the fragrance of the law in the years after the destruction of the sacred place.

The Christians went on to apply old terms to Christ, their experience of god. Jesus was anointed by Mary "and the odour of the myrrh filled the whole house."[4] Paul mentions a sum of money given to the congregation at Philippi as a pleasant odour, an acceptable sacrifice, pleasing to god.[5] In Ephesians v 2 the words ὀσμὴ εὐωδίας are also linked to the sacrifice, ὁ χριστος... παρέδωκεν ἑαυτον ὑπὲρ ἡμων προσφορὰν καὶ θυσίαν τῷ θεῷ εἰς ὀσμὴν εὐωδίας. Whatever the correct explanation of this sentence may be, it is clear that the author concurs with the phrase that he knows from his Greek bible (Θυσία) ὀσμὴ εὐωδίας τῷ κυρίῳ לריח ניחח ליהוה. The concept that life and death are connected to the divine fragrance can be found in 2 Cor. ii 14-16. The fragrance of Christ is spread abroad by Paul and his disciples. The apostle calls them and himself the "sweet savour of Christ" [6] and by virtue of being this they represent for those with whom they associate the chance of life or death.

[1] Ad Numb. xv 7; xviii 17; xxviii 8 a. o.
[2] bTaᶜanit 7a.
[3] Translation of M. Simon, Soncino ed., 1939.
[4] John xii 3 f.; comp. Mark xiv 3 f.
[5] Philipp. iv 18.
χριστοῦ εὐωδία ἐσμὲν τῷ θεῷ. Comp. also H. Vorwahl, AfR 31, [1934], p. 400 f.

Whether in these texts "the progressive liberalization in biblical thought from an anthropomorphic concept of god" becomes clear—as DELLING urges [1]—seems to me unproven. The early Christian might have kept to the Jewish concept of a dual possibility, life or death, obedience or apostacy,[2] they concurred with the Old Testament terminology about sacrifice in the terminology of the Setuagint.

LOHMEYER, who deals with the Israelite religion in a short passage,[3] seeks to prove that Yhwh only reveals himself in an unrestricted way, without a real shape or form. "Wie darum der Gedanke, Jahwe könne sich in göttlich leiblicher Gestalt auf Erden offenbaren, israelitischer Religiösität fremd ist, so begegnet auch nirgends das Symbol des göttlichen Duftes als einer Form seiner Epiphanie." [4] In this way LOHMEYER is in agreement with the majority of students of the bible who restrict the anthropomorphic concept of god to those senses which can most easily be spiritualized: sight, hearing, touch. The sense of smell and taste are dropped. It seems to me that by doing this, one sets up a barrier to aspects of belief occurring in ancient Israel, and also in forms of belief which concur with Old Testament concepts.

The noun ריח, "fragrance," as well as the verb ריח, that only occurs in the Hif., is rather rare in the Hebrew texts which survived. ריח occurs both in the cult and secularly; קטרת, the ascending smoke, and also the savour burnt with the sacrifice, is exclusively a cultic word. Elsewhere [5] I tried to fix the meaning of ריח and of the verb הריח. It became clear that ריח, "fragrance," in all cases means *smell given out*, odour proceding from. I restrict myself here to some examples. In Jerem. xlviii 11 Moab is compared to wine that has not been poured out from one barrel to another, "so it kept its taste and its bouquet, ריח, did not change." [6] In the Song of Songs ריח occurs eight times with the meaning scent that emanates, ointments.[7] In Dan. iii 27 the story is told that Daniel's friends emerged from the fire unharmed, without even their clothes smelling of burning, ריח נור.[8] I did not deal with the divine fragrance in the above mentioned study, although

---

[1] *Art. cit.*

[2] Comp. the contrast Ormuzd and Ahriman in the Persian concept.

[3] *Op. cit.*, p. 25 f. See also J. ZIEGLER, *Dulcedo Dei*, Münster 1937, p. 8.

[4] *Ibidem*, p. 25.

[5] In *Words and Meanings*, essays presented to David Winton THOMAS, Cambridge 1968, pp. 29-38.

[6] *Ibidem*, p. 32.

[7] *Ibidem*, p. 31 f.

[7] *Ibidem*, p. 32.

there were two passages discussed which could serve as an introduction to such an examination.

In Exod. xxx 22 ff. two instructions are given, one about how to make a certain sort of ointment, with which the objects in the temple and the priests had to be anointed, vv. 22-30; and one about how to make a certain sort of sweet-smelling fragrance to be used in the sanctuary, vv. 34-36. The ointment as well as the perfume are said to be absolutely holy. Anyone making it for secular use shall be cut off from his people, a regulation and punishment which clearly underline the cultic character of the given recipes for this ointment and perfume. In the last verse of the chapter the verb הריח is used: "whoever makes any like it to perfume with shall be cut off from his people." [1]

The second passage which I think can help us to arrive at a meaning for הריח with god as the subject is Isa. xi 3b. Sanhedrin 93b contains a quotation of the verse, describing the messiah who can judge by smelling with his nose. Likewise in Christian writings Isa. xi 3 is applied to the messiah who will not judge *secundam aspectum oculorum* but his judgement, i.e. his smell, will be *in timore domini*.[2] It is understandable that scholars have sought for figurative meanings, or have altered the text, or even left it untranslated. When the meaning, fixed in the other passages, is taken as "scent given forth," we must translate our verse as follows: "and his giving forth scent (is done) with the fear of the Lord." The new prince possesses the quality of one who honours god's will and this is noticeable in him just as a fragrance spreads itself.[3]

God is the subject of the verb הריח in more passages. In Am. v 21 the verb occurs with בְּ, as in the two passages just dealt with. The prophet makes god's judgement known. Yhwh hates the cultic feasts of the people. If the feast days were Yhwh's, then his odour, his life-bringing strength, would be made manifest in the cultic celebrations. But now, says Yhwh, I shall withhold my odour at your feast days. What you call the day of Yhwh, a day of light, i.e. life, shall be a day of darkness, i.e. destruction. The intransitive meaning of the verb here too bears a sense which completely fits the context.

In 1 Sam. xxvi 19 the verb is followed by מנחה, vocalized in the masoretic reading as *minḥā*, meal sacrifice. The ancient translations were already aware of this reading. The Septuagint and the Targum

---

[1] *Ibidem*, p. 36 f.
[2] *Ibidem*, p. 30.
[3] *Ibidem*, p. 34 f.

add a suffix, and translate: "may he (god) smell your burnt sacrifice"
(G^B); other Greek MSS take "your burnt-offering" as the subject,
and apparently assume an intransitive meaning [1]; "may he (Yhwh)
accept my offer," Tg. In the Hebrew text Yhwh is certainly the
subject. David thinks himself wrongly being persecuted by Saul. He
says to the king: If Yhwh sets you against me, he may smell a burnt-
offering—a somewhat strange expression. If we take the verb to be
transitive, the sentence would mean: may god smell the sacrifice
and through that come into a favourable frame of mind concerning
David. If an intransitive meaning for the verb is taken, the translation
would run: "may he emanate the odour of the burnt-offering,"
also a rather odd expression. The connection between odour and
sacrifice is normal and this might have been the reason that as early
as the third century B.C. the word מנחה was vocalized as *minḥā*. The
differences in the tradition of the text possibly point to the fact that
difficulty was felt quite early.

However, it is possible to read the word differently, not as *minḥā*
but *menūḥā* which occurs in, among others, Jerem. xlv 3, 2 Sam. xiv 17
with the meaning "solace," "respite," "reassurance." 1 Sam. xxvi 19
could then be translated: "may he (Yhwh) give solace," a free translation of "may he emanate the fragrance of reassurance." If no solace
from Yhwh's part will come to David, then he will be forced to leave
the land where Yhwh is served, urged to worship other gods in a
strange land. But if Saul is set up against David, not by Yhwh but by
men, then they are the reason for his exile, by which he will be depriv-
ed from the privileges of worshipping Yhwh. Such people are accursed
in Yhwh's sight.

The god who emanates no odour because he will not accept the
sacrifice, is the god who withdraws from the people, withholding his life-
bringing strength. It has already been shown in dealing with Amos,
chapter v, that this judgement means that the day of Yhwh is as a day
of darkness. The verb הריח occurs with לא in Lev. xxvi 31 where it runs
parallel to "to ruin" and "to destroy." The preceding verse contains a
condemnation: the cultic places and the objects in use for the cult will
be destroyed. "I will lay your cities in ruin, destroy your sanctuaries
and not smell of the fragrance which is wont to bring you satisfaction."

Here we come across the term ריח ניחח rendered in Greek by ὀσμὴ
εὐωδίας, sweet-smelling fragrance. This term occurs very frequently:

---

[1] In the *Greek-English Lexicon* of LIDDELL & SCOTT an intransitive meaning of
the verb ὀσφραίνομαι is not recorded.

with Noah's sacrifice after the Flood, Gen. viii 21; thrice in Exodus xxix, vv. 18, 25, 41; seventeen times in Leviticus,[1] with the exception of xxvi 31 always in connection with sacrifices, either with or without a *lamed* preceding, and always followed by the expression ליהוה; Numbers uses the term eighteen times [2]; except for xxviii 2 all these passages are connected with the expression ליהוה and occur in connection with sacrifice. In Numb. xxviii 2 the Israelites are commanded to fulfil their sacrificial duties at the appointed time, "my sacrifice, my bread, ..., my fragrance of satisfaction." Ezekiel uses the term four times. The text of Ezek. xx 41 supports, in my opinion, the meaning expressed above and runs: "I shall show myself favourably with the fragrance of reassurance when I bring you out from among the nations and gather you together from the countries where you have been scattered" ...though it must be noted that the verb used here, רצא, also occurs with the meaning: to be satisfied with. In the preceding verse the same verb is used, "there (in the land of Palestine) on the mount of my temple shall I accept them with favour." This verse too is about sacrifices. Yhwh shall show himself as the saviour of the people in (בְּ) what he will do for the exiles: the return to Palestine, the restoration of the temple. The reason for the exile is seen by Ezekiel in the worship of other gods instead of Yhwh in the land that the Israelites had received from Yhwh. Verse 28 of the same chapter contains the reproach that they used every high place and every green tree—the cultic places of the gods—to make sacrifices, offerings which distressed Yhwh, a scent which reassured them and their libations. In Ezek. vi 13 and xvi 19 the expression ריח ניחח is used in the same sense. Instead of ליהוה we find here לכל גלוליהם, a contumelious appelation of the foreign gods.

ניחח is an infinitive Poʿlel of נוח, a mode often indicating the causative of the Qal. BARTH translates it with "Annehmlichkeit," [3] BAUER-LEANDER with "Befriedigung, Behagen, Wohlgefallen." [4] The translation which do not follow the Septuagint, ὀσμὴ εὐωδίας, sweet, pleasant scent, or the Vulgate, *odor suavitatis*, render ניחח by "apaisant"; "odeur apaisante" (DHORME [5]), "Beruhigungsgeruch" (among

---

[1] i 9. 13. 17; ii 2. 9. 12; iv 31; vi 8. 14; viii 21. 28; xvii 6; xxiii 13. 18; xxvi 31.

[2] xv 3. 7. 10. 13. 14. 24; xviii 17; xxviii 2. 6. 8. 13. 24. 27; xxix 2. 6. 8. 13. 36.

[3] J. BARTH, *Die Nominalbildung in den semitischen Sprachen*, 2nd ed. Leipzig 1894, p. 210 f.

[4] H. BAUER und P. LEANDER, *Historische Grammatik der hebräischen Sprache*, Halle, 1918.

[5] *La Bible*, Bibliothèque de la Pléiade, 1956.

others Von Rad,[1] Ringgren [2]), "soothing odor" (Speiser [3]). It is obvious that the expression belongs to the cultic language. The fragrance, perfume, scent of which it is said that it is "reassuring," bringing about a state of appeasement, well-being, is a definition of various sacrifices, and can even be used instead of sacrifice.[4]

The question forces itself on us: who is pleased, appeased, or brought to a state of appeasement, the divinity or the believer? We have become used to thinking of this question as superfluous. Sacrifices brought by believers are usually taken to be attempts to bring the divinity to a favourable mood. The story of Noah's sacrifice after the Flood [5] seems to bring about an immediate decision: Yhwh smelled a soothing savour—though I must add here that many translators, making efforts to repel the idea that Noah could sooth god, have cheerfully taken over the rendering of the ancient versions: sweet-smelling fragrance—and Yhwh takes a favourable decision for mankind. He will not continue to curse the earth. This interpretation is supported by some lines of the Babylonian story of the Flood.[6] Utnapishtim offered a sacrifice, poured out a libation, and burned fragrant materials, "sweet cane, cedar, and myrtle." When the gods smelled the sweet savour, they gathered like flies on (*or*, over) the sacrificer.[7]

---

[1] *Op. cit.*

[2] *Israelitische Religion*, Stuttgart 1963, p. 154.

[3] The Anchor Bible, *Genesis*, 1964, p. 50; "pleasing odour", M. Weinfeld, *Deuteronomy and the Deuteronomic School*, Oxford 1972, p. 210.

[4] Comp. too Ben Sira xxxv 8 (ed. Ziegler, Göttingen 1965): the sacrifice of the righteous "oils"—anoints, makes greasy—the altar and its fragrance—εὐ-ωδία—comes to the Most High. A variant of εὐωδία is εὐδοκία, "favour, goodwill." xlv 16: Aaron as anointed priest is chosen to bring sacrifices, in the Greek text "fragrance and sweet scent," in the Hebrew text: to burn ריח ניחח. In the Ethiopic *Ascension of Isaiah*, vi 17, we read: "and the fragrance of the spirit was on them" (R. H. Charles, *The Ascension of Isaiah*, translated from the Ethiopic version, which together with the new Greek fragment, the Latin versions and the Latin translation of the Slavonic, is here published in full, London 1900, p. 46). Charles thinks of an error, εὐωδία instead of εὐδοκία. I owe Dr W. Baars for drawing my attention to this passage.

[5] Gen. viii 21.

[6] Gilgamesh epic, Tabl. XI, lines 155 ff. See A. Heidel, *The Gilgamesh Epic and Old Testament Parallels*, Chicago 1946, in particular pp. 255 ff. Cf. W. G. Lambert and A. R. Millard, *Atra-ḫasis*, The Babylonian Story of the Flood, Oxford 1969, pp. 98 f. See R. Labat's recent translation in *Les religions du Proche-Orient*, 1970, p. 217.

[7] The author of the Babylonian epic makes the impression that Homer often makes: He does not take the gods seriously. There seems to be a gap between the believers and this literature.

The old Babylonian Prayer of a divination priest, from which ll. 15 and 16 are used as motto of this paper, mentions pure cedar used by the priest in his ritual act. Herewith the priest is insistently inviting the gods whose support he needs. Fragrance is both an act of the priest as well as a condition for the divine revelation.[1]

Noah's offering after the Flood when the earth was once again green is characterized by what he is offering, "clean beasts and birds of every kind." His sacrifice is no propitiation nor an expression of gratitude. Noah's offering of specimina of life saved from the destruction is his acknowledgment that life is god's property. The obvious meaning of ריח is "scent which emanates from." The meaning of הריח can be fixed with some certainty in agreement with the meaning of ריח. I suggest a double meaning of the verb, *to smell* and *to give smell*, to emanate a fragrance.[2] And it deserves to be pondered, in my opinion, to substitute the traditional translation of Gen. viii 21 for: "And Yhwh spread a smell of peace, reassurance, security."

The term ריח ניחח appeared to be a technical term in sacrificial practice. It expresses, I think, that the divinity accepts the sacrifice as his own. When, as in many passages, there also follows ליהוה, this does not indicate that Yhwh is addressed, i.e. receiver of the offering. "To Yhwh" or "for Yhwh" is a completely superfluous piece of information. The meaning is: the sacrifice is Yhwh's. God recognizes the offer as his own. The action of the believer becomes a divine action. It is god himself who has given the directives about what and how the offering ought to be. And the satisfying fragrance is experienced by the believer as the fragrance of his god.

God's fragrance was not an unknown concept in ancient Israel, neither a preposterous concept. Similar phenomena in other ancient religions help us to understand the meaning which the believer attached to fragrant sacrifices. God's fragrance indicated his appearance, and he reveals himself as the giver of life and vitality for both nature and man. When the early Christians used the term "Christ's fragrance" they payed homage to him as the divine presence and strength entirely in keeping with Old Testament belief.

---

[1] I am indebted to Professor FRANKENA for bringing this text to my notice.
[2] Comp. my remarks in *Words and Meanings, op. cit.* p. 38. The evidence of verbs with both a transitive and an intransitive sense is worthy of a separate treatment.

DIE BEDEUTUNG DER GROSSEN SCHRIFT-
PROPHETIE FÜR DAS ALTTESTAMENTLICHE
REDEN VON GOTT

VON

WALTHER ZIMMERLI
Göttingen

I

Die grosse Prophetie stellt ein für das Israel des Alten Testamentes besonders eigentümliches Element dar. Man kann dieses Element unter der Frage nach den Auswirkungen, die es auf den Gang der Geschichte Israels gehabt hat, bewerten. Man wird dann feststellen, dass es ein Ferment der Unruhe gewesen ist. Es hat innenpolitischen Umsturz angezettelt.[1] An anderer Stelle wieder ist es den Machthabern gelungen, die von ihm erzeugte Unruhe unter Kontrolle zu halten.[2] Man kann weiter feststellen, dass „Israel" die Katastrophe des sog. babylonischen Exils schwerlich durchgestanden hätte, wenn es nicht durch die vorausgehende prophetische Verkündigung auf diese vorbereitet, in der Zeit der tiefsten Erniedrigung durch prophetisches Wort gehärtet und zum Ausschauen nach neuen Ufern zugerüstet worden wäre.

Mit diesen geschichtlichen und geistesgeschichtlichen Bewertungen ist aber das Proprium der Prophetie, d.h. die eigentliche Aussage, in der sie gehört sein will, noch nicht getroffen. Die Propheten wissen sich als die von Jahwe her Aufgescheuchten und Gesandten, die nicht ein eigenes politisches Programm zu verfolgen und es etwa gar in eigener Aktivität auszugestalten haben. Das unterscheidet sie zutiefst vom Propheten des Islam. Sie haben immer wieder in einer auffallenden Kurzfristigkeit ihres Auftrages Jahwes Tun und seinen konkreten Willen in konkrete Situationen hinein zu verkündigen. So kennen sie daneben Zeiten des Schweigens und des Wartens.[3] Eine ausdrückliche

---

[1] 2 Reg. ix 1 ff., dazu 1 Reg. xix 16.
[2] Amos wird ausgewiesen (vii 12 f.), Jeremia geschlagen und in den Block gelegt (xx 1 f.), verhaftet (xxxvii 11-16) und in eine Zisterne geworfen (xxxviii 1-6).
[3] Is. viii 16-18, vgl. auch das Schweigen Jeremias zur Zeit der deuteronomischen Reform.

Reflexion über die Grenze prophetischer Verantwortlichkeit findet sich bei dem späten Propheten Ezechiel.[1]

Will man darum das Proprium der Prophetie erfassen, so wird man dem Auftrag, unter dem sie sich gesandt wissen, nachzugehen haben. Der Frage, welche Bedeutung das prophetische Tun und Reden innerhalb des sonstigen alttestamentlichen Redens von Tat und Wort Jahwes hat, soll im Folgenden nachgegangen werden.

II

Die grosse Prophetie Israels ist keineswegs unvorbereitet vom Himmel gefallen. Sie wächst aus einem Muttergrund heraus, für den sich religionsgeschichtliche Parallelen [2] finden und der sich in manchen Erscheinungen auch in Israel selber über die Zeit der Hochprophetie hinaus erkennen lässt.

1 Sam. ix, wo sich die Gestalt des Sehers (רֹאֶה) mit derjenigen des Propheten (נָבִיא) berührt,[3] weiss zu erzählen, dass man beim Seher Auskunft über Dinge des Alltags, die dem Auge des gewöhnlichen Menschen verhüllt blieben, einholte. Saul fragt bei Samuel nach dem Verbleib der entlaufenen Eselinnen. Noch die Neh. vi 14 erwähnte Prophetin Noadja und „die anderen Propheten," die dem Statthalter Nehemia durch ihre Voraussagen Furcht einjagen wollen, scheinen Gestalten zu sein, die es mit solchem unmittelbaren Vorhersagen an einen Einzelnen zu tun haben.

In 1 Sam. x 5, 10 ist daneben von einer Prophetenbande die Rede, die unter dem Spiel von Instrumenten in wildem Gebaren von dem gottesdienstlichen Platz eines Ortes herunterkommt. In der Prophetin Mirjam, die mit dem Tamburin den singenden Frauen nach der Vernichtung der ägyptischen Verfolger voranzieht,[4] scheint der Vorläufer, und in den von der späten Chronik erwähnten Tempelsängern, deren Tun als נבא bezeichnet wird,[5] der späte Nachfolger in solchem Tun zu erkennen zu sein. Man stösst hier am deutlichsten auf eine Art

---

[1] Sie ist schon in dem: „Ob sie hören oder ob sie es lassen" von ii 5, 7; iii 11 zu verspüren, tritt aber offen heraus in den Ausführungen von iii 17-21 und xxxiii 1-9.

[2] Vgl. dazu etwa G. HÖLSCHER, *Die Profeten*, Leipzig 1914, 129-143; A. GUILLAUME, *Prophétie et Divination*, Paris 1941 passim; A. NEHER, *L'essence du prophétisme*, Paris 1955, 17-81; J. LINDBLOM, *Prophecy in Ancient Israel*, Oxford 1962, 1-46.

[3] 1 Sam. ix 9.

[4] Ex. xv 20 f.

[5] 1 Chr. xxv 1, wo mit Q(G V T) zu lesen ist הנבאים בכנרות בנבלים ובמצלתים und 3 הנבא על הדות והלל ליהוה.

beamteter Kultprophetie.[1] Was Elia- und Elisageschichten von der
Fähigkeit des Propheten, Kranke zu heilen, berichten,[2] ragt selbst in
die Jesajalegende hinein.[3] Man wird sich fragen, ob nicht auch das
Tun der Prophetinnen, die Ez. xiii 17-23 beschreibt, wenn dieses
auch sichtlich noch mit allerlei magischen Praktiken verbrämt ist, in
den Kontext solchen gesundheitlichen „Bindens und Lösens" hinein-
gehört.

Es ist nicht mit Sicherheit auszumachen, wie breit dieses „unpoli-
tische" Tun prophetischer Gottesmänner als Untergrund durch Israels
ganze Geschichte hin da ist. In den Berichten des Alten Testamentes
tritt demgegenüber die Prophetie stärker heraus, die es mit dem
Jahwevolk und seinen Vertretern in dessen politischen Entscheidungen zu tun hat. Im Alten Testament ist dieses sicher in besonderer
Weise durch die Tatsache bestimmt, dass Israel seines Gottes Handeln
von den Anfängen im Exodusgeschehen her in besonderer Weise in
seinen geschichtlichen Begegnungen erfuhr. Doch hat dieses auch in
den Maribriefen, die eine Fülle von dem König gegebenen „prophetischen" Bescheiden erkennen lassen, eine Entsprechung.[4]

III

Es ist nun aber für die alttestamentliche Prophetie weiter kenn-
zeichnend, dass sie schon früh den im politischen und militärischen
Bereich Führenden in Israel nicht nur mit Einzelweisungen zur Seite
trat,[5] sondern seit dem Aufkommen eines Königtums für dessen Bestehen im Lichte des Jahwewillens eine kritische Verantwortung über-
nahm.

So sehen wir schon gleich in den Anfängen des Königtums die Gestalt Samuels, wie immer diese geschichtlich näher zu kennzeichnen
sein mag, zunächst an der geistigen Legitimierung dieses neuen Amtes
beteiligt,[6] in der Folge dann aber, aus Anlass des nicht eingehaltenen
Banngebotes in einem Jahwekrieg in scharfer Wendung gegen dieses
Königtum.[7] In anderer Weise ist der Prophet Nathan, über dessen
Herkunft leider Bestimmtes nicht auszumachen ist, an der Gründung

---

[1] A. J. JOHNSON, *The Cultic Prophet in Ancient Israel*, 2nd ed. Cardiff 1962.
[2] 1 Reg. xvii 17-24; 2 Reg. i 6; iv 18-37; v 1-14; xiii 20-21.
[3] 2 Reg. xx 1-11; Jes. xxxviii.
[4] F. ELLERMEIER, *Prophetie in Mari und Israel*, Herzberg 1968.
[5] 1 Sam. xxii 5.
[6] 1 Sam. ix-xii.
[7] 1 Sam. xv.

der davidischen Dynastie beteiligt.[1] Der gleiche Nathan tritt David, wie dieser zwei elementare Ordnungen im Jahwevolk durch Ehebruch und Mord verletzt hat, in kritischem Gerichtswort entgegen.[2]

Die geschichtlichen Angaben der Königsbücher wissen für das Nordreich, das den altisraelitischen Traditionen enger verbunden blieb als das davidische Jerusalem, von mehrfachen weiteren Eingriffen der Propheten bei Thronwechseln. Bleibt hier in der frühen Königszeit manches geschichtlich im Dunkel, so wird das Geschehen in seinen geschichtlichen Umrissen in der Eliazeit klarer fassbar.[3] Die Nabothgeschichte in 1 Reg. xxi zeigt zunächst einen kritischen Angriff Elias auf Ahab, der sich durchaus mit dem Angriff Nathans auf David vergleichen lässt. Im feigen Mord an Naboth und den ungerechten Machenschaften zur Besitzergreifung des Landanteils Naboths sind wiederum Grundordnungen des Jahwevolkes durch das Königshaus verletzt.[4] Zugleich aber wird sichtbar, dass nun der Angriff des Propheten auf das Königshaus totaler zu werden beginnt. Die Revolte Jehus, die zur Ausmordung der ganzen Dynastie Omris und auch einiger Glieder des mit dieser verschwägerten judäischen Königshauses führt,[5] kann kaum ohne einen erheblichen Anteil der Prophetenkreise um Elia-Elisa verstanden werden.

Nach dem Gesetz von Challenge and Response gewinnt die prophetische Kritik angesichts der stark tyrisch-kanaanäisch orientierten Religionspolitik des Hauses Ahabs, besonders der tyrischen Prinzessin Isebel, die Härte eines Totalangriffes auf das ganze Königshaus. Die Dimension der prophetischen Polemik weitet sich hier angesichts der Breite baalistischer Gefährdung des von den Omriden beherrschten Landes spürbar aus.

Darin aber liegt wohl schon ein deutlicher Unterschied zu dem vor, was auch in den Maritexten an Gottesbotschaft gegen einen Herrscher zu erkennen ist. Geht es dort noch um Einzelvergehen, dass der Herrscher es versäumte, den Gott zu befragen, dass er ein Opfer nicht gebracht, ein Haus zu bauen plante, das er nicht bauen sollte [6] u.s.w., so

---

[1] 2 Sam. vii.

[2] 2 Sam. xii, vgl. auch die Worte Gads in 2 Sam. xxiv.

[3] Vgl. aber auch O. H. STECK, *Ueberlieferung und Zeitgeschichte in den Elia-Erzählungen*, WMANT 26, Neukirchen 1968.

[4] Ungerechte Machenschaften, um sich in den Besitz eines Gutes zu bringen, sind nach J. HERRMANN, „Das zehnte Gebot," *Sellin-Festschrift*, Leipzig 1927, 69-82 in dem חמד des letzten Dekaloggebotes nach Ex. xx 17 verboten.

[5] 2 Reg. ix 27 f., auch x 13 f.

[6] Vgl. die Texte A 15; ARM(T) II 90 und ARMT XIII 112 bei ELLERMEIER (vgl. S. 50, Anm. 4).

ist hier im Raum des Jahweglaubens, wo dem Herrscher ein einziger göttlicher Herr mit einem bestimmten, umgreifenden Rechtswillen gegenübersteht, der Angriff auf die Existenz der Dynastie und seine Begründung umfassend geworden.[1]

IV

Seinen weitesten Horizont erreicht dieser Angriff aber erst mit dem Auftreten der Schriftpropheten. Nochmals möchte man geneigt sein, das Gesetz von Challenge and Response zu zitieren. Die Weltgeschichte fordert das Gesamtvolk Israel heraus—bei Amos noch in seltsamer Witterung zu einer Zeit vorausgenommen, in welcher der billige Alltagsverstand davon noch nichts geahnt haben wird, bei Jesaja dann voll entfaltet.

In dieser weltgeschichtlichen Kampfsituation der Völker aber geht es nicht mehr nur um das Bestehen dieses oder jenes Königshauses und die Erhaltung bestimmter dynastischer Prärogativen innerhalb des Volkes. Gewiss ist auch bei Amos noch die Drohung zu hören: „Jerobeam wird durchs Schwert getötet werden," [2] und Amos wird vor allem um dieses Angriffes willen des Landes verwiesen. Aber darüber hinaus ist bei ihm nun das ungleich Vollere zu hören: „Israel wird in die Verbannung geführt werden, weg von seinem Lande." [3] Und noch schärfer ist die Formulierung, die im Jahwewort der vierten Vision des Propheten zu vernehmen ist: „Das Ende ist gekommen über mein Volk Israel. Ich werde nicht mehr (schonend) an ihm vorbeigehen." [4]

Hier ist die Hülle gesprengt. Es geht nicht mehr nur um einen Kleinbescheid in einer Alltagsfrage, auch nicht mehr nur um einen Bescheid in einer politischen Einzelsituation lokaler Gefährdung oder das Verhalten eines einzelnen Königs, sondern um das Ganze von Sein oder Nichtsein Israels, des Volkes Jahwes.

---

[1] Bei aller Kritik in Einzelfragen fehlt in Mari dieser umfassende Angriff, der die Dynastie als ganze in Frage stellt. In dem am Horizont heraufziehenden Kampf Zimri-Lims gegen Hammurapi, der mit dem Untergang Maris endete, sagt der Prophet dem König von Mari nach ARMT XIII 23 den Sieg an. Ebenso ermahnt ARMT XIII 114 den König im gleichen Zusammenhang zur Furchtlosigkeit. Vgl. weiter A 4260; X 6; X 8 und X 10. Auch der schärfste Brief ARM X 50 mit seiner Warnung vor einem Kriegszug will den König vor dem Verderben bewahren und kann keinesfalls mit ELLERMEIER S. 147 als „unbedingte, unbegründete Unheilsankündigung" verstanden werden.

[2] Am. vii 11, vgl. auch v. 9.

[3] Am. vii 11, 17.

[4] Am. viii 2.

Aber auch dieses ist ganz deutlich: Es geht dabei nicht nur um eine geschichtsimmanente Prognose, die der Prophet dem Volke zu stellen hat, etwa im Stile einer Ankündigung des „Untergangs des Abendlandes." Vielmehr geht es hier um die unausweichliche Konfrontation Israels mit Jahwe. Nicht ein auch abgelöst zu betrachtendes Ereignis im Kampf der Völker der Welt wird hier angekündigt, sondern ein Ereignis, das sich zwischen Jahwe und seinem Volk Israel vollzieht. Allerdings ist dieses Geschehen nun eben kein innerlichheimliches Geschehen in einer religiösen Gedanken oder Gesinnungswelt hinter den Dingen der Völkergeschichte, sondern, sosehr es ein Geschehen ist, in dem Jahwe mit seinem Volke redet, ist es doch zugleich ganz und gar ein Geschichtsgeschehen in der Völkerwelt.[1] Wie sehr aber dieses Geschichtsgeschehen ganz und gar Geschehen zwischen Jahwe und seinem Volke ist, bei dem Jahwes Stimme nicht durch die Stimme eines irdischen Grossmachtvolkes übertönt sein will, zeigt sich in der eigentümlichen Erscheinung, dass Amos für den Vollzug der Deportation Israels und seines „Endes" keine Grossmacht ausdrücklich namhaft macht. Mag die deportierende und das „Ende" verursachende Grossmacht in der Folge sein, wer sie will,[2] entscheidend ist, dass Israel darin die Begegnung mit seinem Gott erfährt und erkennt.[3]

Das bleibt aber auch da die Leitlinie des Verstehens, wo mit Namen benannte Grossmächte dann in der Tat in der Geschichte aufzutreten beginnen: die Assyrer in den Tagen Hoseas, Jesajas und Michas, der neubabylonische König Nebukadnezar in den Tagen Jeremias und Ezechiels. Darin, dass sich das zuerst bei Amos [4] auftauchende Theologumenon vom „Tage Jahwes" im weiteren auch bei Jesaja,[5] bei Jeremias Zeitgenossen Zephanja,[6] bei Ezechiel,[7] und dann bis hinunter in die schon apokalyptisch gefärbte Prophetie Joels findet, ist gesichert, dass auch bei ihnen das Geschehen der politischen Kata-

---

[1] Zu dieser Struktur alttestamentlichen Glaubens vgl. W. Zimmerli, *Die Weltlichkeit des Alten Testamentes*, Göttingen 1971.

[2] Die gleiche Unbestimmtheit der geschichtlichen Androhung ist auch noch bei Hosea zu finden, wenn er in IX 3 androht: „Ephraim muss zurück nach Aegypten und in Assur werden sie Unreines essen." Von da her besteht keine Notwendigkeit, in Js. vii 18 die Erwähnung der Aegypter neben Assur zu eliminieren, so etwa H. Wildberger, *Jesaja*, BK X Neukirchen 1969, 303.

[3] Am. iv 12 formuliert dieses, mag der Vers nun von Amos selber stammen oder nicht, sehr klar.

[4] Am. v 18-20.

[5] Is. ii 12-17.

[6] Zeph. i f.

[7] Ez. vii; xiii 5, auch die sekundäre Einheit xxx 1 ff.

strophe Israels in der Dimension einer Begegnung mit dem Gotte Israels, der nun als sein Richter im geschichtlichen Geschehen auftritt, steht. Der „Tag Jahwes" ist auf jeden Fall der Tag der Begegnung mit Jahwe.

V

Für Jesaja scheint nun allerdings eine Einschränkung notwendig zu werden. So gewaltig bei ihm die Schilderung des „Tages Jahwes" dasteht, so ist doch bei ihm das Wort vom „Ende," das von Amos her seine nachdrücklichste Auslegung in Ez. vii erfährt, nicht zu hören. Dafür verbindet sich in seinem Wort je und dann mit der Ankündigung der tiefen Demütigung Jerusalems und Judas der Hinweis auf das Tun dessen, der auf dem Zion wohnt,[1] der seinen geheimnisvollen, des Menschen Augen nicht durchschaubaren „wunderbaren Plan" ausführt.[2] In diesem behält auf jeden Fall der Zion, nicht als ein brutum factum der Geographie, sondern als ein von Jahwe zeichenhaft gesetztes Element seine besondere Bedeutung. „Siehe, ich lege in Zion einen Fundamentstein, einen *bohan*-Stein, einen kostbaren Fundament-Eckstein. Wer glaubt wird nicht weichen." [3] Darin wird sichtbar, dass Jahwe auf Erden, inmitten seines Volkes, wie sehr ihm dieses auch immer wieder entläuft und allem Anschein nach rettungslos in sein eigenes Verderben hineinrennt, ein letztes Ziel der Vollendung unverrückt im Auge behält. In anderer Weise formulieren Js. i 21-26, wie Jahwe durch die Glut eines vernichtenden Feuers hindurch das Ziel der Ausschmelzung einer reinen Gottesstadt, die den Namen „Rechtsburg, treue Stadt" verdienen wird, verfolgt. Darf Is. ix 1-6, was mir nicht verboten erscheint, ebenfalls als jesajanisch angesprochen werden, so wird hier darüber hinaus sichtbar, dass zu der Zukunft, auf welche Jahwes Planen zugeht, auch der wahre Davidide, in dem der prophetische Gottesspruch von 2 Sam. vii eine überraschend überhöhte Einlösung erfährt, gehört.

Aber Jesaja steht nicht allein. Es muss ihm auf jeden Fall Hosea, so sehr dieser aus einer ganz anderen Traditions-Vorgeschichte herkommt, zur Seite gestellt werden. Gewiss, hier ist nicht vom Zion und vom kommenden Davididen [4] mit dem vierfachen [5] neuen Königs-

---

[1] Is. viii 18.

[2] Is. xxviii 29, zum „Plan" v 19; xiv 24-27, zum „Wunderbaren" bes. xxix 14.

[3] Is. xxviii 16.

[4] Die Erwähnung Davids in Hos. iii 5 stammt nicht vom Propheten selber.

[5] In Is. ix f. 5 ist kein 5. Thronname zu rekonstruieren, vgl. dazu *VT* 22 (1972), S. 249-252.

namen die Rede. Hier ist es die altisraelitische Ueberlieferung vom
Auszug aus Aegypten, dem Zug durch die Wüste und der Gabe des
Landes Kanaan. So sieht er denn den Vollzug des Gerichtes, das
Israels Existenz bedrohen wird, in der Gestalt einer neuen Hinaus-
treibung in die Wüste, zurück hinter die Gabe des geschenkten Landes.[1] Aber er sieht in anderer Form, in der Sache aber ganz ebenso wie
Jesaja Jahwe in seinem Richten mit einem Werk befasst, hinter dem
sich ein neues Aufrichten des gerichtswürdigen Volkes ergeben könnte. „Von der Wüste her"[2] wird Jahwe Israel dann wieder seine Weinberge geben und das böse Tal Achor, durch das es einst unter böser
Versündigung ins Land hineingezogen ist, zum Ort eines neuen Ein-
zuges, zur „Pforte der Hoffnung" machen. Ganz elementar, in einem
irrationalen Ausbruch der Liebe Jahwes kommt es in Hos. xi 8 f. zum
Ausdruck, dass Jahwe sein Volk nicht preisgeben möchte: „Wie könnte ich dich hingeben, Ephraim, dich ausliefern, Israel! Wie könnte ich
dich hingeben wie Admah, dich machen wie Zeboim. In mir kehrt
sich mein Herz um, mein Erbarmen ist entbrannt. Ich will meinen
heissen Zorn nicht vollstrecken, will Ephraim nicht wieder verderben." Wieder in anderer Weise spricht das die zweite, biographisch so
gar nicht mit der ersten in Kap. i abzustimmende Ehegeschichte von
Kap. iii aus, dass Jahwe sein Volk, das er liebt, in eine strenge Karenz
und Klausur führen wird, in der es zu Ende ist mit all den Gaben, die
es zur Zeit so leichtfertig missachtet und nicht mehr als Jahwes Gaben
anerkennt—eine Karenz und Klausur aber, durch die hin Gottes Erziehung eine weitere Zukunft mit seinem Volke im Sinne hat.

Ob auch des Judäers Amos Worte über die harte Verkündigung
vom Ende Israels hinaus in eine weitere Zukunft weisen, ist mehr als
fraglich. Die beiden Schlussworte Am. ix 11 f. und 13-15 sind ohne
Anhalt in des Propheten sonstiger Verkündigung, soweit sie uns über-
liefert ist, und doch wohl fremder Hand zugehörig. Ueber das „Vielleicht" einer möglichen Gnade über dem „Rest Josephs," wenn dieser
sich zum Gehorsam zurückfände,[3] scheint des Amos Verkündigung,
die es in jedem Falle auch mit dem lebendigen Gott und nicht mit
einem Fatum des End-Schicksals zu tun hat, nicht hinaus zu gehen.

Ebenso ist nicht mit Sicherheit auszumachen, ob der Zeitgenosse

---

[1] Hos. ii 16; xii 10. Daneben reden viii 13 und ix 3 auch von einer „Rückkehr"
nach Aegypten. Das ist eine andere Form der Zurücknahme der heilsgeschicht-
lichen Führung.

[2] Das משם von Hos. ii 17 bezieht sich auf das המדבר von ii 16.

[3] Am. V 15, von H. W. WOLFF, *Amos*, BK XIV-2, Neukirchen 1969, 274 f. als
Zusatz beurteilt.

Jesajas, Micha, aus der Landstadt Moreseth-Gath von kommender Zukunft seines Volkes, und etwa gar wie Jesaja von der Erwartung eines kommenden Retters (von Bethlehem her) redet. Zwingend ist allerdings die Ursprünglichkeit des „messianischen" Wortes Mi. v 1-3 [1] dem Propheten nicht abzusprechen. Und wenn ALT [2] mit seiner Rekonstruktion des Textes von Mi. ii 1-5 im Rechte sein sollte, so würde nach diesem Worte der Judäer Micha, der vom Lande herkommt, nach einer neuen, gerechten Landverteilung Ausschau halten.

VI

An dieser Stelle gilt es nun aber hinüberzufragen in das übrige Alte Testament, um dann klarzustellen, wie sich das prophetische Reden von Jahwe zu dem verhält, was dort zu hören ist.

Nun ist es sicher gewagt, umfassend von *einem* Reden des sonstigen Alten Testamentes von Jahwe zu sprechen. Hat doch die neuere Forschung, die auf kritische Differenzierung aus ist, zur Genüge deutlich machen können, wie verschiedenartig im einzelnen an den verschiedenen Orten geredet wird. So redet etwa die priesterliche Welt, die in der erzählenden Priesterschrift im Pentateuch, dem Heiligkeitsgesetz und anderen in der Priestersphäre entstandenen Gesetzen (und im Priesterpropheten Ezechiel) zu Gehör kommt, eine sehr andere Sprache als der jahwistische Erzähler, der Gesetzgeber im Bundesbuch und die deuteronomische und deuteronomistische Welt. Und doch kann auch hier etwas Aehnliches festgestellt werden, wie eben im Nebeneinander der von so verschiedenen Orten und Traditionshintergründen her sprechenden Propheten Jesaja und Hosea. Da, wo sie von Jahwes Wort über Israel, auf das hin auch die prophetische Rede konvergiert, sprechen, da befinden sich ihre Aussagen in auffallender Nähe zueinander.

Das mag an den beiden grossen Geschichtsberichten, die vom Anfang der Welt her beginnend Jahwes Absicht mit Israel deutlich zu machen versuchen, sichtbar gemacht werden. Der Jahwist schildert, nachdem er nur skizzenhaft die anfängliche Gestaltung der Welt durch יהוה אלהים gezeichnet hatte, die düsteren Anfangsgeschehnisse der Menschengeschichte. Anhebend mit der Vergehung im Gottesgarten,[3]

---

[1] Der ursprüngliche Text hat hier eine Ueberarbeitung erfahren.

[2] A. ALT, „Micha II 1-5. ΓΗΣ ΑΝΑΔΑΣΜΟΣ in Juda." *Interpretationes ad Vetus Testamentum pertinentes Sigmundo Mowinckel septuagenario missae*, Oslo 1955, 13-23 (= *Kleine Schriften* III, München 1959, 373-381).

[3] Gen. iii.

über die Kain- und Lamechgeschichte,[1] die Engelehen,[2] in denen die
Tradition vom Heroenzeitalter in spezifisch alttestamentlicher Weise
verarbeitet wird [3] und in denen der Erzähler die Ursache der grossen
Flut sehen wird, führt sein Bericht zu der geballten Menschenmasse
von Babylon. In ihrem Bau des Turmes, der bis zum Himmel reichen,
und der Riesenstadt, die die Masse zusammenhalten soll, sucht diese
sich einen Namen zu machen und Zukunft zu sichern. In ihrer Zerstreuung durch die Länder hin erntet diese Menschheit von Gott her,
was sie gesät.[4] Da aber greift Jahwe nochmals in seine Welt ein. Dem
Herausgerufenen, Abraham, verheisst er den Anfang einer neuen Geschichte.[5] Mehren will er diesen Einzelnen. Ein Land will er ihm
geben. Des Jahwisten eigenster Akzent aber ist in dem auffallend
hartnäckig gebrauchten Wort „Segen-segnen" zu hören, das sich im
Kopfstück des Berichtes über diese neue Geschichte findet. Ein Segen
soll Abraham in der zuvor vom Wort „Fluch" gekennzeichneten
Welt [6] werden. Der Horizont ist dabei ausgeweitet auf „alle Ge-
schlechter der Erde." Und wenn hier festgestellt wird, dass Jahwe
dem Abraham einen grossen Namen machen will,[7] so steht das deutlich im Gegenlicht zu jenen Turmbauern, die sich selber einen Namen
machen wollten. So steht das Wort „Segen" über dem Ahnen Israels
und in ihm über Israel selber.

Ganz anders erzählt die Priesterschrift von den Anfängen der Welt.
Breit ausladend wird berichtet, wie Gott in sechs Tagen den kunst-
vollen Weltenbau aufführt, um am 7. Tage zu ruhen.[8] Jedes Ohr in
Israel hört hier, wenn schon kein Gebot formuliert wird, die Gründung des Sabbat-Ruhetages, an dem Israel einst teilbekommen wird.
Noch aber ist Israel nicht da. Stattdessen wird auch hier von der
Katastrophe der grossen Flut erzählt, in der Gott nach 10 Menschen-
generationen Gericht über das gewalttätig gewordene Menschenge-
schlecht halten muss. In einem ausdrücklichen Bundschluss mit Noah,[9]
dem allein Geretteten, verspricht Gott die Erhaltung auch der sündig
gewordenen Menschheit, die aber auf jeden Fall wenigstens einige

---

[1] Gen. iv.
[2] Gen. vi 1-4.
[3] Diese taucht noch in Ez. xxxii 27 auf. Dazu *BK* XIII, 1969, 789 f.
[4] Gen. xi 1-9.
[5] Gen. xii 1-3.
[6] Gen. iii 14. 17; iv 11, auch ix 25.
[7] Gen. xii 2.
[8] Gen. i 1-ii 4a.
[9] Gen. ix 1-17.

elementare Blutordnungen einhalten soll. Wenn Blut vergossen wird, dann soll Menschenblut geahndet, Tierblut aber auf keinen Fall genossen werden. Als Zehnter nach Noah tritt in einer schon weit in die Völker verzweigten Menschheit Abraham, der Ahne Israels auf. Auch hier treten in der feierlichen Bundeszusage Gottes [1] Mehrungs- und Landverheissung, die alten Elemente der Abrahamüberlieferung, auf. Ueber sie wird als das eigentümlich priesterliche Interpretationselement nicht das Wort vom Segen, wie beim Jahwisten, ausgesprochen, sondern die Zusage: „Ich will dein Gott sein," was sofort auch auf das Volk, das von Abraham herkommen wird, ausgeweitet ist.[2] Diese Zusage ist auch hier in der Zusage eines „ewigen Bundes" verankert. Hinter ihr ist schon zu ahnen, was dann in den Tagen des Mose nach dem Bericht des Priesters wirklich werden wird: Das grosse Volk, aufgebrochen zu dem ihm verheissenen Lande hin, am Gottesberg seinem Gott begegnend, der nun verheisst, im „Zelt der Begegnung," das Mose in des Volkes Mitte errichten soll, selber in der Mitte seines Volkes gegenwärtig zu sein.[3] So schildert der Priester die besondere Würde, die Israel eigen ist. Jahwes Volk ist es und Jahwe ist sein Gott für alle Zeiten.[4]

VII

Das Wort der Propheten klingt neben den Aussagen, nach denen Israel das Volk des Segens und Jahwes eigenes Volk ist, eigentümlich schrill. Ja, es scheint, wenn Hosea eine Tochter auf Jahwes Geheiss „Nicht-Erbarm" (—„denn ich werde mich des Hauses Israel nicht mehr erbarmen, dass ich ihm vergeben würde")[5] und einen Sohn „Nicht-mein-Volk" (—„denn ihr seid nicht mein Volk und ich werde nicht mehr für euch dasein"),[6] nennt, als ob Jahwe sein früheres Wort völlig zurückgenommen hätte.

Welche Bedeutung kann dann aber das Wort der grossen Propheten im Alten Testament haben? Ist angesichts des eben Gesagten nicht

---

[1] Gen. xvii.

[2] Gen. xvii 7 f.

[3] Ex. xxix 45 f.

[4] Zu dieser „Bundesformel" vgl. R. SMEND, *Die Bundesformel*, ThSt 68, Zürich 1963.

[5] Hos. i 6.

[6] Hos. i 9. Dazu H. W. WOLFF, *Hosea* BK XIV-1 Neukirchen 1961, 23 f. Möglicherweise ist allerdings statt des אהיה לכם von MT ursprüngliches אלהיכם zu lesen, was auf die volle Bundesformel führen würde.

einfach die volle Unverträglichkeit des Prophetenwortes mit der sonstigen Aussage des Alten Testamentes vom Jahwewort über Israel festzustellen?

Bevor eine Antwort auf diese Frage versucht wird, muss noch eine Linie der prophetischen Verkündigung, die bisher erst beiläufig sichtbar wurde, ausgezogen werden.

Die Propheten waren nicht nur Menschen, welche die kommende Katastrophe mit ihrem stärker geschärften Sinn witterten. Sie suchten Israel auch die innere Ratio des Kommenden deutlich zu machen. In den Angriffen eines Nathan und Elia gegen David und Ahab wurden dem König je zwei elementare Ordnungen, die im Dekalog ihre knappste Formulierung erfahren haben [1] und die vom König verletzt worden waren, entgegengehalten. Bei Amos kann man einmal sehen, dass er das Verbot der Pfändung von Gewändern, das im Bundesbuch zu finden ist, sehr konkret in seiner Anklage anführt.[2] Im weiteren konkretisiert er allerdings die Verletzungen der Regel der Barmherzigkeit gegen den Nächsten durchaus selbständig, wenn er etwa den unverantwortlichen Luxus, der in Samaria geübt wird, anprangert, Dinge, die in den älteren Gebotssammlungen so nicht ausdrücklich erwähnt sind. Man hat daraus gemeint schliessen zu können, dass bei Amos nicht von einer Bindung an das alte Recht Israels geredet werden könne,[3] dass hier eine neuartige freie, charismatische Neuinterpretation des Gesetzes geschehe,[4] oder dass hier eben das allgemeinmenschliche Wissen um das Rechte zur Sprache gebracht werde.[5] Nun ist es aber auch durchaus schon bei der Vor-Schriftprophetie zu erkennen, dass sie, in sinngemässer Konkretisierung israelitischer Rechtsanschauung, ihre Angriffe führt. Das gilt nicht nur da, wo das im älteren Recht Israels nirgends kodifiziert niedergelegte Banngebot verletzt wird,[6] sondern ebenso da, wo David seine Volkszählung veranstaltet,[7] was in keinem älteren Gesetz ausdrücklich verboten wird,

---

[1] Im 6., 7. und 10. Gebot, vgl. dazu S. 51, Anm. 4.

[2] Am. ii 8, dazu Ex. xxii 25. Die von R. BACH, „Gottesrecht und weltliches Recht in der Verkündigung des Propheten Amos". *Festschrift G. Dehn*, Neukirchen 1957, 23-34 vertretene These, dass Amos ganz im alten apodiktischen Recht verwurzelt sei, lässt sich in dieser Strenge wohl nicht erweisen.

[3] K. KOCH, „Die Entstehung der sozialen Kritik bei den Propheten." *Probleme biblischer Theologie, Festschrift für G. von Rad*, München 1971, 236-257.

[4] G. VON RAD, *Theologie des Alten Testaments* II, München 1965 4. Aufl. 426. 434.

[5] H. H. SCHMID, „Amos. Zur Frage nach der ‚geistigen Heimat' des Propheten." *Wort und Dienst. Jahrbuch der Kirchlichen Hochschule Bethel*. N.F. 10, Bethel 1969, 85-103.

[6] 1 Sam. xv; 1 Reg. xx 35-43.

[7] 2 Sam. xxiv.

aber sichtlich dem altisraelitischen Empfinden vom Herrscherwillen Jahwes widerspricht. Insofern ist Amos mit seinen Angriffen kein absoluter Neuerer. Bei Hosea (und Jeremia) ist es dann ausdrücklich zu sehen, wie bestimmte geformte Rechtsreihen, die an dekalogische Formulierung erinnern, geradezu zitiert werden können.[1] Demgegenüber ist es bei Jesaja vor allem der Hinweis auf die verletzte Majestät Jahwes—im innen- wie im aussenpolitischen Bereich—, die Jahwes richtendes Einschreiten notwendig macht.[2]

In steigender Härte wird dabei die völlige Unfähigkeit des Volkes zu echter Hinwendung zu Jahwe und seinem konkreten Willen zum Ausdruck gebracht. Jesaja redet vom „Nicht-Wollen" des Volkes der widerspenstigen Söhne.[3] Jeremia schildert, wie er in den Strassen Jerusalems bei Kleinen und Grossen vergeblich nach einem sucht, der Recht täte.[4] Er kann das unheimliche Bild prägen, dass sein Volk sich so wenig ändern kann wie ein Mohr seine Haut und ein Panther sein Fell ändern kann.[5]

Die stärkste Zuspitzung aber erfährt diese Aussage von der schlechthinigen Unfähigkeit Israels und Jerusalems, seines Gottes Gebot zu halten, in den Aussagen Ezechiels. Die grossen Bildreden von Kap. xvi und xxiii zeichnen es in der Dimension des Geschichtsablaufes, wie in Jerusalem und Israel von den Anfängen her keine reine Stelle zu finden ist, an der Jerusalem und Israel Recht getan hätten. Ez. xx 1-31 sagt das gleiche ohne Bildverkleidung. Das Bildwort vom unbrauchbaren Rebenholz Ez. xv formuliert es geradezu ontologisch, wie unbrauchbar, nur noch fürs Feuer brauchbar, Jerusalem ist. Und in einer an Hos. iv 1 f. (und Jer. vii 9) erinnernden Weise stellen Ez. xxii 1ff. das gleiche erneut in einer nicht mehr zu überbietenden Steigerung dar, indem sie der „Blutstadt" Jerusalem einen Gebotskatalog vorhalten und bei jedem Einzelgebot das Verfehlen des Gehorsams feststellen. Man hat den Eindruck, dass hier jede „geschichtliche Gerechtigkeit" fehlt. Von einem Jahwe gehorsamen Rest, wie man ihn für Jerusalem nach den Erzählungen von Jer. xxxvi ff. immer-

---

[1] Hos. iv 2 lässt sicher nicht zwingend auf den in Ex. xx belegten Gesamtdekalog zurückschliessen. Darin ist L. PERLITT, *Bundestheologie im Alten Testament*, WMANT 36, Neukirchen 1969, 98 Anm. 6 recht zu geben. Doch handelt es sich hier auf der anderen Seite sicher auch nicht einfach um eine beliebig zusammengestellte Gruppe von Vergehungen. Vgl. weiter Jer. vii 9.

[2] Vgl. etwa das auffahrende מלכם von Is. iii 15 für den innenpolitischen und xxxi 1-3 für den aussenpolitischen Bereich.

[3] Is. xxviii 12; xxx 9 (15), xxx 1; i 4.

[4] Jer. v 1 ff.

[5] Jer. xiii 23.

hin in einzelnen, dem Propheten Jeremia nahestehenen Gruppen noch konstatieren möchte und wie auch Ez. ix 4 ihn erwarten lässt, ist hier keine Spur mehr zu erkennen.

In solchem Messen Israels und Jerusalems am Rechtswillen Jahwes bringt die grosse Prophetie durchaus ein genuines Element auch des sonstigen Alten Testamentes zur Geltung. Die Berufung Israels ist nie eine unverbindliche Einladung gewesen, sondern hat dieses von früh an mit einem fordernden Rechtswillen Jahwes verbunden. Die radikale Eliminierung jeder Bundeswirklichkeit aus dem älteren Israel [1] vermag ebensowenig zu überzeugen wie die völlige Trennung von Bund und Gebot vor der deuteronomischen Zeit.[2] Wie immer es sich mit der Bedeutsamkeit gerade der Bundeskategorie im älteren Israel verhalten mag, es ist nicht zu verkennen, dass sich Israel in seinem Glauben an Jahwe von früh her auch einem fordernden Willen verpflichtet weiss.[3]

Es ist nun allerdings das Neuartige in der Hochprophetie, dass dieser Wille in einer unerbittlichen Schärfe angemeldet und die nahende Katastrophe mit der Verletzung dieses Willens verbunden wird.

VIII

Diese Katastrophe hat sich sukzessive in den Ereignissen von 733, 721, 597 und 587 ereignet.

Hier aber geschieht das etwa von Amos oder auch von der vorexilischen Verkündigung Ezechiels her Unerwartete, dass im Zeitpunkt der grossen Katastrophe, nachdem der in Jerusalem noch politisch übriggebliebene Rest „Israels" verbannt, im Davidhaus das unter der Verheissung stehende Geschlecht des irdischen Gesalbten Israels endgültig aus der Königsherrschaft verstossen und im Tempel der nach der Verkündigung des (im Sinne der Reform Josias interpretierten) Deuteronomiums allein legitime Ort der Anbetung in Schutt und Asche gesunken ist, gerade aus dem Munde der Prophetie ganz voll eine Verkündigung aufbricht, die neue Zukunft ansagt. Ist es bei Jeremia möglicherweise nur die verhaltene Erwartung, dass man „in diesem Lande wieder einmal Häuser und Aecker und Weinberge kaufen" werde [4] und dass der Neuanfang bei den nach Babylonien Exilier-

---

[1] So PERLITT l.c. (S. 60, Anm. 4).

[2] E. GERSTENBERGER, „Covenant and Commandment," *JBL* 84, 1965, 38-51.

[3] Das gilt, auch wenn man die Hypertrophie der Argumentation mit dem „Bundesformular," gegen die PERLITT mit Recht angeht, nicht mitmachen kann.

[4] Jer. xxxii 15.

ten liegen werde,[1] so ist ausgerechnet bei dem härtesten Verkündiger der radikalen Unfähigkeit Israels, wirklich als Jahwes Volk zu bestehen, bei Ezechiel, die volle Aussage neuen Lebens aus dem Tode,[2] der Rückholung der in die Länder Versprengten ins Land und einer neuen Gegenwart Jahwes inmitten seines Volkes zu vernehmen.[3] Die Versuche, Ezechiel jede Zukunftsverkündigung abzusprechen,[4] scheitern zunächst an der so ausgesprochen ezechielischen Vision Ez. xxxvii 1-14 und der auf sie folgenden Zeichenhandlung.[5] Ueber xx 32 ff. hin, die dann dem Propheten schwerlich zwingend abgesprochen werden können, ergibt sich die Brücke zu der grossen Schlussvision von Ez. xl-xlviii, von welcher ein Kernelement noch vom Propheten selber stammen könnte.

Das Buch Ezechiel verrät auch die ausdrückliche Reflexion über den Grund dieses Umbruches der Verkündigung. Es ist hier nicht der irrationale Ausbruch der nicht zu dämpfenden Liebe Jahwes zu seinem Volk, der in Hos. xi 8 f. zu hören war. Ebensowenig ist es der Hinweis auf den alles Verstehen des Menschen übersteigenden göttlichen Plan, in dem Zion seine bleibende Bedeutung behält, wie bei Jesaja.[6] In Ez. xxxvi 16 ff. ist es, dem sonstigen Stil Ezechiels entsprechend, das Eifern Jahwes um die Ehre seines Namens. Weil er sich seines Namens „erbarmt,"[7] der durch die Zerstreuung seines Volkes unter die Völker bei diesen zum Spott wird, darum wird er den Tod Israels, so verkündet es die Vision Ez. xxxvii 1-14, aus seiner Schöpfermacht heraus neu zum Leben wenden. „Nicht um euretwillen handle ich, Haus Israel, sondern um meines heiligen Namens willen, den ihr unter den Völkern, zu denen ihr gekommen seid, entweiht habt, und ich werde meinen grossen, unter den Völkern entweihten Namen, den ihr in ihrer Mitte entweiht habt, heiligen. Und die Völker sollen erkennen, dass ich Jahwe bin, spricht der Herr Jahwe, wenn ich mich vor ihren Augen an euch heilig erweise."[8]

---

[1] Jer. xxiv. Die Ursprünglichkeit von xxxi 31-34, wo vom „Neuen Bund" die Rede ist, steht noch stark in der Diskussion und kann hier wohl nicht einfach vorausgesetzt werden.

[2] Ez. xxxvii 1-14.

[3] Ez. xx 32-44; xliii 1-12.

[4] S. HERRMANN, *Die prophetischen Heilserwartungen im Alten Testament*, BWANT 5. F. 5, Stuttgart 1965, 241-291.

[5] *BK* XIII 1969, 890 f. 908.

[6] Das Staunen angesichts der höheren, dem platten Menschenverstand nicht zugänglichen Weisheit der göttlichen Pläne kommt im Bauerngleichnis Is. xxviii 23-29 ganz besonders stark zum Ausdruck.

[7] Ez. xxxvi 21 verwendet das starke Verb חמל.

[8] Ez. xxxvi 22 f.

Was aber bei Ezechiel in dieser herben Formulierung des Propheten, der um das Eifern Jahwes um seinen Namen weiss, zu vernehmen
ist, das setzt sich bei Deuterojesaja in den psalmartig gehaltenen Jubel
angesichts der näherrückenden Befreiung um. Aber auch hier ist es
unverkürzt festgehalten, dass die Wende zu neuem Leben nicht in
einem irgendwie am Volke selber Lebens- oder gar Liebenswerten
begründet ist, sondern allein im freien Entscheid der Barmherzigkeit
Jahwes. „Ich, ich tilge deine Vergehungen aus um meinetwillen und
gedenke deiner Sünden nicht mehr." [1]

IX

Mit diesem erneuten Ja zu Israel rückt aber die Gottesrede, wie die
Propheten sie verkündigen, unversehens wieder nahe an die zuvor
skizzierte übrige Rede des Alten Testamentes von Gott heran. Und
doch ist nicht zu übersehen, dass sie dieser Rede eine neue Tiefen-
dimension gibt. Durch die prophetische Verkündigung und die sie
begleitende Geschichte ist Israel durch die Hölle seiner tiefsten Verlorenheit hindurchgeführt worden—einer Verlorenheit, die nicht nur
die geschichtliche Erniedrigung meinte, sondern seinen Stand vor
Gott in Frage stellte. Alles Eigenrecht und alle Eigengerechtigkeit ist
ihm hier aus den Händen geschlagen worden. Nur als das aus der
freien Barmherzigkeit seines Gottes heraus lebende und von da her zu
neuem Hinhören gerufene Volk kann es sich verstehen, wo es der
Botschaft der Propheten ernstlich standhält.

Ist es nur Zufall, dass gerade da, wo diese freie neue Barmherzigkeit
Jahwes über Israel am jubelndsten verkündet wird, auch die Völkerwelt ausserhalb Israels in einer neuen Weise als von diesem Geschehen
betroffen in Sicht kommt und die Mauern zu ihr hin anfangen niedri-
ger zu werden?

Bei Ezechiel, dem eben erst ins Exil geführten Priester, ist davon,
wenn er schon von einer Erkenntnis, die auch den Völkern zuteil
werden wird, spricht, noch wenig zu sehen.[2] Wohl aber macht der aus
der Welt der Psalmen kommende Deuterojesaja sichtbar, wie angesichts der neuen Tat Jahwes an seinem Volk, die aus der Treue zu
seinem alten Tun stammt, das Licht der Fremdgötter zu verblassen

---

[1] Is. xliii 25.
[2] H. GRAF REVENTLOW, „Die Völker als Jahwes Zeugen bei Ezechiel," *ZAW*
71, 1959, 33-43 setzt hier wohl etwas zu starke Akzente, die bei Deuterojesaja
richtiger am Platze sind.

beginnt und Bewegung in der Völkerwelt auf den Gott hin anhebt, der sich in seinem Tun an Israel erwiesen hat.[1]

Es ist der Beitrag der grossen Schriftprophetie zum alttestamentlichen Reden von Gott, das aus den Völkern herausgeführte, unter die Verheissung des Segens (J) und der Gottesnähe (P) gestellte Volk von jeder Eigengerechtigkeit zu entblössen und ihm den Gott sichtbar zu machen, vor dem der Mensch allein aus der freien Gabe zu leben vermag. Zeuge dieses Gottes zu sein, ist das Volk, das die prophetische Botschaft vernommen, berufen.[2]

---

[1] Vgl. etwa Is. xlv 18-25.
[2] Is. xliii 10, 12.

Berît AND COVENANT IN THE DEUTERONOMISTIC HISTORY

BY

DENNIS J. McCARTHY
Rome

From the point of view of the experience which gives its words their connotations, religious vocabulary can be divided into two classes; (1) terms directly religious in their associations, and (2) those primarily associated with everyday experience. For us (or for me) the first sort is largely connected with cult, a realm of experience consciously connected with religion and religion alone. Thus an example of it in English would be "sacrament." The word has deep meaning and rich associations, but they are religious, and in any context it will introduce a religious coloration. An example of the second sort would be "father." It is deeply rooted in the scriptural religious tradition, but no matter how a person meets this tradition, he normally meets it with rich associations already tied to the word from experience not thought of as specifically religious, and these associations will always be present in the religious context.

Hebrew *berît* belongs to the second class. It was experienced in society in a context larger than the explicitly and exclusively religious. Men made *berîtôt* [1] among themselves, as Jonathan did with David, or David with the northern tribes. Moreover, the word does not seem to have achieved an important position in the Old Testament religious vocabulary until rather late.[2] In other words, *berît* was not merely

---

[1] The use of this odd plural points up a problem of discussion in this area. The traditional translation, "covenant *(Bund)*," has been called into serious question: cf. E. KUTSCH, "Gesetz und Gnade. Probleme des alttestamentlichen Bundesbegriffs," *ZAW.* 79 (1967), pp. 18-35; "Der Begriff ברית in vordeuteronomischer Zeit," *Rost Festschrift. BZAW.* 105, Berlin 1967, pp. 133-143; "Von ברית zu 'Bund'," *Kerygma und Dogma* 14 (1968), pp. 159-182; *THAT* I, cols. 339-352, insisting that the word should be translated by "obligation" *(Verpflichtung)* or the like. To avoid the appearance of prejudging the case I have avoided any translation and used *berît* in the body of this article.

[2] On the rise to prominence of *berît* in the theological vocabulary of the Deuteronomic school see L. PERLITT, *Bundestheologie im Alten Testament.* WMANT 26, Neukirchen 1969, but note that despite PERLITT *berît* was not the exclusive

experienced in a secular context *along with* a religious; historically it had been experienced there for a long time *before* it appeared in the religious context in an important way.

This means that, when it became important in religious vocabulary, it will have carried over connotations it had acquired in its primary context. Hence it is important to study the phenomenon of the secular [1] *bᵉrît*, or more exactly *bᵉrît*-making, for *bᵉrît* was first of all an act (see below, n. 23) to see what associations it has, since these will color its use in religious contexts. This study will deal directly with the reports of secular *bᵉrît*-making in the Deuteronomistic History. For one reason, most mentions of such *bᵉrît*-making occur here or can be dealt with indirectly in relation to texts from the History.[2] Simply in quantitative terms these examples determine the general connotations of the word. Even more important, *bᵉrît* is applied to religious phenomena primarily in the Deuteronomic school, and surely the word so applied carried with it the connotations familiar to that school from the history with which it concerned itself.

A final preliminary note is in order. The modern debate about *bᵉrît* has been posed largely in terms of the questions: Who obliges whom in a *bᵉrît*, and, What kind of obligations are involved in *bᵉrît*, unilateral or multilateral?[3] This study is not aimed directly at these questions.

---

property of that school and its successors. It was used in a modest way at least in religious contexts before Deuteronomy: see my review article in *Biblica* 53 (1972), pp. 110-121.

[1] "Secular" is a problematic word, of course. *bᵉrît* was made "before Yahweh" or under oath, and so was connected with religion at least *in obliquo*, as every aspect of ancient life seems to have been. But *in recto* it could concern connections among men, things apart from the specifically religious sphere of cult and things thought to be primarily an aspect of relations with God. There is a real distinction between these two aspects of *bᵉrît* so that "secular" seems a valid as well as convenient designation of the second.

[2] In fact 17 of 21 (or 22) examples. There are thirteen mentions of *bᵉrît*-making in Dtr: Jos. ix 1-x 1; 1 Sam. xi 1-3; xviii 1-4; xx 5-8; xx 10-17; xxii 8; xxiii 16-8; 2 Sam. iii 12-21; iii 21; v 1-3; 1 Kings v 26; xv 18-19; xx 32-34; 2 Kings xi 4; xi 17. Each of this set of texts is eparate evidence of the connotations of *krt bᵉrît* because it deals with a different *bᵉrît* or represents a different report of a *bᵉrît* from that presented in another text. The five texts: Ezek. xvii 11-21; Hos. ix 4; xii 2b; 2 Chron. xxiii 1; xxiii 3 can be dealt with in connection with the texts in Dtr.

This leaves only three texts: Gen. xxi 22-32; xxvi 22-33; xxxi 23-xxxii 3 (or 4, if one were to treat separately the J and E elements in xxi 22-32, as he probably should). On these see provisionally D. J. McCARTHY, "Three Covenants in Genesis," *CBQ*. 26 (1964), pp. 179-189. They deserve further study, but there is no space for it here. It will be seen, however, that they confirm the major conclusions from the Deuteronomistic evidence.

[3] See J. BEGRICH, "Berīt. Ein Beitrag zur Erfassung einer alttestamentlichen

It is concerned simply to find out what the texts associate with *krt* *berît*. However, one cannot and should not ignore the *Zeitgeist*, and it will be evident that much that is said relates to these questions.

I. ISRAEL AND THE GIBEONITES (Jos. ix 1-x 1).[1] Joshua *wayya'aś* *lāhem šālôm wayyikrot lāhem berît lehayyôtām*, and the leaders of Israel *wayyiššābe'û lāhem* (ix 15). The agents of Israel are presented as the sole actors in the *berît*-making. The text describes negotiations. The Gibeonites propose a *berît*, justifying this by the fact that they are from afar. Israel objects, and the Gibeonites answer with persuasion: they are Israel's servants. Their identity is questioned anew, and the Gibeonites reassert their points: they are strangers and servants. It is on this understanding that they are given a *berît* granting them life.[2] *Berît* is correlative with the words and acts connected with its making. What follows shows this. When Gibeon is found actually to be nearby, only one of the elements involved in the negotiations is altered. Servitude remains in new conditions. The result is not an end of *berît* and its obligations, but alteration of them. The relation of servitude is still there, and Gibeon can appeal to it (x 6).

Thus the obligations actually involved in this *berît* turn out to be effectively bilateral. Israel guarantees Gibeon and Gibeon serves Israel, even though Israel's representatives are presented as the sole actors in the actual *berît*-making. But, in fact, the text does not stick quite consistently to this view of the action. x 1b says: *hišlîmû yošbê gib'ôn* *'et-yiśrā'ēl*. That is, the Gibeonites did just exactly what ix 15a presents Joshua as doing alone in making the *berît!* It may well be that x 1b is a memory of a tradition which presented the Gibeonite *berît* as an

---

Denkform," *ZAW.* 60 (1944), pp. 1-11; A. JEPSEN, "Berith. Ein Bcitrag zur Theologie der Exilzeit," *Rudolph Festschrift*, Tübingen 1961, pp. 161-179; and the articles of E. KUTSCH mentioned in n. 1.

[1] For the text see M. NOTH, *Josua, HAT* I-7, pp. 53-60: it is a combination of traditions which cannot be analyzed into parallel sources. The present combination of traditions is pre-Deuteronomic and it gives a coherent view of *berît*-making. It is, therefore, valid evidence for the connotations of *berît* at a relatively early date. J. LIVER, "The Literary History of Joshua IX," *JSS* 8 (1963), 227-243, analyzes the text into an ancient tradition of friendship with Gibeon altered to give it an anti-Gibeonite cast during Saul's efforts to destroy Canaanite enclaves such as Gibeon. One may not accept his reconstruction in detail, but he makes some important points. One, relevant here, is his recognition of the bilateral character of the *berît* (pp. 227, 235).

[2] The grant of life is associated with ancient treaties. See J. WIJNGAARDS, "Death and resurrection in Covenantal Context (Hos. vi 2)," *VT.* 17 (1967), pp. 226-239. It is associated with *berît* in Jos. ix 15; 1 Kings xx 32; and, apparently, 1 Sam. xx 14, and implied in *berît* contexts in 1 Sam. xi 1-3 and xx 7-8 (see below, p. 70, n. 3).

explicitly two-sided affair.[1] This may allow interesting historical specu-
lation, but the present form of the text is significant in itself for the
connotations of *berît*. It shows that a relatively early form of the tradition could already ascribe a *berît*-making to Joshua alone and then
calmly present the same action as the Gibeonites' work. The terminology, in other words, is not very rigid. What it asserts in any given
place should not be pressed *in sensu negante* without further ado. The
text can pass from attributing the act to one party to attributing it to
another without embarrassment.

Conclusions from the report of the Gibeonite *berît*: 1) There is an
extensive report of negotiations which work out bilateral obligations.
2) There is no explicit statement defining these obligations. 3) Joshua
is the only subject of the phrase *krt berît*, but x 1b has the Gibeonites
performing what is in fact the same action.

II. JABESH-GILEAD AND NAHASH (1 Sam. xi 1-3). The men of
Jabesh-Gilead make a proposal: with a *berît* they will serve Nahash.
He does not reject this entirely, but he adds cruel and humiliating
terms. Even in his contempt he allows a counter-proposal.

Conclusions from this report: 1) There are negotiations involving
service and implying that this is a condition for a grant of life. 2) There
is not explicit statement of the *berît* obligations. 3) Nahash is the
subject requested to *krt berît*.

III. JONATHAN AND DAVID, 1 (1 Sam. xviii 1-4; xx 5-8). It is generally accepted that in this first *berît* involving the heroes Jonathan is
the agent. He binds himself to David by a symbolic gift of clothes and
weapons. He is granting fellowship.[2] No doubt, but in clause actually
mentioning *berît* both Jonathan and David are agents, both subjects
of the verb *wayyikrot*.[3] In the midst of a description of *berît*-making
where all the emphasis is on what Jonathan feels and does the text

---

[1] On the history of the Gibeonite *berît* see J. BLENKINSOPP, "Are There Traces
of the Gibeonite Covenant in Deuteronomy?", *CBQ*. 28 (1966), pp. 207-219, and
J. M. GRINTZ, "The Treaty of Joshua and the Gibeonites," *JAOS*. 86 (1966),
pp. 113-126. It is true that *šlm* relates x 1b to ix 15a, not *krt berît*, but in ix 15
"make peace" is perfectly parallel with two other expressions for creating an
obligation. It is not credible that the Gibeonites could be thought of as subjects
of one member of the triad and not the others. Further, *šlm* is integral to *berît*:
cf. 1 Kings v 26; Gen. xxvi 28-30.

[2] *Lebensgemeinschaft*. So BEGRICH, *ZAW*. 60 (1944), p. 1; A. JEPSEN, *Rudolph
Festschrift*, p. 163; E. KUTSCH, *ZAW*. 79 (1967), p. 26, n. 29; *Rost Festschrift*,
p. 135, n. 12.

[3] The singular verb with a double subject in xviii 3a is perfectly acceptable
grammar, and the text needs no emendation. For the construction see Gen. ix 23;
discussed in JOÜON, *Grammaire de l'hebreu biblique*, 150q.

still takes the action as somehow attributable to David as well as Jonathan. One can conceive of explanations of this as some sort of correction of the history. E.g., the writer may not wish to leave the great David in an inferior position. This simply means that for him *berît* and *berît*-making are such that he is free to write in this way. There is nothing fixed in the process or vocabulary to prohibit him from making David subject of the *krt berît* phrase when he wishes, even though all else point to a *berît* simply granted to him. The *berît* is not totally one-sided. The all-important initial act at least is attributable to both parties.

This is even clearer in 2 Sam. xx 8, where David says that Jonathan has "brought him into a *berît*" *(biberît yhwh hēbē'tā 'et-ʿabdekā)*. This does not prove that David acted in the *berît*-making. The usage is figurative, and the hifil could be declarative. Theoretically the sentence could simply mean that Jonathan has affirmed that David is within the figurative area of his *berît*. An English paraphrase could be: "thou hast brought thy servant under thy protection." However, actual usage is against this interpretation. Ezek. xvii 13 says that Nebuchadnezzar *wayyābē'* Zedekiah *beʾālā*. This stands in synonymous parallelism with *wayyikrot 'ittô berît*. And xvii 18 equates the oath and *berît* with giving one's hand, i.e., with the *act* signifying assent. *Hēbî'*, then, in the context of *berît*, is not just declarative. It means to cause one to do something which commits him to the *berît*. This is not to create a state of *berît* by unilateral fiat. It means one move the other to do something.[1] He may not be entirely eager to do it, but he does it.

In our case there is no reason to doubt David's willingness to go into the *berît*. In any case, he is active. He follows Jonathan's lead. 1 Sam. xx 8 thus shows that the use of *krt berît* in xvii 3 is correct. It is not a rather careless generalizing expression. It describes what

---

[1] Ezekiel's use of the root *bô'* in relation to *berît* shows this and more. In xvi 8 *wā'ābô biberît 'et-* describes Yahweh's entering into *berît* with Jerusalem. His act realizes the *berît*. This use of the kal stem is the correlative of the use of the hifil in xvii 13, and the correlatives produce a picture. The more powerful person simply acts. The weaker is acted upon. He is made to do something, and yet he also does something. This is complex, but it is realistic. The more forceful of several persons involved together usually is more active in determining the nature of a connection. In the first moment, the weaker undergoes the influence of the stronger but he too must *act* under this influence. There is no leading without following. The use of the Hebrew verb thus conforms to experience. But experience also shows that influence is two-sided. The weaker can move the stronger, and this is accounted for in Hebrew usage too: cf. 1 Sam. xx 17 (MT) where a troubled Jonathan makes David swear *(hāšbîaʿ)*.

bᵉrît-making involved here, a two-sided activity, with Jonathan leading, perhaps, and David following, but both acting.

The *bᵉrît* obligation might still be unilateral though the act of *bᵉrît*-
making was not. But consider xx 8 again. David appeals to the *bᵉrît*.
It obliges Jonathan to show *ḥesed*, to protect faithfully his partner.
This might be an appeal to an obligation incumbent on Jonathan
alone, but there is more. David appeals as Jonathan's *ʿebed*. He puts
himself in a subordinate relationship to Jonathan, and this is as closely
associated with the *bᵉrît* as is *ḥesed*. Indeed, it is only here, in an explicit
appeal to *bᵉrît*, that David styles himself Jonathan's *ʿebed!* It is the
retainer who has a right to the lord's protection.[1]

Moreover, 2 Sam. xviii 1-4 puts much emphasis on Jonathan's
ʾaʰᵃᵉbâ for David. This means love, to be sure, but it is a love which
is associated with treaty and covenantal contexts. This means, as
Moran has shown,[2] that the love which is the basis of the first Jonathan-David *bᵉrît*, whatever else it may include, has two major implications. It involves loyalty *(ḥesed)* and service (cf. *ʿebed*), the very things
appealed to in connection with *bᵉrît* in 2 Sam. xx 7-8. This confirms
the close connection between the two as they appear there, and more
probably, their correlation. The love on which the Jonathan-David
bᵉrît is based implies what David makes explicit: reciprocal obligations.

Thus much of the vocabulary of this *bᵉrît* is attached to biblical
tradition. Still, one can hardly fail to notice a special atmosphere about
it. It is a fellowship of warriors. It is a very personal relationship—note
the emphasis on love. The lord is a gift-giver. The retainer commits
his very life into the lord's hands.[3] It involves obligations one can
appeal to, but these are in no way made explicit in the *bᵉrît*-making.
This combination of factors is unique in Old Testament *bᵉrîtôt*, but
it is by no means without parallel. It is, in fact, an example of the
heroic friendship.

Such associations of heroes are part of the heroic tradition from
Gilgamesh and Enkidu through Roland and Oliver down to its imita-
tion in stories like Fennimore Cooper's *Leatherstocking Tales!* They
have fairly definite and consistent characteristics and a natural setting
in a specific stage of society. Typically they involve a lord and a

---

[1] Though JEPSEN, *Rudolph Festschrift*, p. 163, interprets this in just the opposite
sense.

[2] "The Ancient Near Eastern Background of the Love of God in Deuteronomy," *CBQ* 25 (1963), pp. 77-87, especially p. 82, n. 33.

[3] Note xx 7b, where David puts his life in Jonathan's hands. He returns it to
the lord who, in the convention, grants life with *bᵉrît*.

favorite member of his *comitatus*. The lord is a gift-giver, correlative duties of protection and service are taken for granted, life itself is committed to the association, and the friendship involved is indeed a love surpassing the love of women. Such associations are normally described in the literature of the so-called heroic ages, and these are usually ages when a nomadic group is beginning to come to terms with settled life in an invaded land but has not forgotten its tribal past.[1] In this setting certain familial and personal aspects of relationship are emphasized over more political and impersonal ones. And all this is exactly the situation of Israel under Saul. The *bᵉrît* of Jonathan and David, then, describes a heroic friendship in its proper setting. The special connotations which this adds to the word *bᵉrît* must be remembered if we are to feel its full resonance.

Conclusions from the report of the first Jonathan-David *bᵉrît:* 1) There were no negotiations, but Jonathan had come to love David before the *bᵉrît* was made. 2) There is no explicit statement of *bᵉrît* obligations, but these were taken for granted and so could be explicitly appealed to. They were bilateral. 3) Both parties are subjects of the phrase *krt bᵉrît*. 4) The special features of the *bᵉrît* mark it as the unique biblical example of a heroic friendship.

IV. JONATHAN AND DAVID, 2 (1 Sam. xx 11-17; xxiii 16-18). The first passage certainly deals with a formal connection between Jonathan and David, but the text is a problem. In 14-16 Jonathan's troubles and desires are not clearly expressed, and at the crucial point, the oath in 17, MT has Jonathan making David swear while LXX has Jonathan doing the swearing. Must we then reject MT? Many do so, and for two principle reasons. First, the text is supposed to be concerned with

---

[1] The term *comitatus* comes, of course, from Tacitus' classic description of the heroic band in the *Germania*. Old Germanic poetry, e.g., in Anglo-Saxon, *Beowulf*, *The Seafarer*, *Finnsburg Fragment*, is another indispensable source for the background of heroic society and its literature which are reflected in many elements of the David story besides the Jonathan *bᵉrît*. See also C. M. BOWRA, *Heroic Poetry*, London 1961, pp. 65, 476-507. H. J. STOEBE, "Gedenken zur Heldensage in den Samuelbüchern," *Rost Festschrift*, 208-218, sees the matter rather differently. He seems to take the Jonathan-David association as described in 1 Sam. xviii 1-4 to be altered by more popular, unheroic elements. However, it is difficult to accept exact distinctions between heroic saga, popular *(bauerlich)* saga etc. in such a small sample of literature as Samuel, and indeed the Bible, offers. Neither does the distinction itself allow for the variety within the strict heroic tradition itself. It concentrates too much on the aristocratic element, while BOWRA has shown that there are primitive and proletarian traditions that may properly be called heroic. In any case, the friendship of Jonathan and David is paralled in the heroic tradition even in its most limited sense.

David's need for help. Hence it is more appropriate that Jonathan swear to stand by him. Secondly, the appeal to love (17b) is a motive for Jonathan to act, not David.[1] The first argument seems to miss the point. 12-13 show Jonathan's willingness to help David, but the next verses show him as a man troubled by the danger which David's rise presents to him and his. He wants reassurance in return for his help and so it is fitting that he adjure David. As for the love, as we have seen, it is connected with *berît*, and it implies fidelity and service. This is a proper basis for an appeal for reassurance in a new situation with the positions of the parties reversed. This is the more fitting in that xviii 1 shows that the disposition, the love, is larger than the act which formally ratifies it. It exists before that act.

Thus it is hardly necessary to turn to LXX. MT remains problematic in details, but it gives a picture sufficiently complete and coherent. Jonathan binds David by oath to an obligation defined by his pleas for himself and his family. And he binds him *again (wayyôsep)*. In the text this "again" can only refer back to xviii 3-4. No other *berît* has been reported. That is, MT 1 Sam. xx 16-17 assumes that the first Jonathan-David *berît* involved a binding oath on David's part. So it confirms our analysis of xviii 1-4; xx 7-8: Jonathan appears as the chief mover of the *berît*-making, but David had his part in the action.

In fact MT xx 10-17 may well reveal the steps involved in the process of *berît*-making. Jonathan urges the action. The expression *wayyikrot 'im* taken by itself might even mean "imposed a *berît* on" David or the like. However, the continuation of the process rules this out. It is no simple, one-sided act. David is made to do something, to take an oath.[2] One might describe the process in parliamentary

---

[1] The arguments are given in detail in H. P. SMITH, *Samuel. ICC*, Edinburgh 1899, pp. 187-189, and S. R. DRIVER, *Notes on the Hebrew Text of the Books of Samuel*,[2] Oxford 1913; W. CASPARI, *Die Samuelbücher. KAT* VII, Leipzig 1926, p. 259, adopts the LXX reading but insists that the oath is *gegenseitig;* cf. pp. 251-252, 258. MT 16a *wayyikrot yehônātān 'im-bêt dāwid* is a standard ellipsis for *krt berît* (cf. 1 Sam. xi 2; xxii 8). LXX has no reference to *diathēkē*. This is not an argument for preferring the MT text, but it means that only MT is directly relevant to a discussion of the connotation of *berît*. It shows what Hebrew could connect with it. LXX refers only to an oath, which is not necessarily identified with *berît* at all.

[2] The close parallel to 16a in xxii 8a (or perhaps reference: n.b. the ellipsis of *berît* and the allusion to David's family, not to David directly, in both texts) is a further argument. Saul complains about Jonathan's initiatives with David: his making *berît* is parallel to stirring him up! He has made David do something (on the emphasis on David's *action* here see A. WEISER, "Die Legitimation des Königs David," *VT*. 16 (1966), 332). Note the use of the hifil in xx 17a also; like Ezekiel's *hēbî'* it implies a complex action with two subjects.

language. Jonathan moves a *berît* and David accepts it. The mutuality is confirmed by 1 Sam. xx 42 where Jonathan says that both he and David have sworn. The only thing in the text this can refer to is the account in xx 20-17. The pattern resembles the earlier *berît*. The action is complex, not one-sided. One side may do more than the other, but both are agents.

There is also an element of definition. Jonathan's speech tells what it is all about. Mutual obligations are adumbrated. Jonathan will keep David informed as long as he is in danger, and David will protect Jonathan when he has come to power.

The other report of a Jonathan-David *berît*, 1 Sam. xxiii 16-18 seems to be a tradition parallel to that in xx 10-17. The circumstances are the same. Jonathan comes to David who is in hiding. He proposes a *berît*, and his proposal covers the same points: Jonathan alludes to David's danger but admits his coming supremacy and calls for respect for his own position. The act of *berît*-making is reported more simply, but clearly both parties are agents: *wayyikretû šenêhem berît*.[1]

The whole report is clear and succinct. One might imagine an editor tidying up the disorder of xx 10-17. But if that were the case, why did he not do something in that text itself? And why repeat it here in a position where it is rather out of place? Surely we have here an alternate tradition of the affair. In any case, whether as a parallel or, less likely, a re-interpretation, 1 Sam. xxiii 16-18 confirms the view that emerges from MT xx 10-17. Hebrew tradition saw the later Jonathan-David *berît* as a bilateral thing both in its making and in its content.

Conclusions from the second Jonathan-David *berît:* 1) Strictly speaking there are no negotiations, but the urgency of Jonathan's language in 1 Sam. xx 12-15 accords with the tradition associating persuasion and so negotiation of a kind with *berît*. 2) There is a statement defining mutual *berît* obligations. 3) Both parties act in the *berît*-making, and in 1 Sam. xxiii 18 both are subjects of the phrase *krt berît*.

V. DAVID AND ISRAEL (2 Sam. iii 21; v 1-3). Both texts mention *berît* in connection with David's accession to kingship over the northern tribes. It is a single act seen from different points of view.[2]

---

[1] Perhaps a technical phrase for mutual *berît*-making. It recurs for the *berît* between the equal and friendly sovereigns Solomon and Hiram: 1 Kings v 26. The tradition of mutual *berît* with Tyre is alluded to again in Am. i 9: *berît 'aḥîm*. *'aḥ* was the normal way allied kings of equal status described themselves in the ancient near east.

[2] Not the points of view of different historians but of a single tradition. 2 Sam. iii 21 and v 3 belong to the same strand (cf. L. ROST, "Die Überlieferung von der

Each party is represented as acting: in iii 21 all Israel *wayyikretû berît* *'itteḵā*, i.e., with David, and in v 3 David *wayyikrot lahem berît*. Perhaps these correlatives indicate that Israel imposes an obligation on David and he formally accepts it, for, it is said, *krt berît* with *'et* or *'im* means "impose an obligation on" *(verpflichten)* and with *le-*, "accept *(über-nehmen)* an obligation." [1] This might be, but the case is complicated. Even though one were to grant that the obligation involved was one-sided,[2] the repetition of the phrases reporting the act means that things were not entirely one-sided. Both parties were agents, active *berît-*makers, though their activities may have been different. At least the act of *berît-*making, which produces and conditions all that follows, was bipartite.

However, there is a problem even with the obligation involved. No doubt in actual fact David undertook express obligations to respect the liberties of Israel. The theory of the *Königsvertrag* is pertinent, and it would justify the assumption that David really undertook to foster Israel's "Heil, Frieden, Wohlstand, Leben." [3] But this

Thronnachfolge Davids," *Das kleine Credo*, Heidelberg 1965, p. 238; not even CASPARI, *KAT* VII, who has a most detailed source analysis, separates these verses).

[1] The normal usage for mutual *berît* would have been *bên... ûbên*. This description of the use of the prepositions is given by E. KUTSCH, *THAT* I, cols. 343-346; *ZAW*. 79 (1967), p. 24, n. 26. However, A. JEPSEN, *Rudolph Festschrift*, 172, asserts that there is no differentiation in the use of the prepositions. J. MAIER, "Urim und Tummim," *Kairos* 11 (1969), pp. 23-24, thinks that *le-* is used when one "...eine Verpflichtung gegenüber einem anderen eingeht," that is, he agrees with KUTSCH to this extent, but finds the use of *'im-* and *'et-* neutral. In fact, it is difficult to maintain distinctions, at least in the materials under discussion in this article, and MAIER himself says that in 2 Sam. v 3 *krt berît le-* concerns a "...Vertrag... in dem wohl Rechte und Pflichten des Königs festgelegt waren." Thus the ties are two-sided, and this is surely the correct interpretation of the text, as we shall see.

[2] So A. JEPSEN, *Rudolph Festschrift*, pp. 163-164, and E. KUTSCH, *THAT* I, col. 343. In *ZAW*. 79 (1967), p. 26, n. 33 KUTSCH took the two passages together as a possible exception to his rules for the use of *'et-* and *le-* in that they would express bilateral *berît* with these prepositions, but he already was leaning to JEPSEN's view.

[3] Quoted from A. JEPSEN, *Rudolph Festschrift*, p. 164. But the *Königsvertrag* cannot be understood simply as a one-sided obligation imposed on the king to limit his power. In the *Vertrag* the people had to submit to the royal power except as limited by the specific agreement. Thus, the total context of the classic case, 1 Sam. x 17-25, includes 1 Sam. viii. The people subject themselves to a king who can tax, carry out public works, make war and peace, even though only within the limits defined by the "constitution" alluded to in x 25. Hos. ix 4 might be further evidence that Israel's royal *berît* was bilateral both in the content of its obligations and in the act which realized it. The text is cryptic—it could be no more than a reflection on perjury as a common crime—but mention of the king in ix 3 inclines one to think of the *Königsvertrag* (cf. H. W. WOLFF, *Hosea. BKAT* XIV-1, p. 227). If this the reference it indicates that in the *Vertrag* the people of Israel bound

is not what the text of Sam. actually associates with *krt berît* here. The act is the conclusion of lively negotiations. The terms which give the obligation under oath [1] a concrete content have been hammered out. The outlines of the process are simplified but clear. Abner, on David's behalf, deals with the tribes (2 Sam. iii 17-18). This results in a readiness to make a *berît*. Two things are explicit: readiness for the *berît*-making, and admission of David's supremacy (iii 21). When the *berît* is actually made it is accompanied by the statement summing up the results of the negotiations (vlb-2). The emphasis is entirely on David's power. Israel accepts him as king and war-leader (v 2; cf. iii 17) and recognizes his divine election (2 Sam. v 2; cf. iii 18). This may not reflect the total historical reality, but it is what colors *berît* as it stands in the text. David is taking over mastery over Israel. David's "obligation" is to rule and guide!

Thus the posited normal usage of *krt berît 'et-* and *le-* is actually reversed: Israel comes to David who reigns when it makes a *berît* with *('et-)* him, and he becomes their shepherd and leader when he makes a *berît* for *(le-)* them. This may be the result of development. Perhaps the terminology reflects an earlier stage when the roles were more or less reversed. One can imagine an accord in which Israel was presented as imposing limiting obligations on David's power and he acknowledging the limits. This might have been expressed in precise

---

themselves to something (*debārîm* surely indicates the contents, the things sworn to; cf. the semantic parallels *awātu* and *memiyaš* in Akkadian and Hittite treaties), and they were subjects of the phrase *krt berît*. Thus the people had a part in the *berît* exactly parallel to that presumed for the king. See also J. MAIER, *Kairos* 11 (1969), pp. 25, 30, on the royal *berît* as a conferral of power which, though it might be limited, was still related to divine powers. On the *Königsvertrag* in general sed G. FOHRER, "Der Vertrag zwischen König und Volk in Israel," *ZAW*. 71 (1959), pp. 1-22. Concerning the actual historical basis of the picture of kingship, and particularly that of David, see A. WEISER, *VT*. 16 (1966), pp. 335-337, 349-350: passages like 2 Sam. v 2 which emphasize the divine origin of royal power are the work of the author of the history put into the mouths of his characters. They serve to justify the claims of the Davidids. Weiser places this interpretation of history in the time of Solomon. He is no doubt correct in seeing interpretation and not historical reporting at work—though the interpretation doubtless had a solid basis in history—and his dating is persuasive. Even if the interpretation is later than Solomonic times, it is pre-Deuteronomic, and once more offers evidence for connotations of *berît* in an early era.

[1] Even though oath *(nšb')* is not mentioned, *krt berît* by itself signifies an especially solemn oath. Originally it seems to have been a ritual, "acted-out" conditional curse on oneself (cf. D. J. McCARTHY, *Treaty and Covenant. Analecta biblica* 21, Rome 1963, pp. 52-57; E. KUTSCH, *ZAW*. 79 [1967], pp. 20-21), but it came to mean a solemn act of commitment even when there was no such rite, as in 1 Sam. xviii 3; xx 16 etc.

terminology with *krt bᵉrît ᵓet-* and *lᵉ-* attributed to the appropriate subjects. Even so, one should note, each of the parties would be an active subject of the phrase *krt bᵉrît*. But this, though perhaps probable, is not the way *krt bᵉrît* is used in the text. The writer actually reverses the usage. For him *bᵉrît*-making no longer involved a precisely fixed vocabulary, if it ever had.[1]

Conclusions from the David-Israel *bᵉrît:* 1) It was prepared for by negotiations. Presumably each party conceded something, but in the text everything is in David's favor. 2) The statement summing up the negotiations defines the *bᵉrît* obligations. It is an affirmation of David's supremacy. 3) Both parties are subjects of the phrase *krt bᵉrît*.

VI. AHAB AND BEN-HADAD (1 Kings xx 31-34). According to this report Ahab has defeated Ben-Hadad and the latter sues for peace. His ministers offer his submission: *ᶜabdᵉkā ben-hᵃᵉdad*, and plead for his life: *tᵉḥî-naᵓ napšî*. Ahab responds generously: Ben-Hadad is not his servant but his brother. Encouraged by this, Ben-Hadad himself appears and proposes terms. Ahab accepts them and grants a *bᵉrît*.[2]

---

[1] 1 Kings xv 19 is another example of the fluidity of the terminology. The text uses *bên... ûbên* of a bilateral *bᵉrît* in 19a and then slips into *bᵉrît ᵓet-* in 19b for the connection between Israel and Damascus which was even more certainly two-sided than the *bᵉrît* between insignificant Judah and Damascus mentioned in 19a. On the actual situation see A. JEPSEN, "Israel und Damascus," *AfO.* 14 (1941-44), 153-172, especially p. 154.

[2] It is not necessary to alter the text here, reading *tᵉšallᵉḥēnî* for MT *ᵓᵃᵉšallᵉḥekā*, as suggested (but not preferred) by A. JEPSEN, *Rudolph Festschrift*, p. 164, and accepted by E. KUTSCH, *Rost Festschrift*, p. 135. A. S. VAN DER WOUDE, "I Reg XX 34," *ZAW.* 76 (1964), pp. 188-191, has shown that *šlḥ* can mean "give," and on this basis he can translate 34aβ-b with Ben-Hadad remaining the subject: "Ich will (sie; scl. die Städte und Basare) dir unter feierlicher Zusicherung *(babbᵉrît)* schenken,' und er die feierliche Zusage gab und (sie) ihm schenkte." This avoids the problems of the unannounced changes of subject which plague the verse in all other interpretations without violence to the text. Even the ellipsis of the direct object of *šlḥ* (understanding as the object what has just been mentioned) is paralleled with *šlḥ*, "give," in Ugaritic texts cited by VAN DER WOUDE. This interpretation leaves the weaker party tying himself to the stronger by *krt bᵉrît lᵉ-*, but it should be noted that the obligations involved are still bilateral. Differently P. A. H. DE BOER in *Hebräische Wortforschung. Festschrift W. Banmgartner*, SVT 16 (1967), p. 28, who translates: "ich will dich freilassen auf Verpflichtung, (bedingt)," conditionally. The example of the weaker making the *bᵉrît* is paralled in Hos. xii 2b. There Ephraim *yikrotû bᵉrît ᶜim-aššûr*. However, the prophetic text raises another problem with the use of the prepositions because it certainly means that Ephraim put itself under obligation to Assyria, and *krt ᶜim* is supposed to mean "put an obligation on" another. Hosea's text, of course, implies diplomatic dealings (cf. D. J. MCCARTHY, Hosea xii 2: Covenant by Oil, *VT.* 14 [1964], pp. 215-221), but the prophet is concerned with what Ephraim has done, not how it did it, and there is little more about the connotations of *bᵉrît*, e.g., about the unilaterality or bilaterality of the obligations involved, to be gained from the explicit information

This is a miniature picture of the way such things must have worked. Negotiations were needed, as is normal when two persons are settling something important involving them both. There is some technical language. As we have seen, the grant of life is part of the tradition. *'ebed* designates the inferior party (cf. David in 1 Sam. xx 7-8), and *'aḥ* an approximate equal (e.g., Israel and Tyre; cf. above, n. 18). That is, in formal terms Ben-Hadad acknowledges defeat and Ahab accepts reality: a single defeat is not the end of a power like Damascus. These negotiations result in a definite statement of the obligations accepted by each party. Ben-Hadad restores territory and makes commercial concessions, and in return Ahab frees him to rule his kingdom. Unlike any of the examples we have examined previously, there is no indication that more than one party acts in the *berît*-making. Ahab makes it for Ben-Hadad.

Conclusions from the report of the Ahab—Ben-Hadad *berît:* 1) The text describes, in technical vocabulary, the negotiations in which obligations were formulated. 2) There is a statement defining the obligations, which affect both parties. 3) Only one party is the subject of the phrase *krt berît*.

VII. Jehoiada and Joash (2 Kings xi; 2 Chron. xxiii).

There are two *berîtôt* described here, but we can avoid repetition in the comparison of Kings and Chronicles by treating them together. 2 Kings xi 4b simply says that Jehoiada *wayyikrot lahem berît wayyašba' 'otām*. Is this perfectly synonymous parallelism? It is possible. Passages like Jos. ix 14-15; Gen. xx 31-32; and xxvi 28 show a tendency to multiply expressions for the action by which men establish an obligation. However, the contexts of these passages are not exact equivalents of the verse in Kings. They are stories concerned with *berît*-making as such. Periphrasis in describing the matter of central interest is natural. In Kings the *berît*-making is but an incident in an account of violent action directly concerned with something else. The priest decides on a coup, summons the guard officers to the temple, *krt lahem berît*, causes them to take an oath, and reveals the king.

The story hurries forward. There is no pausing. There is no time for pleonasm. Every clause moves the action forward—unless the author forgets and repeats himself in 4b. Why should he? It fits the style and the occasion to read *krt berît* as being a step in the action different from the oath. What might it be? We have found negotiations

---

in the text. One assumes that the benefits accrued largely to Assyria, but this is an assumption.

normal procedure in connection with *berît*. Perhaps here *krt berît* is metonymy referring to this element. One might translate "came to terms with," or, with *NEB*, "made an agreement with." This is surely what did take place. Jehoiada made a deal with the "colonels" which was to their advantage and fostered his plan. Such is the way of conspiracies. This seems the most natural interpretation of the text, and it would imply that the officers' oath obliged them to the mutually advantageous deal they had worked out. Or one might take *wayyikrot lahem berît* to refer to Jehoiada's counter-commitment to the officers' oaths. He binds himself to them as they to him.[1] Again, as a simple matter of fact, this the way it must have been, however it may have been described. In either interpretation the *berît* is not one-sided. A deal on mutual advantageous terms is part of the picture, or each party joins as subject in the complex act which ratifies a commitment.

In xx 17b the *berît* is *bên hammelek ûbên hā'ām*. The *berît*-maker, the subject of the phrase *krt berît*, is the priest, Jehoiada. The text makes no statement about the obligations involved, but if *bên... ûbên* has its common meaning, they are incumbent on both parties. This is meager information, but perhaps Chronicles can add to it.

2 Chron. xxiii 1 begins like 2 Kings xi 4a: "In the seventh year Jehoiada took the officers," but at this point it takes a new direction with "...into a *berît* with himself." xxiii 2 is new material describing the extension of the conspiracy into Judah, but 3 returns to the parallel in 2 Kings xi 4b with *wayyikrot berît*. But the Chronicler has already put Jehoiada's *berît* with the officers into his first verse so that at this point he puts in the *berît* between the people and Joash. Having described this *berît* here, when his story reaches the point parallel with 2 Kings xi 17b, he omits further mention of it.[2]

In the course of all this the Chronicler makes clear that the first *berît* is a conspiracy. Jehoiada takes the officers into it with himself. This is as clear a description of *berît* as a relationship as one could wish, the more striking in that by the Chronicler's time *berît* had become closely identified with law. The second *berît* is differently described too. The congregation itself, not the priest makes the *berît* with *('im)* the king, and there is a statement about the king immedi-

---

[1] Differently E. KUTSCH, *ZAW.* 79 (1967), p. 24, because of the parallel with *wayyašba'*. Our version saves the "probability rule" that *le*- points to an obligation the subject takes on himself toward another.

[2] Hence its omission in xxiii 16 is no argument against the authenticity of the clause in Kings, a fact already widely accepted on other grounds.

ately after the mention of b^erît-making. Such a statement has been connected with b^erît so often that it is not surprising here. The only unusual thing is that it follows the report of the action rather than precedes. The Chronicler inverts the usual order because he is following the text of 2 Kings xi 4 so closely. There, naturally, Jehoiada is said to wait until he has made b^erît and bound the officers by oath; then "he showed them the king's son..." Chronicler models his statement: "Behold the king's son..." on this clause so that his statement follows the mention of b^erît itself.

The content of the statement recalls that in 2 Sam. iii 21 and v 2 in its emphasis on the royal power: "he shall reign as Yahweh promised to David's family." Royal power and divine election: this b^erît covers the same ground as that of David with Israel. It goes beyond 2 Kings xi 17b: for the Chronicler, the b^erît between the people and the king leaves the latter clearly and explicitly overlord.[1] Is this simply because he wishes to insist on the supremacy of the house of his hero, David? Or did b^erît, even one which establishes a king who is of David's house and the object of Yahweh's promise, self-evidently include limits on the power it conferred? Perhaps both factors, and others as well were at work. In any event, the writer could use 'im in the place of bên... ûbên, and he could use it of a b^erît implying relations of lordship and subjection. Neither the conception nor the terminology of b^erît was so fixed as to prevent him from such a change.[2]

Conclusions from the report of b^erîtôt in 2 Kings xi:

A. Jehoiada and the officers: 1) Negotiations are indicated in 4b, (an interpretation confirmed by 2 Chron. xxiii 1. 2) There is no statement of any obligation (though the negotiations must have involved a *quid pro quo*). 3) Jehoiada is the subject of the phrase *krt b^erît*, but the officers take an oath. Both parties, then, are active.

B. Joash and the people: 1) No negotiations are mentioned. 2) There is no definition of b^erît obligations (but 2 Chron. xxiii 3b describes them in terms of traditional royal power. 3) The subject of

---

[1] Differently E. KUTSCH, *THAT* I, col. 344, no. 5.

[2] Probably the Chronicler's report is simply an elaboration of his source in Kings: see J. M. MYERS, *II Chronicles. Anchor Bible* 13, New York, p. 131. The way his variations grow out of details in the text of Kings seems to confirm this. If it is so, his interpretation is noteworthy not so much because of its antiquity but because of its presenting b^erît in terms of a two-sided relationship (which is what the text of Kings points to in our opinion) when the habit of his time would have led him to turn it into law.

the phrase *krt b*ᵉ*rît* is Jehoiada (but 2 Chron. xxiii 3a changes this to the congregation).

VIII. ABNER AND DAVID (2 Sam. iii 12-21). The report of the *b*ᵉ*rît* is incomplete. It is the only one of any length which lacks a direct affirmation the "he-they made a *b*ᵉ*rît*." Nor is there any summary statement defining the major *b*ᵉ*rît* obligations. These lacunae may occur because the story is interested in David and Israel, and Abner enters only in relation to this central interest. Still, we have something. Abner asks David to make him a *b*ᵉ*rît*. Then, there are negotiations, which all seem to work to David's benefit. This seems very one-sided. David is the sole subject of the phrase *krt b*ᵉ*rît*. He takes on no obligations explicitly mentioned. Perhaps he is simply taking Abner into his service.[1]

Now, it is clear that this leaves out a great deal. Abner was negotiating from strength. He was the power in Israel, and he knew it.[2] An able condottiere will have used such a position to his advantage. His price surely included the command of David's army, this was surely granted, and it led the displaced Joab to murder him.[3] But this is deduction. It is what we can reasonably see as the history behind the text. The problem is: Was talk about *b*ᵉ*rît*-making inevitably associated with things that would bring like ideas to the mind of the writer and his audience? In other words, did *b*ᵉ*rît*-making accompanied by bargaining necessarily imply a *quid pro quo?* On the evidence of the texts examined before this one, it would seem that it did. That is, the general character of *b*ᵉ*rît*-making as it appears in Dtr supports the conclusions which historical probability induce us to draw from this text. But the text is not explicit in the matter.

A final point: it is unusual that there is not report that *b*ᵉ*rît* was made. However, the banquet in iii 20 seems to be the equivalent.[4]

---

[1] E. KUTSCH, *Rost Festschrift*, p. 136: "...er (David) ihn in Pflicht nimmt."

[2] This is apparent in his ironic question in iii 12: "to whom does a country belong?" I.e., to the shadow king or real commander of its forces? He can bring Israel to David. He and David know it, and his immediate success show they are right.

[3] So H. W. HERTZBERG, *I and II Samuel*, Philadelphia 1964, pp. 258, 260.

[4] See the affirmation of the act: he-they made *b*ᵉ*rît* in Jos. ix 15; 1 Sam. xviii 3; xx 16-17; xxiii 18; 2 Sam. v 3; 1 Kings xx 34 (and note 2 Chron. xxiii 3, where the allusion in 2 Kings xi 17 has been turned unto a report with the affirmation; the report in 1 Sam. xi 1-3 has no affirmation of the fact, but the act never took place!). See also Gen. xxi 27, 32; in xxvi 30 and xxxi 53b-54 the act is reported through an equivalent expression. Hence the quasi-certainty that 2 Sam. iii 20b is an allusion to the action which formally realized *b*ᵉ*rît*.

Immediately it is done Abner sets out to bring Israel under David's sway. This is his *berît* obligation and it is now in force. We have seen synonyms used along with *krt berît* to affirm the *berît*-making. Here one seems to be substituted. This is interesting in itself, and the symbolism of the equivalent used is important. David has taken Abner into his family for his service *and* for his protection.

SUMMARY

I. *Type of source:* We have seen six reports of *berît*-making as such, that is, stories which are entirely concerned with the process as their central theme. We have six texts which speak of *berît*-making as part of another theme which is the central interest. Other references are more or less passing allusions. It is worth noting these distinctions because they condition the kind and the quantity of information we can expect. The direct reports are the most important, and must be noticed as such.[1]

II. *Elements characteristically associated with* berît-*making:*

A. *Negotiations:* elements of persuasion, proposal, and counter-proposal are characteristic. These are found in all the regular reports except the first Jonathan-David *berît*, a personal association where negotiation was unneeded and indeed out of place, and 1 Sam. xxiii 16-18, a succinct report paralleling xx 10-17 which does imply the negotiations. Note that all the reports of *berît*-making in Genesis have negotiations.[2]

B. *Terms:* 1) *formulations* which state what one or both parties were to do as a result of the negotiations are common.[3] Again, the feature is paralleled in the Genesis reports.

2) However, the terms may be left *unformulated* in this strict. sense. However, they appear clearly in the course of the negotiations (Jos.

---

[1] Direct reports: Jos. ix 1-x 1; 1 Sam. xviii 1-4 (with xx 6-8); xx 10-17; xxiii 16-16; 2 Sam. iii 21; v 1-3; 1 Kings xx 32-34; incidental in other reports: 1 Sam. xi 1-3; 2 Sam. iii 12-21 (about the rise of Saul and David respectively); 1 Kings v 26 (about Solomon's greatness); 1 Kings xv 18-19 (incident in a war report); 2 Kings xi 4, 17 (incidents in the report of the restoration of the Davidids; 2 Chron. xxiii 1-3 turns these into reports); allusion: 1 Sam. xxii 8; Hos. ix 4 (in a prophetic reflection); Hos. xii 12b, and Ezek. xvii 11-21 (in prophetic reproaches).

[2] Gen. xxi 22-32; xxvi 22-33; xxxi 23-xxxii 3.

[3] Cf. 1 Sam. xx 12-15; xxiii 17; 2 Sam. v 2 (cf. iii 17-18); 1 Kings xx 34. 1 Kings xv 18-19 shows that the parties knew clearly what was expected of one another; 2 Chron. xxiii 3 provides a formulation for the incident in 2 Kings xi 17, showing how oppropriate the feature was felt to be.

ix 6-13; 1 Sam. xi 1-2), in appeals to the *berît* (1 Sam. xx 7-8; cf.
1 Kings xv 18-19), in the equality of the parties (1 Kings v 26; 2 Kings
xi 17—though 2 Chron. xxiii 3 formulates the terms and removes the
parity here), or in the kind of association involved (2 Kings xi 4:
fellow conspirators; cf. the interpretation in 2 Chron. xxiii 1-2). The
prophetic texts, Hos. ix 4 and Ezek. xvii 11-21, complain of broken
obligations, but only Ezekiel gives any concrete content to this. Hos.
xii 2b reproaches the *fact* of *berît*-making, not the terms involved, so
that the conclusion that they were a one-sided obligation on Ephraim
is a deduction.

3) The terms, whether formulated or alluded to, are *usually bilateral*,
that is, they indicate duties incumbent in some way or another on
both parties (service in return for the grant of life, service in return
for protection, help in war in return for payment etc.).[1] So too in
Gen. xxi 22-32 and xxxi 32-xxxii 3 the *berîtôt* are explicitly bilateral.
This is implicit in Gen. xxvi 22-33.

4) *Occasionally obligations are unilateral*, that is, they empower or tie
but one party: in 2 Sam. v 3 David assumes leadership over Israel
(compare 2 Chron. xxiii 3: the enthronement *berît* seems to concern
divinely-ordained sovereignty), in 2 Sam. iii 12-21 Abner submits to
David (if we discount implications of mutuality in 20), and in Ezek.
xvii 11-21 Zedekiah is Nebuchadnezzar's vassal. Possibly also in Hos.
ix 4, but the prophet is reproving one party and simply says nothing
about another, and in Hos. xii 12b, and Ephraim's obligation must be
deduced (see number 3 above).

C. *Relationships: berît*-making usually occurs when a relationship
already exists. Jonathan already loves David, David is already the
destined head of Israel (note 1 Sam. xx 13, 15; xxiii 17, as well as
2 Sam. iii 18; v 2), or a state of inferiority already exists and is accepted
by Gibeon, by Jabesh-Gilead, and by Ben-Hadad. The pre-existent
relationship is characteristic of the Genesis reports also: Gen. xxi 23
and xxvi 29 insist on the peace and good relations already in force;
Gen. xxxi 43 on family connections.

D. *Social usage:* in certain situations the terms seem to have been
self-evident. A hopeless or a defeated party was to serve in return for

---

[1] This is true of all *berîtôt* reported except the David-Israel example (2 Sam. v 3),
all noticed incidentally except that of David with Abner (2 Sam. iii 12-21, and
here 20 may imply the mutual obligations of a *paterfamilias* and a retainer admitted
to the *familia* in a formal meal); and of Joash and the people (2 Kings xi 17) *as
(re)interpreted in* 2 Chron. xxiii 3 (for the distinctions: reports, incidental reports,
and allusions, see above, p. 81, n. 1).

the grant of life (Jos. ix 1-x 1; 1 Sam. xi 1-2; 1 Kings xx 32). The heroic friendship also involved service and life but in a very different atmosphere.

E. *The act* of *berît*-making: the report regularly states that the act took place (see above, p. 80, n. 4).

F. *Variety of agents:* this is simply bewildering. There can be a third party agent (2 Kings xi 17), one agent (1 Sam. xi 1; 2 Sam. iii 12—but both of these are proposals to make *berît*, not real affirmations of the act itself; 1 Kings xx 34), one apparent agent with the other party finally involved (Jos. ix 15; x 1; 1 Kings xi 4), two parties seem to have approximately equal roles (1 Sam. xxiii 18; 2 Sam. iii 21; v 3; 1 Kings v 26), or two parties, one of whom seems to do more than the other (1 Sam. xviii 3-4 [cf. xx 8]; xx 17-18; Ezek. xvii 11-21—note that a hifil is usually used). This becomes even more complex if one tries to relate agancy to unilaterality and multilaterality. There is no correlation! There are bilateral *berîtôt* with one agent (1 Sam. xi 1; 1 Kings xx 34), with two (1 Sam. xxiii 18; 1 Kings v 26) with two agents, one more active than the other (1 Sam. xviii 3-4; xx 16-17), with a third party as agent (2 Kings xi 17), or with an apparent single agent who turns out to have a partner (Jos. ix 15-x 1; 2 Kings xi 4). Then there are unilateral *berîtôt* with but one agent—though none of the examples is conclusive—(Hos. ix 4; xii 2b; 2 Sam. iii 12-21), with two agents (2 Sam. iii 21-v 3), or with two agents, one more active than the other (Ezek. xvii 11-21). Among other things, this complexity means that in the cases treated there is no rule about the primary agent of *berît*. He need not be more or less powerful than the other party, and in any case he does not act alone. It is interesting that the move toward *berît*-making usually comes from the inferior, but not always: cf. 1 Sam. xviii 1-4 and 2 Kings xi 4. These are special cases, and indeed the complex character of *berît*-making cannot be understood unless we observe the great variety in kinds of *berît* and in the situations in which it is made. This deserves a special study in itself.

If the reader finds this obscure and confusing, this is because it is so.[1] The texts simply do not concern themselves with relating unilateral terms to single agents, or with any other consistent combination of these factors.[2] This is important for the question of unilaterality.

---

[1] The only way to make the situation clear is to put it on a graph with lines for one party, two-party etc. crossing those for unilateral etc. This does not lend itself to print, and what it makes clear is that there is no clarity.

[2] This confusion or indifference accounts for the irregular use of the preposi-

No berît *is one-sided unless the obligation is incumbent on one party and one party makes the* berît. The first point needs no explanation. The second is clear when we reflect that the act realizes and so conditions the obligation. Even if it is incumbent on but one party, there is no *berît* obligation unless there is a *berît* act, and as long as the latter involves both parties the obligation is somehow dependent on them both.

Conclusions. krt berît originally referred to a specific act, but it came to mean a solemn commitment in general. The reports concerning such commitments normally start from the fact of a relationship. They normally include a record of negotiations, formulation of terms, and a statement that the act of making *berît* was actually performed. Thus the negotiations end with a solemn ratification of the terms. The terms normally apply to both parties, and the act is commonly the work of both. Indeed, even unilateral terms could depend on a common act. In these circumstances it seems impossible that *berît* not acquire an association with ideas of relationship. It is tied up with a complex of recognized relationships, active relations (negotiations), terms which relate one party to another, and a common act. The word *berît* carries these overtones. It is relational.

This is confirmed by some of the parallels with the act in the texts studied. It is paired with *šalôm* (cf. above, n. 8). That is, it is paired with a state of "peace," "unity," "completion." *šalôm* is hard to translate, but it is relational. The act is also paired with kingship (1 Sam. iii 5). David makes *berît* and becomes king. He acquires an enduring status which is a relationship: one is king *of* something. *A pari*, the *berît* made is enduring and relational. Another kind of *berît* involves the relation of love, and *berît* can make one a servant or a brother, that is, put one in a state of enduring relationship. So one appeals to the servant relationship (Jos. x 6). Again, one is *in* a *berît*, and he appeals to this, to the relationship in which the obligations obtain (1 Sam. xx 7-8).

Secular *berît*, then, as described in Dtr (and in Genesis) is as clearly tied to relation as to obligation. Indeed, the two are inseparable. Obligation is a relational word too. With regard to translation, then:

---

tions. If there is no concern to coordinate agent and obligation, then it is no wonder that krt berît *le*-/*ʿim*-/*ʾet*- show no consistent differentiation in their use in this sample (see comments on 1 Sam. xx 16; xxii 8; 2 Sam. iii 21; v 3; 1 Kings xx 34, for ex.). Even bên... ûbên, the most firm fixed prepositional usage, is equated with *ʾet*- in 1 Kings xv 19 (and with *ʿim* if we compare 2 Kings xi 17 with 2 Chron. xxiii 3). The sample, of course, is too small to establish tules for probable useage, but it does indicate exceptions.

relation and obligation, commitment and action, these are what we mean by covenant.[1] The traditional translation can stand. With regard to its religious use: *berît*, when applied to the relation of man to God, must carry some of its rich associations with complex relationships with it. These were surely modified and others added, but they cannot have been lost.

---

[1] See *The Oxford English Dictionary*: "covenant" means, in addition to "agreement," "undertaking, pledge or promise of one of the parties," "an agreement... or promise of legal validity," "a clause of such an agreement," and, in older usage, "vow" and "matter agreed upon... or promised." Thus, as well as the *relation* itself, it can mean the *action* of undertaking it or the *content* (obligation) undertaken. It can be *multilateral*: "agreement," or *unilateral* "promise or undertaking of one party." This range of meaning, which is not due to theological usage, is very close to that of secular *berît*. I do not presume to judge definitively whether this is true of the traditional translations in other languages, e.g., *Bund, alliance*. They do seem, to an outsider, to concern rather more the aspect of relation than that of content or action, but this study would seem to indicate that a substitute should not on this account overemphasize these other aspects at the expense of the relational.

THE PASSOVER SACRIFICE

BY

MENAHEM HARAN
Jerusalem

I. The Distinctive Features of the Passover and its Supposed Origin

The passover sacrifice is mentioned indirectly in all the Pentateuchal sets of laws: in the Book of the Covenant (Exod. xxiii 18) and the Smaller Book of the Covenant (Exod. xxxiv 25)—as we shall demonstrate later on; within the framework of the Priestly Source, i.e. in the calendar of "the sacred occasions" (Lev. xxiii 5) and in the list of additional sacrifices offered up during the year (Num. xxviii 16); also in the code of Deuteronomy, where a number of details relating to this sacrifice are cited (Deut. xvi 1-7).

1

The actual traits, however, of the offering are specified in "narrative" passages constituting a part of the story of the exodus. These are two in number: a detailed P passage (Exod. xii 1-20; and the appendix at the end of this chapter, vv. 43-50) and a J passage (ibid. 21-27). The Rabbinic sages understood these passages as referring mainly to the passover offered up in Egypt in contradistinction to the permanent passover referred to in other sections (Mekhilta to Exod. xii 3; B. T. Pesaḥim 96a *et al.*), and they were followed by the medieval commentators and a number of moderns.[1] Indeed, one cannot deny that these passages are said to be spoken in Egypt and the accomplishment of the sacrifice is inseparable from the story of the deliverance itself. As the story has it, the signs of the blood of the sacrifice that was presented in Egypt caused Yahweh to pass over the houses of the Israelites, when he smote all the first-born of man and beast on the eve of the exodus (Exod. xii 12-13, 23). By this, the name of the

---

[1] Like A. Ehrlich, U. Cassuto, and even A. Kahana; needless to say, a commentator like S. D. Luzzatto adopted this interpretation.

sacrifice is also explained—פסח הוא ליהוה, "It is the passover sacrifice to Yahweh," because on that night he *passed over* the houses of the Israelites (ibid. 11, 27).[1] The very offering of the first passover sacrifice rescued, then, the Israelites from the catastrophe and also enabled them to leave that country (cf. Num. xxxiii 3). Nevertheless, it cannot be doubted that the first sacrifice presumably serves as a model for the future and that in every generation the details of the sacrificial rite have to be repeated in exactly the same manner. There is no indication that any distinction should be made between the Egyptian passover and that which would be offered up in future generations. Express notes concerning the validity of the sacrifice for the ages to come are even appended to the P (Exod. xii 14, 17) and J (ibid. 24-27) passages. Similarly it is stated in the continuation of the P passage that just as the first night was "a night of vigil for the Lord" so it must remain one of vigil "for all the people of Israel throughout their generations" (ibid. 42). This means to say that the account of the preparation of the first sacrifice becomes a statute, or, in other words, the presentation of the law against the background of the exodus furnishes the broad aetiological explanation of the dramatic features of the sacrifice. Needless to say, the two passages are only parallel literary formulations of a single theme. A mention should further be made of the P statute regarding the duty of observing the Second Passover incumbent on anyone who was "defiled by a corpse or on a long journey" at the proper time. This law, too, is prescribed in a narrative framework (Num. ix 1-14).

Following are the features that characterize the passover offering and the dramatic gesticulations connected with its preparation. According to the P passage (Exod. xii 1-14) this sacrifice is to be offered up on an exact date in the year, namely the fourteenth of the first month, and is to be slaughtered at twilight (on this detail cf. Lev. xxiii 18; Num. ix 3, xxviii 16). The offering is held in readiness from the tenth of the month, and is eaten by the members of the household

---

[1] The phrase פסח (הוא] ליהוה, occurs in this form in all the sources (see further Exod. xii 48; Lev. xxiii 5; Num. ix 10, 14, xxviii 16; Deut. xvi 1-2; 2 Kings xxiii 21, 23). Possibly it contains an intimation of the pagan origin of the ceremony. We find similar locutions such as חג המצות ליהוה "the feast of unleavened bread to Yahweh" (Lev. xxiii 6; cf. Exod. xii 14, xiii 6); חג הסכות ... ליהוה, "the feast of booths to Yahweh" (Lev. xxiii 34; cf. ibid. 41; Num. xxix 12); חג שבעות ליהוה אלהיך, "the feast of weeks to Yahweh your God" (Deut. xvi 10); cf. also Exod. xxxii 5. Possibly the rituals of the pilgrimage festivals, too, being bound up with agriculture and settled conditions of life, have pagan origins.

together, or by them and their neighbours. It is brought from the
flock only, of the sheep or of the goats, and the animal must be without
blemish, a male and a year old.[1] Its blood must be smeared on the two
doorposts and on the lintel of the house. The eating takes place at
night, after the sacrifice has been roasted over the fire, "its head, legs,
and entrails"—it is not to be eaten raw or cooked with water—and it
is accompanied by unleavened bread and bitter herbs. Nothing of it
should be left over until morning. The eating itself is done hurriedly
and is accompanied by dramatic-theatrical gestures: loins girded,
sandals on the feet, a staff in the hand. In the appendix to this passage
are added the instructions that only the circumcised may be included
among those partaking of the passover, that none of its flesh may be
taken outside the house and that not a bone of it may be broken (cf.
Num. ix 11-12).

The J passage (Exod. xii 21-27) in no way contradicts the descriptions given in P. In a number of particulars it fully agrees with P: the
passover is to be brought from the flock, is prepared according to
families, and its blood is applied to the two doorposts. On the other
hand it contains several details not specified in the P passage: only
here is it explained that the blood of the sacrifice is to be collected in
a basin,[2] and that a bunch of hyssop is to be used for daubing the
blood on the entrance of the house,[3] and that no one may go out of
the door of the house till morning (in the parallel account we find only
the prohibition not to leave any part of the offering until morning).
It appears that if we are to extract as many details as possible of the
drama of the passover sacrifice, we must combine the two accounts.
Both refer to the same happening, only neither of them embraces all
the details, which means that they actually complement each other.

---

[1] According to P (Lev. xxii 23) "an ox or a sheep with a limb extended or
contracted" may be presented as a free-will offering, but not for a vow (and *a
fortiori* not for a thanksgiving or a public sacrifice). At any rate, the status of the
passover is higher than that of a free-will offering.

[2] Hebrew: *saf*, a vessel for holding liquids (cf. 2 Sam. xvii 28; 1 Kings vii 50;
2 Kings xii 14 *et al.*). But the LXX understood the word in the sense of the
threshold of the door, rendering it in Exod. xii 22: παρὰ τὴν θύραν.

[3] We find hyssop also used in the purification from leprosy, for sprinkling
blood (Lev. xiv 4-7, 49-52), and in the purification from defilement by the dead,
for the sprinkling of the water of lustration (Num. xix 6, 18-19). While the
psalmist declares: "Purge me with hyssop and I shall be clean" (Ps. li 9). On its
botanical identity see M. ZOHARY, *Encyc. Miqra'it*, I, coll. 185-186. Its identification with the plant called in Arabic زَعْتَر or صَعْتَر was already suggested by SAADIA
GAON (cf. Y. KAPAḤ, פירושי רס״ג על התורה, Jerusalem 1963, *ad loc.*) and IBN-
EZRA, in his commentary to Exod. xii 22.

All these aspects jointly produce a most "strange" and extraordinary pattern. Suffice it to point out that the very eating at night is the complete reverse of the customary procedure in the biblical times (even with regard to secular slaughtering). And of all the various categories of sacrifice there is not a single oblation that must be eaten just at night-time, save the passover—just as there is not a night in the whole year on which it is obligatory to eat sacrificial flesh except the one that begins on the fourteenth of the first month at twilight. How much more so is the entire picture strange, seeing that the eating at night is only one facet out of a unique complex of ritual peculiarities.

2

The dramatic traits that embellish the passover contain a number of clear indications of its nomadic origin. The pointers are as follows: the collective participation in the preparation and eating of the sacrifice; the bringing of the offering specifically from the flock, not from the herd; the eating at night, which is the distinctive time of nomads; the consumption of the sacrifice in the form of roast only, not raw or boiled with water; the special emphasis given to the rôle of the blood and the particular use made of it in connection with this sacrifice; likewise the hurried eating of the metal accompanied by the theatrical gestures. It was once suggested that originally this sacrifice had a purificatory significance, and that the use of hyssop for the application of the blood to the lintel and doorposts should also be comprehended as pointing thereto. On the other hand, a number of scholars have sought to base themselves particularly on J's evidence in Exod. xii 21-27 in stating that primarily this was an apotropaic rite of applying blood to the lintel and doorposts for protection against plagues— without a sacrifice or the consumption of flesh (which are not mentioned in the J passage).[1]

---

[1] The interpretation of the passover as a purificatory sacrifice was proposed by H. EWALD, *Die Alterthümer des Volkes Israel*[3], Göttingen 1866, pp. 460-461. This conception is based on the premise that the P sections of the Pentateuch are not late (in contradiction to the view subsequently accepted by the WELLHAUSEN school). The theory that the passover was an apotropaic ritual of merely smearing blood was advanced, e.g., by K. MARTI, *Geschichte der israelitischen Religion*[4], Strasburg 1903, pp. 40-41; and I. BENZINGER, *Encyc. Biblica*, III, London 1902, coll. 3594-3595. More recently H. J. KRAUS has adopted an interpretation akin to this (*Gottesdienst in Israel*[2], Munich 1962, p. 62), and he, too, relies principally on Exod. xii 21-27. Views similar to these two, in a somewhat confused form, were already expressed by W. J. MOULTON, *Dictionary of the Bible*, III, Edinburgh 1900, pp. 688-

Now it is incontestable that the passover ritual as a whole contains an apotropaic element. Nevertheless, it must be stated that the theories mentioned stress unduly one detail out of the entire picture, or seek to base themselves on a single evidence, while ignoring the other evidence, which parallels and complements it, namely that of P. If we do not wish to view the matter in distorted perspective, it is better to look at the entire picture as reflected in all the sources and concede the indications of the passover's nomadic origin, possibly also its basic connection with this season of the year (as well as with the day of the full moon) without hastily making further speculations.[1] The primary connection of the passover offering with nomadic conditions of life differentiates it from the feast of unleavened bread, which as a distinctly agricultural festival (of the beginning of the barley harvest) had its place only in settled conditions of life. The nexus between the sacrifice and the festival does not emanate in this instance from the basic character of the two, but is the result of circumstances.

In D's account of the passover a number of its authentic characteristics have been excised. True, even according to this description the passover is prepared at night (Deut. xvi 1, 4, 6-7) and eaten before morning (ibid. 4), but it is brought from the flock and the herd (ibid. 2), and is boiled (ibid. 7). Boiling is the form in which settled inhabitants are accustomed to prepare meat for food (cf. Jud. vi 19; 1 Sam. ii 13; Ezek. xlvi 24 *et al.*). In D's description, therefore, the sacrifice is depicted in a flatter and more even form than that given to it in the other sources.[2] In addition, D emphasizes that the passover must be presented at the chosen place only (Deut. xvi 5-7).

3

With regard to the passover celebrations mentioned in the historical books we would note briefly that the narrative concerning the pass-

---

689. The apotropaic element in the passover sacrifice is also pointed out by S. E. LOEWENSTAMM, *The Tradition of the Exodus in its Development* (Hebrew), Jerusalem 1965, pp. 84-88, 93-94.

[1] One of the latest scholars to use the evidence of P is actually L. ROST, *Das kleine Credo und andere Studien zum AT*, Heidelberg 1965, pp. 101-106. ROST describes the passover as an apotropaic celebration of nomadic herdsmen before they start out on their annual journey. The celebration was held at the beginning of the year, at full moon, in the season when the nomads were accustomed to move their camps from the desert areas to the settled districts. KRAUS *(loc. cit.)* seems to accept ROST's explanation as well.

[2] On the excision of some ancient features of the passover in D's portrayal cf. also M. WEINFELD, *Tarbiz* XXXI, 1962, p. 5.

over offered up by the Israelites at Gilgal, on the eve of the cessation of the manna (Jos. v 10-11), is P's. Josiah's passover was kept, it would appear, in the spirit of D, following upon this king's reforms and as the climax thereof, and in the Book of Kings a number of Deuteronomistic expansions were attached to the story of this passover (2 Kings xxiii 21-23). But in the parallel description in 2 Chron. xxxv 1-19, it is depicted synthetically and with the help of ingredients from both D and P: it is offered up from the flock and the herd, but is handled by the priests and the Levites (the latter prepare it for themselves and for both the priests and the singers and door-keepers). Likewise, the Chronicler's statement: "And they cooked *(wayebaššelû)* the passover lamb *with fire* according to the ordinance" (ibid. 13), is simply an attempt to combine the two expressions: "You shall boil it *(ûbiššalta)* and eat it" (Deut. xvi 7) and the emphatic injunction to roast it over *the fire* (Exod. xii 8-9). Probably this account contains a projection of the usages obtaining in the preparation of the passover current in the time of the chronicler himself, when the Pentateuch had already been combined and published in its entirety, but the midrashic tradition that was due to take shape in Rabbinic interpretation did not yet exist.[1]

A similar observation may be made concerning Hezekiah's passover, in whose preparation the priests and Levites take part, and on account of the defilement of the priests and the people and the fact that many of the people were at a distance from Jerusalem they even keep the celebration on the fourteenth of the second month (2 Chron. xxx 1-20), in complete accord with the law of Num. ix 1-14. In the case of Josiah's passover (2 Chron. xxxv 12-13) and so, too, with regard to Hezekiah's celebration (ibid. xxx 5, 16, 18) the Chronicler even expressly bases himself on "Scripture"—"as it is written in the book of Moses," and in "the law of Moses the man of God," "according to the ordinance." Similarly, the passover that, according to Ezra vi 19-21, was kept by those who had returned from captivity to Zion was patterned in con-

---

[1] The Talmudic *halakha* bases itself on Exod. xii 3-5, 21 only and ordains that the passover—both that of Egypt and the regular passover—should be presented from the flock alone (Mekhilta *ad loc.;* P. T. Pesaḥim viii, 3 *et al.*). The legalistic conception of the Pseudepigrapha also rules thus (Jubilees xlix 3). The mention of the herd in Deut. xvi 2 is expounded by the Talmudic sages as referring to the festal sacrifice (Sifrē *ad loc.;* M. Pesaḥim vi, 3-4), or to "the remainder of the passover" (i.e. a lamb that was set aside to be a passover sacrifice, but was lost and another was offered up in its stead, and subsequently the lost sheep was found), which is presented as a peace-offering (B. T. Pesaḥim 70b).

formity with the conception of the Chronicler and belongs to the same category.

II. WELLHAUSEN'S VIEW AND THE EVIDENCE IN THE SOURCES PRECEDING D

Is the passover mentioned in the sources preceding D (and P)? In this respect WELLHAUSEN expressed a most surprising opinion, whose impact has not disappeared from scholarship to this day. He argued that D was the first of all the Pentateuchal sources to recognize the passover sacrifice and the first in which the word *pesaḥ*, "passover" itself came to be mentioned. In Exod. xxxiv 25 (which, in the opinion of many scholars, including WELLHAUSEN, is part of the "Cultic Decalogue") the passover is not referred to, because the correct reading of this verse is given in Exod. xxiii 18 (where, in truth, the word "passover" does not occur).[1] While the verse Exod. xxiii 18 itself cannot *allude* to the passover (even without mentioning the name), because the Book of the Covenant, which comprises this verse, recognizes the law of the first-born (Exod. xxii 29-30) and in WELLHAUSEN's view the offering of the firstlings is the ancient form of the passover.[2] The difficulty represented by Exod. xii 21-27 he tends to resolve by arguing that this is a mere late addition to JE, or to the P passage preceding it.[3]

The passover, claims WELLHAUSEN, is only a later incarnation of the offering of the firstlings of the cattle, which is one of the most ancient institutions of the biblical cult. According to the biblical tradition the oblation from the firstlings of the flock was already brought by Abel himself, the first shepherd in the world (Gen. iv 4). WELLHAUSEN posits that before the Israelites went out of Egypt they asked permission to go and slaughter the first-born of the sheep, but since the Egyptians did not accede to this request, they were punished in respect to their own first-born. The fact that according to Exod. xiii 11-16 (apparently an E section) the obligation to offer up the firstlings was imposed upon the Israelites only when they left Egypt he would dismiss with the claim that the passage has undergone Deuteronomistic

---

[1] J. WELLHAUSEN, *Prolegomena*[6], Berlin 1927, pp. 82-85.

[2] Cf. *ibid.*, p. 88.

[3] See *idem, Die Composition des Hexateuchs*[4], Berlin 1963, pp. 73-75. About the same time K. BUDDE already argued against WELLHAUSEN on this point ("Die Gesetzgebung der mittleren Bücher des Pentateuchs," *ZAW* XI, 1891, pp. 197-200).

revision.[1] As for the verses Exod. xiii 1-2, in which, again, it is stated that the sacrifice of the firstlings was established in Israel only upon their leaving Egypt, apparently there is no need to pay any attention to them, since they belong to P, which is taken to be late. Until the appearance of D there were, then, only firstlings, which were offered up during the month of Abib. In WELLHAUSEN's view the sacrifice of the firstlings was not fundamentally an agricultural but a nomadic institution, and the fact that in principle it was also incumbent on human first-born is explained by him as one of the later distortions of this institution. D was the first to call this sacrifice "passover," and when it speaks of the passover that is to be offered from the flock and the herd (Deut. xvi 2), D actually refers to the firstlings of the flock and the herd. D was also the first to relate this oblation to the festival of unleavened bread and to make it a memorial to the exodus. In P the practice was still further removed from its authentic sources, but remained connected with the festival of unleavened bread and linked to the recollection of the departure from Egypt.[2]

The forced character of this hypothesis is quite evident and there is no need for a lengthy refutation. It is entirely based on the supposition that J and E do not recognize or mention the passover but only the offering of the firstlings. However, the truth of the matter is that Exod. xii 21-27 is not a later addition, and most scholars cannot but admit that this passage belongs essentially to J or to E (the arguments in favour of J appear stronger), and we have already seen that it is a simple parallel to the narrative of P.[3] Moreover, we shall show further on that even the Books of the Covenant, which are the codes of laws of J and E, already recognize the passover, and since alongside this oblation J and E also know of the existence of the offering of the firstlings, it is not to be doubted that these are two different sacrifices.

---

[1] WELLHAUSEN, *Prolegomena*[6], p. 84.

[2] See *ibid.*, pp. 82-89, 97-98. WELLHAUSEN's view was particularly followed by W. ROBERTSON SMITH, *The Religion of the Semites*[2], (New York 1956), pp. 464-465.

[3] At most there may be found in the second half of this passage traces of Deuteronomic nuances, from "You shall observe this rite" onward (vv. 24-27[1]). This will undoubtedly be argued by those scholars, including WELLHAUSEN, who claim that there was Deuteronomistic editing of the Tetrateuch, that is, of JE (see e.g. H. HOLZINGER, *Einleitung in den Hexateuch*, Freiburg 1893, pp. 485, 492; *idem*, *Exodus*, KHC, Tübingen 1900, p. 34). But there is still a possibility to posit that this is a manifestation of a "proto-Deuteronomic" style, indications of which are discernible here and there in the body of JE (to be sure, much more in E than in J); on this point cf. below, p. 113, n. 1. At all events, in the first half of this passage (vv. 21-23) there is no trace even of such nuances.

The flocks and herds give birth chiefly in the spring time, and hence the firstlings are mentioned in the same context as the passover and festival of unleavened bread; but the offering of the firstlings as such has no fixed time and may be brought even outside its season. This is actually stated in Exod. xxii 29 in regard to the firstling of oxen and sheep: "Seven days it shall be with its dam; on the eighth day you shall give it to me." [1] As against this, the passover, as is clearly seen also in J's account in Exod. xii 21-27, is a different offering in its character and in all its features.

Furthermore, assuming that there exists a direct and continuous line of development leading from the first-born to the passover one fails to understand why the separation itself between the passover and the firstling occurred in P and the first-born was preserved as a discrete sacrifice (Exod. xiii 1-2; Lev. xxvii 26-27; Num. xviii 15-18), just as it is distinguished from the passover also in D (Deut. xii 6, 17, xiv 23, xv 19-23), and, in point of fact, even in J and E themselves (only this WELLHAUSEN did not admit). For if the sacrifice of the first-born evolved into the passover, it would not have continued to exist in a distinctive form. In all the disparaging remarks about P's logic in

---

[1] With regard to this verse it was argued (W. NOWACK, *Lehrbuch der hebräischen Archäologie*, II, Freiburg 1894, p. 147) that it is a late addition in accordance with Lev. xxii 27, dating from the time when the passover sacrifice and the offering of the first-born were already separated from each other. But this view is quite groundless, apart from the dubious conjecture concerning a genetic relationship between the first-born and the passover. The verse in the Book of the Covenant speaks of firstlings of cattle, while Lev. xxii 27 (which belongs to H) refers to every sacrifice brought from the cattle. In other words, even though Exod. xxii 29 sets no fixed time for the offering up of the firstling, there is an obligation not to delay its presentation but to sacrifice it to the Lord immediately after its eighth day. As against this, in D there is no such demand and according to the assumption the Israelite has to offer up the first-born of his cattle when he comes to the chosen place (Deut. xv 19-20). Likewise in P and in H there is no such demand concerning the firstling, for Lev. xxii 27 indicates the minimum time after which it is permissible to sacrifice *any* beast that was born: "And from the eighth day *on* it shall be acceptable as an offering by fire to the Lord" (but there is no obligation necessarily to offer it up). The reason is that the views of D and P (as well as that of H) are based on the centralization of worship, and in such circumstances it is impossible to obligate the Israelite to make the fatiguing journey to the temple every time that a firstling of his cattle is born, and it is preferable that he should offer it up when he comes there on a pilgrimage festival. But the Book of the Covenant can impose such a duty, because when there are many temples available, no special trouble is involved in this sacrifice (cf. S. R. DRIVER, *Exodus*, Cambridge 1918, *ad loc.*). This means to say that the humanitarian law of letting the calf or lamb remain "with its mother" eight days after its birth, is integrated into the Book of the Covenant and the Holiness Code in various ways, as a common legal heritage that was related to prevalent custom.

connection with the passover descriptions and concerning the scant historical worth that can be ascribed to these portrayals,[1] I have found no answer to this point. The assumption that the sacrifice of the first-born was originally a nomadic institution, which only in one of its later transformations was expanded to include human first-born, is also a mere hypothesis.

To be sure, not all scholars have followed the peculiar view of WELLHAUSEN, for most concede that Exod. xii 21-27 appertains to one of the non-priestly sources. Nevertheless, the many who grant the existence of the passover offering in J, namely in Exod. xii 21-27, are not prepared to admit that this sacrifice is also mentioned in Exod. xxiii 18 (i.e. in the Book of the Covenant) and in Exod. xxxiv 25 (i.e. in the Smaller Book of the Covenant, which is not a "Cultic Dec-alogue"). Only one of these two verses (Exod. xxxiv 25) speaks explic-itly of *zebaḥ ḥag happāsaḥ*, "the sacrifice of the feast of the passover"; hence it is possible to claim that the parallel verse (Exod. xxiii 18) does not refer to this sacrifice but to any ordinary sacrifice.[2] On the other hand, the law that occurs in both these verses is divided into two instructions; consequently, it may be claimed that even Exod. xxxiv 25 itself does not allude entirely to the passover but only the second instruction therein does ("Neither shall the sacrifice of the feast of the passover be left until the morning").[3] Some scholars, indeed, maintain that the whole of Exod. xxxiv 25, including both its injunctions, refers to the passover,[4] while others give this interpretation also to Exod. xxiii 18, only this view is based in their case on preference given to the recension of Exod. xxxiv 25 (the reverse of WELLHAUSEN's argu-ment) or by regarding Exod. xxxiv 25 as the earlier source from which Exod. xxiii 18 (together with the adjacent verses) was, as it were, derived.[5]

---

[1] WELLHAUSEN, *Prolegomena*[6], pp. 97-98.

[2] See e.g. the remarks of A. DILLMANN, S. R. DRIVER, U. CASSUTO, M. NOTH, in their commentaries, *ad loc.*

[3] This was assumed by e.g. DRIVER and NOTH, in their commentaries to Exo-dus. But previously DRIVER was apparently inclined to the opinion that both verses in their entirety refer to passover and the feast of unleavened bread. See S. R. DRIVER, *Deuteronomy*, ICC, Edinburgh 1902 (1951), pp. vii, 190.

[4] This is admitted, among others, by H. HOLZINGER, B. BAENTSCH, G. BEER-K. GALLING, in their commentaries to Exodus, *ad loc.*

[5] See especially the commentary of BEER and GALLING, *ad loc.* Indeed, all who regard Exod. xxxiv 17-26 as a "Cultic Decalogue" are compelled to prefer it to Exod. xxiii 14-19, because according to this premise Exod. xxxiv 18 ff. constitutes a part of the Decalogue, whose continuity is not to be broken. R. DE VAUX concedes that Exod. xxiii 18 and likewise Exod. xxxiv 25 must refer to the passover

We are sure that the connection as well as the difference between
the two above-mentioned verses, and similarly between the pericopes
Exod. xxiii 14-19 and xxxiv 18-26 as a whole, are not to be explained
by clerical dependence, by the assumption that the one might have
been copied from the other. They are two parallel and independent
literary formulations of the same legal material. There are no divergences between them that can be explained as copying errors in the
one case or the other; but all the differences can be satisfactorily explained if we posit that two scribes committed to writing fixed dicta
that had been given their form by oral inculcation. The two parallel
formulations are still close, therefore, to the language of the inculcation and declamation of this material, and the purport of the two
verses, to all intents and purposes, is the same. In truth, both refer
to the passover sacrifice, as we shall demonstrate below. This means
that even the collections of laws earlier than D recognize, definitely
enough, this offering. Furthermore, they also recognize it already as
an adjunct of the festival of unleavened bread and as one of the
sacrifices offered up in temples.

III. The Injunctions Recurring in Exod. xxiii 18, xxxiv 25

Following are the two verses appearing in parallel forms in the
Books of the Covenant, each one of which is divided into two instructions:

[I] לא תזבח על חמץ דם זבחי [II] ולא ילין חלב חגי עד בקר: Ex. xxiii 18

[I] לא תשחט על חמץ דם זבחי [II] ולא ילין לבקר זבח חג הפסח. Ex. xxxiv 25

1

The sense of the first injunction is: You shall not offer (or, You shall
not slaughter) my sacrifice (i.e. the passover sacrifice) so long as you
have not removed every leavened thing. This point is expressed in the
priestly section Exod. xii 1-20: From the moment that the passover
lamb has been slaughtered, it is obligatory to begin eating unleavened
bread and no *śeʾōr*, leaven may be left over in the houses (ibid. 15, 18).
The passover sacrifice itself is eaten together with unleavened bread
and bitter herbs (ibid. 8; Num. ix 11). Undoubtedly this premise

---

sacrifice, only he finds in them Deuteronomic editing (*Les Institutions de l'a.T.*, II,
Paris 1960, p. 386). KRAUS makes a somewhat similar admission (*op. cit.*, p. 62).

underlies the injunction in the Books of the Covenant and is also explicitly stated in D (Deut. xvi 3-4). This is how the verse was explained also by the Talmudic sages: You shall not slaughter the passover lamb while unleavened bread is still present (Mekhilta to Exod. xxiii 18; B. T. Pesaḥim 63a *et al.*), and they were followed by the medieval commentators, who correctly hit here the real meaning of the text.

Critical commentators who claim that this instruction refers to all the sacrifices are of opinion that the verse speaks here of the meal offering accompanying animal sacrifice, which may not be leavened.[1] This is explained in the priestly regulation (Lev. ii 11, vi 10), though the priestly regulation is somewhat more lenient in the case of loaves of thanksgiving offering, which do include cakes of leavened bread (ibid. vii 13). However, scholars seem to have failed to pay attention to a small detail, namely that the meal offering accompanying the animal sacrifice is subsidiary to it, and if the verses Exod. xxiii 18, xxxiv 25 had referred to that meal offering, the text should have read: You shall not burn (or put, or bring) unleavened bread *on* [the blood of] my sacrifice.[2] In respect of the two loaves of Pentecost, which are of primary importance, the burnt offerings being subsidiary to them, the text reads: "You shall offer up with [literally *on*] the bread seven lambs a year old without blemish... And the priest shall wave them with [literally *on*] the bread of the first fruits" etc. (Lev. xxiii 18-20). But the verses Exod. xxiii 18, xxxiv 25, had they referred to the meal offering which is subsidiary to the sacrifice, would not have been formulated as they are: "You shall not offer/slaughter *upon* leavened bread." Furthermore, the context of the verses and the juxtaposition of their members incline one to posit that just as the second member speaks of the passover (see further on), so the first member also refers to the selfsame offering, even though it is not specified by name.

---

[1] Cf. above, p. 95, n. 2. CASSUTO regards this as an anti-Canaanite trend, since unleavened bread was not considered holy among the Canaanites.

[2] No argument can be brought from the statement with regard to the loaves of the thanksgiving offering: "With [literary *on*] cakes of unleavened bread he shall bring his sacrifice" (Lev. vii 13), since that verse speaks of bringing, הקריב (not slaughtering, שחט or sacrificing, זבח) and the reference is to cakes and wafers of unleavened bread, which are placed *upon* the leavened loaves. The order of offering in the case of peace-offerings of thanksgiving, as explained in the text is as follows: the cakes and wafers of unleavened bread are offered על זבח, התודה "upon the sacrifice of thanksgiving," or, more exactly, על חלות לחם חמץ, "on the cakes of leavened bread" that were placed upon the sacrifice of the thanksgiving. In other words, the unleavened bread is offered on the leavened bread, and the leavened bread on the sacrifice (see ibid. 12-13).

The phrase דם זבחי, "blood of my sacrifice," for its part, is intrinsically difficult, and all the commentators have been hard put to it to suggest a solution, for we do not find דם as the object of the verbs זבח and שחט. The best suggestion is to regard the noun in the construct as having adjectival force, and the meaning of the expression would be "blood sacrifice." Thus we find רע מעלליכם (Isa. i 16)—"your evil doings"; קומת ארזיו (ibid. xxxvii 24)—"its tall cedars." [1] But even this suggestion is subject to doubt.

2

The sense of the second injunction is: You shall not delay the sacrifice of the passover till morning (i.e. finish it during the night). That the reference in this injunction is specifically to the passover we are able to deduce, *inter alia*, from the express mention of the name passover in one of the two parallel versions (Exod. xxxiv 25).[2] True, this verse reads: זבח חג הפסח, "The sacrifice of the *feast* of passover," and nowhere else in the Bible is the term "feast" applied to the passover, for the feast is only "the feast of unleavened bread." Nevertheless, the mention of the passover is original in this verse, as we shall see later. The obligation to finish the eating of the flesh of the passover before morning is explicitly stated in a passage of P (Exod. xii 8, 10) and in D (Deut. xvi 4, 7), and indirectly, but indubitably, even in a section of J (Exod. xii 22). It is this duty that underlies this instruction, as was correctly understood by some medieval (non-critical) expositors, who grasped here the plain meaning of the text.[3]

The precept not to delay the passover until the morning finds expression in the two parallel instructions with slight verbal variations: in Exod. xxiii 18 there is an injunction not to delay the burning of the *fat parts* of the festal offering, that is, of the passover, and thereby expression is given to the obligation to eat the sacrifice in the course of the night, for the sacrificers are not permitted to begin eating until the fat has been burnt on the altar (cf. 1 Sam. ii 15-16). Nor should

---

[1] Cf. CASSUTO's commentary, *ad loc.*

[2] Among those who interpreted this law in a general sense (not as referring specifically to the passover) there were some who argued that this direction was formulated at the time when the passover was the principal sacrifice of Israelite worshop (see DRIVER's commentary, p. 245). But this argument is altogether improbable.

[3] This is the interpretation given by RASHBAM and S. D. LUZZATTO. Others (RASHI, IBN-EZRA, NAḤMANIDES) explained this injunction as referring to the burnt- and peace-offerings of all the feasts.

one suppose that the fat should be burnt, but the eating should be postponed to the following day, for there is no reason to keep the flesh after its consumption has been permitted. This means to say that if the dictum enjoins the Israelites not to hold up the disposal of the fat of the sacrifice during the night, it does so only on the premise that the sacrificers are obliged to eat the offering in the course of that night. Whereas Exod. xxxiv 25 speaks of the sacrifice itself and enjoins not to hold it up, that is, not to delay its implementation, including the burning of the fat and the consumption of the offering, until the morning. Consequently, the verbal variations do not involve a substantive difference of meaning, and both formulations refer in effect to the same thing.

Those who claim that in Exod. xxiii 18 this instruction refers to all the sacrifices, interpret it to mean that the burning of the fat (and by implication, the consumption of the flesh) may not be postponed to the following day, so that the sacrifice should not become invalidated after it had been slaughtered. They liken it to the P law that ordains that the sacrifice of the thanksgiving must be eaten "on the day that he offers his sacrifice" and no part of it may be left "until morning" (Lev. vii 15, xxii 29-30).[1] It appears that the expression "until morning," which occurs both in the formulation of the law in Exod. xxiii 18 and in that of the priestly laws in Lev. vii 15, xxii 30, led the scholars to suppose that the same subject was being dealt with in both cases. But upon examination it becomes evident that there is no room here for analogy. First of all it must not be forgotten that the law of P itself is lenient in respect of votive and freewill offerings, which may be eaten in the course of two days and become "foul" only on the third day (Lev. vii 16-18).[2] One wonders, therefore, why the non-priestly law of Exod. xxiii 18 saw fit to demand something that was not even required by P, which as a rule is the more stringent in such matters. Nor is it to be supposed that the law of Exod. xxiii 18 refers to what is called in P sacrifices of thanksgiving, for even in such a case we should have found a more lenient ruling outside P (especially when the actual distinction between votive and free-will offerings and sacrifices of thanksgiving does not exist outside P).

---

[1] See e.g. DRIVER's commentary, p. 246; cf. A. DILLMANN, *Exodus*³, KeH Leipzig 1897, p. 279.

[2] Lev. xix 5-8 likewise refers to votive and free-will offerings, for it also permits them to be eaten till the third day, even though they are termed here indefinitely *zebaḥ šᵉlamîm*, "sacrifice of peace-offerings," because most of the peace-offering sacrifices were presented as votive or free-will offerings.

Furthermore, even in regard to the thanksgiving offering, which is
to be eaten in one day, the priestly law prescribes: ... ביום קרבנו יֵאָכֵל,
"[And the flesh...] shall be eaten *on the day* of his offering, he shall not
leave any of it until morning"; ... ביום ההוא יֵאָכֵל, "It shall be eaten
on the same *day*, you shall leave non of it until morning" (Lev. vii 15,
xxii 30). With regard to the votive and free-will sacrifices, which are
eaten in the course of two days, the text expresses itself in similar
fashion: ביום הקריבו את זבחו יֵאָכֵל וממחרת ···, "It shall be eaten
on the day that he offers his sacrifice, and on the morrow... but what
remains of the flesh of the sacrifice on the third day shall be burned
with fire; if any of the flesh of his sacrifice of peace-offering is eaten
on the third day, he who offers it shall not be accepted" etc.;
ביום זבחכם יֵאָכֵל וממחרת, "It shall be eaten *the* same *day* you offer it, or
on the morrow" etc. (Lev. vii 16-18, xix 6-7). The reason for this is
clear: all the sacrifices (except the passover) must be eaten during the
day, and the text comes to enjoin that the end of their consumption
must not be postponed to other days. The nights are not taken into
account for the completion of the eating of the sacrifice, since as a rule
the night was not a time for eating. But the direction in Exod. xxiii 18,
xxxiv 25 states: לא ילין ... עד בקר, "shall not be left lying [literally,
not spend the night] until morning"; ולא ילין לבקר, "shall not be left
lying until morning." The root לין employed in the verses clearly
attests an action that takes place *at night* and the prohibition is not to
postpone it till the morning. The difference in the circumstances, which
is reflected in the linguistic divergences, is also clear enough—viz,
that the sacrifice dealt with here, in contrast to the regular peace-
offerings, is slaughtered in the evening (in D's terminology "at sun-
set"; P's term is "at twilight") and eaten at night; hence it was proper
to enjoin that its fat and flesh should not be held over until morning.
In contrast to the votive, free-will, and thanksgiving peace-offerings,
which are mentioned in the priestly legislation, in contrast to all the
sacrifices offered throughout the year, here a night sacrifice is implied,
but there is only one such sacrifice in the year, and that is the passover.
It may, therefore, be said that the expression לא ילין, "shall not be
left lying through night" betrays the particular character of the sacrifice alluded to in these verses, that it is specifically a night sacrifice.

In other words, this instruction refers to exactly the same point that
is treated in the accounts of P: the passover offering is not to be left
lying until morning—that is to say, it must be eaten at night and
nothing of it is to be left over till morning, and anything that remains

untill morning must be burnt by fire, all as prescribed in Exod. xii 8, 10; Num. ix 12. Scholars seem to have been prevented from realizing this because of the *damnosa hereditas* of the consensus that P is exceedingly late. In J's account ostensibly it is not specified that the passover must be eaten by morning, but only that one may not go out of the door of the house until morning (Exod. xii 22); yet, the palpable identity of these two statements cannot be doubted.[1] This being so, it can lend an additional weight to our contention that the first instruction refers only to the *eating* of the leavened bread, which is forbidden from the moment that the passover lamb is slaughtered—a point which is also expressed, as we have said, in the descriptions of P (ibid. 15, 18).

IV. The Ancient Nucleus of the Passover Law in D

If the preceding proofs do not suffice to determine the correct significance of the injunctions in Exod. xxiii 18, xxxiv 25 they are further augmented by the decisive testimony of D.

1

It is a common feature of Deuteronomy that it does not formulate its laws (nor the narrative portions of its discourses) in an entirely new phraseology or in its own specific diction. Frequently its statements are constructed on an ancient nucleus, on a kind of verbal foundation found ready to hand, to which D adds its own particular contribution—special emphases due to differences of conception, or didactic and parenetic statements in its typical manner and style. Often we are able to remove the embellishment and reveal the brief and ancient kernel of the law, since this kernel appears in a similar form, and at times even in entirely identical words, in other legal sections,

---

[1] It may be pointed out even more precisely that the expression לא תשחט, "You shall not slaughter" (Exod. xxxiv 25) corresponds to J's expression in Exod. xii 21 ושחטו הפסח, "And slaughter the passover," and P's expression in Exod. xii 6 ושחטו אותו כל קהל עדת ישראל, "And all the aggregate community of the Israelites shall slaughter it." Furthermore, in both sources the text immediately proceeds to speak of the use to which the blood is to be put (ibid. 7, 22), and it is not impossible that it has a certain connection with the idiom דם זבחי, "the blood of my sacrifice" in the Books of the Covenant. Similarly, the statement זבח הוא ליהוה, "It is a sacrifice to Yahweh" may be analogous to the designations זבחי, "my sacrifice," זבח ... הפסח, "sacrifice... of the feast of passover" in Exod. xxiii 18, xxxiv 25.

that are earlier than D. For example, the law of the slave is built in D (Deut. xv 12-18) on three verses of the ancient statute cited in the Book of the Covenant, namely the opening verse and the two closing verses (Exod. xxi 2, 5-6). The nucleus of the law concerning the appointment of judges and the maintenance of justice (Deut. xvi 18-20) occurs with literal exactness in the Book of the Covenant (Exod. xxiii 6, 8). The injunctions "None shall appear before me empty-handed," "Three times a year all your males shall appear before the Sovereign, the Lord," which are found in Exod. xxiii 15, 17, xxxiv 20, 23 also appear verbatim and in the same context in D, but in the reverse order and with a number of expansions (Deut. xvi 16). On the other hand, the prohibition "You shall not boil a kid in its mother's milk," which is mentioned in Exod. xxiii 19, xxxiv 26, re-emerges in D without any expansions, but divorced from the context of the festivals and related to a different theme—that of forbidden foods (Deut. xiv 21). This nucleus is cited, then, without additions, but before it found its way into D is was removed from its first context and integrated into a new topic.

Many scholars are of the opinion that such verbal contacts attest that D derived most of its laws directly from the earlier codes, particularly from the Book of the Covenant (Exod. xx 20—xxiii 33).[1] This view is linked to a broader conception that postulates that JE were available to the author of D, and just as he drew upon those sources for the composition of the "historical" -narrative reviews incorporated in his discourses (Deut. i 6—iii 29, ix 8—x 11), so he based his legislation on the collections of laws contained in those sources. However, in this form the theory does not do justice to all the facts. It is a rule that I have found confirmed in the course of repeated examinations of the narrative sections of the Pentateuch, that only E was lying before the author of D,[2] and since the Book of the Covenant is the law code of E, it is not impossible that it, too, was known to the author of D. And yet, it is difficult to suppose that D's author drew his legal material directly from the Book of the Covenant. It is a manifest fact that ever so many laws comprised in the Book of the Covenant, which disclose no particular trend, are not cited in the code

---

[1] One of the first to give comprehensive expression to this view was A. KUENEN (*Historisch-Kritische Einleitung in die Bücher des AT*, I, Leipzig 1887, pp. 159-161). Subsequently it recurs frequently in the writings of scholars. Cf. HOLZINGER, *Hexateuch*, pp. 302-303 and the references there.

[2] For the present one may consult my study: "The Exodus Routes in the Pentateuchal Sources" (Hebrew) *Tarbiẓ* XL, 1971, pp. 113-143.

of D, and, contrariwise, very many regulations cited in the latter and which are also undoubtedly founded on ancient nuclei, have no basis or root in the statutes incorporated in the Book of the Covenant. Furthermore, there is such a great difference between the two codes in respect of the arrangement of the legal material, that it does not stand to reason that D's code was compiled by direct recourse to the Book of the Covenant. It would be much more accurate to say that D had access of his own, without the help of an intermediary, to the legal material that was preserved and transmitted by a long tradition, the material of which a part, in an older literary crystalization, is also found in the Book of the Covenant.[1] Accordingly, the author of D availed himself of the narrative framework of E for constructing a number of sections in the discourses of Moses, but he made a fresh approach to the legal material that was embedded, in part, in the heart of this framework. He needed this new approach in order to emphasize the distinctness of the Second Covenant, which, in his view, the Lord made with Israel in the steppes of Moab east of the Jordan, "in addition to the covenant which he had made with them at Horeb" (Deut. xxviii 69; cf. i 5).

Thus, it is not from the Book of the Covenant that D extracted the ancient kernels of his laws, but from that very source that at an earlier stage furnished the Book of the Covenant itself with its basic material (and even in the Book of the Covenant those nuclei are sometimes enveloped in a number of expansions). But this does not alter the actual fact that brief verbal and largely identical nuclei of those laws are sometimes cited in the code of D (wrapped in large expansions) and in the Book of the Covenant (much more exposed). This fact will help us to confirm the meaning of the instructions that concern us, in the form which they take in Exod. xxiii 18, xxxiv 25, since they, too, are incorporated in D.

2

The passage in D devoted to the passover and the feast of unleavened bread (Deut. xvi 1-8) is divisible into three segments: an introduction, which is an injunction to observe the presentation of the passover

---

[1] This view is actually held by e.g. C. STEUERNAGEL (*Deuteronomium*[2], GHK, Göttingen 1923, p. 40), only that in his opinion several expansions that occurred in D led to the interpolation in D of verses similar to those of the Book of the Covenant. A close view is also adopted by Y. KAUFMANN (*Toledôt Ha'emûnah Hayyiśre'elît*, I, 54-58), who speaks of "a rich legal literature" that was current among the Israelites.

in the month of Abib (v. 1); a hurried description of how to sacrifice
the passover and to link to it the eating of unleavened bread seven
days (vv. 2-4); an ordinance to sacrifice the passover in the chosen
place only and an iterated command to eat unleavened bread during
the six remaining days after returning home (vv. 5-8). Now the second
segment contains an expansion and "inflation" of the two injunctions
recurring in Exod. xxiii 18, xxxiv 25. The compressed and laconic
version of those verses runs like a golden thread at the heart of the
contents of this segment and actually forms the foundation on which
its ordinances are based. Suffice it to compare the passages in order
to discern the real basis of the matters expressed here by D:

וזבחת פסח ליהוה אלהיך צאן
ובקר ... לא תאכל עליו חמץ
שבעת ימים תאכל עליו מצות לחם
עני ... ולא ילין מן הבשר אשר
תזבח בערב ביום הראשון לבקר

לא תזבח על חמץ דם זבחי ולא ילין חלב
חגי עד בקר

"You shall not offer [the blood of] my
sacrifice so long as anything leavened exists [literary *on anything leavened*]; and the fat of my feast [festal
sacrifice] *shall not be left lying until
morning"* (Exod. xxiii 18)

"You shall offer up the passover for
the Lord your God ⟨from⟩ the flock
or the herd... You shall *not* eat *anything leavened* with it [literary *on it*];
seven days you shall eat unleavened
bread with it, bread of distress...
and *none* of the flesh of what you
offer up on the evening of the first
day *shall be left lying until morning"*
(Deut. xvi 2-4).

לא תשחט על חמץ דם זבחי ולא ילין
לבקר זבח חג הפסח

"You shall not slaughter [the blood
of] my sacrifice so long as anything
leavened exists [literary *on anything
leavened*]; and the *offering* of the feast
of passover *shall not be left lying until
morning"* (Exod. xxxiv 25)

The dependence of this passage of D on the ancient injunctions
cited in Exod. xxiii 18, xxxiv 25 is shown not only by the verbal
pattern formed by the verses, but also by the fact that actually the
excerpt from D does not state more than is contained in those injunctions, except for some slight elaborations, which are dictated in part
by D's particular viewpoint. This, then, is the essential content of the
second segment in the D passage: the passover has to be offered up
from the flock or the herd in the chosen place—nothing leavened may
be eaten with it, only unleavened bread for seven days—its flesh may

not be left lying until morning. The last two points correspond to the two above-mentioned injunctions, while the preceding point (v. 2) serves as a preamble to them. The third segment in the D passage (vv. 5-8) is intended primarily to emphasize that it is an unequivocal obligation to offer up the passover specifically in the chosen place, and the matter is mentioned only in order to inculcate the constant demand of D in respect of the centralization of the cult. Apparently the brief statement concerning the chosen place, contained already in v. 2, was not enough for the author, so that after he had discharged the task of citing the main law and dealing with it (vv. 3-4), he found it necessary to come back to centralization of worship urging it at length (vv. 5-8).

For the sake of exactness it must be mentioned that beside the verbal pattern discernible in the second segment of the D excerpt (vv. 2-4), which resembles the ancient directions in Exod. xxiii 18, xxxiv 25, there is throughout the passage, in addition, a number of stereotyped phrases, which also have parallels in the sources that preceded D, namely in the Book of the Covenant and the section Exod. xiii 3-7, which belongs to E. The following references will illustrate the point:

1.

שמור את חדש האביב ועשית פסח ... כי
בחדש האביב הוציאך יהוה אלהיך
ממצרים לילה

את חג המצות תשמר ... למועד חדש
האביב כי בחדש האביב יצאת ממצרים

"Observe the month of Abid and keep the passover... for in the month of Abid the Lord your God brought you out of Egypt by night" (Deut. xvi 1)

"You shall observe the feast of unleavened bread... at the set time of the month of Abib, for in the month of Abib you came out from Epgyt" (Exod. xxxiv 18; cf. xxiii 15).

2.

שבעת ימים תאכל עליו מצות לחם עני
כי בחפזון יצאת מארץ מצרים

שבעת ימים תאכל מצות כאשר צויתיך
למועד חדש האביב כי בו יצאת ממצרים

"Seven days you shall eat it with un-leavened bread, bread of distress—for you came out of the land of Egypt hurriedly" (ibid. 3).

"Seven days you shall eat unleavened bread as I have commanded you, at the set time in the month of Abib, for in it you came out of Egypt" (Exod. xxiii 15; cf. xxxiv 18, also xiii 3-4, 7).

3.

למען תזכר את יום צאתך מארץ מצרים
כל ימי חייך

זכור את היום הזה אשר יצאתם ממצרים

"That all the days of your life you may remember the day when you came out of the land of Egypt" (ibid. 3).

"Remember this day, in which you came out from Egypt" (Exod. xiii 3).

4.מצות יֵאָכֵל את שבעת הימים ולא יֵרָאֶה לך חמץ ולא יֵרָאֶה לך שאור בכל גבולך

"Unleavened bread shall be eaten *for seven days;* no leavened bread shall be seen with you, *and no leaven shall be seen with you in all your territory*" (ibid. 7).

ולא יֵרָאֶה לך שאור בכל גבולך שבעת ימים

"*No leaven shall be seen with you in all your territory for seven days*" (ibid. 4).

5.שבעת ימים תאכל מצות וביום השביעי חג ליהוה

"Seven *days you shall eat unleavened bread, and on the seventh day* there shall be a pilgrimage-feast *to the Lord*" (ibid. 6).

ששת ימים תאכל מצות וביום השביעי עצרת ליהוה אלהיך

"Six *days you shall eat unleavened bread, and on the seventh day* there shall be a solemn assembly *to the Lord* your God" (ibid. 8).

Note that in the first set of parallels, while the verse in the Book of the Covenant speaks of the feast of unleavened bread, the corresponding verse in D refers to the passover sacrifice, and yet the same expressions are employed in it. In the second set of parallels, the statement about the month of abib evolves in D into one containing an adverb— instead of "for in it (i.e. in the month of Abib) you came out of Egypt" we find "for you came out of the land of Egypt hurriedly," but the essential verbal pattern is preserved. In the fifth set of parallels "seven days" are changed to "xis days"; this is due to D's emphatic requirement that the Israelite should go up on the first day to the chosen place and offer up the passover there (vv. 5-7). Thus, when the man returns home, he has six days left for eating unleavened bread.[1] These variations testify that in D's language the stereotyped phrases are put to "living" use, and that he employs them as material with which to express his notions.[2]

---

[1] This is the simple explanation of the six days of eating unleavened bread mentioned in Deut. xvi 5, although several verses earlier the same passage refers to seven days of eating unleavened bread (ibid. 3). Critical exegetes have experienced difficulty—but quite needlessly—in understanding D's wording here; while the Talmudic sages adopted an exposition of their own (B. T. Pesaḥim 120a; Ḥagiga 18a; Menaḥot 66a).

[2] For the verbal parallels in Deut. xvi 1-8 as a whole cf. the critical commentaries, especially that of S. R. DRIVER. A number of echoes of these stereotyped expressions even found their way into the language of P. With the sentence שבעת, ימים תאכל מצות "Seven days you [sing.] shall eat unleavened bread" (Exod. xiii 6, xxiii 15, xxxiv 18; Deut. xvi 3, 8) compare שבעת ימים מצות תאכלו, "Seven days you [pl.] shall eat unleavened bread" (Exod. xii 15; Lev. xxiii 6). With its variant מצות יֵאָכֵל את שבעת הימים, "Unleavened bread shall be

Now although D's language is replete, throughout this passage, with set expressions found ready to hand, it does not obscure the fact that the second segment (Deut. xvi 2-4) is built principally on the two ancient injunctions that were cited in Exod. xxiii 18, xxxiv 25. As we stated above, not only does the verbal pattern of these directions lie at the base of this segment, but in respect of the passover oblation it does not state (at least in vv. 3-4) more than is to be found in these injunctions. The addition to the content of these injunctions occurs only in v. 2, which is the preamble to the segment, and states that the passover must be brought from the flock or the herd and offered up at the chosen place. The other stereotypes that found their way into this segment, and into the entire passage Deut. xvi 1-8, are connected with the duty to eat unleavened bread and most of them are used here to express this obligation, which remains valid for seven consecutive days (and is a continuation of the sacrifice).

We may, therefore, conclude that if D already understood the two directions that occur in Exod. xxiii 18, xxxiv 25 as referring to passover, and based on them his own instructions regarding this sacrifice, it may be fairly assumed that this is actually their meaning; all the more so when it has become clear to us (above, sec. III) that this connotation inevitably flows from what is stated in the injunctions themselves.

V. The Linguistic Variations in the Two Instructions

Consideration should also be given to the exact wording of the ancient instructions on the passover sacrifice as they were known to the author of D.

The formulation of the first instruction undoubtedly agreed with the phrasing of Exod. xxiii 18: לא תזבח על חמץ, not with that of Exod. xxxiv 25: לא תשחט על חמץ. Although the verb שחט ("slaughter") is specifically applied to the passover in other passages,[1]

---

eaten for the seven days" (Exod. xiii 7) compare שבעת ימים מצות יֵאָכל, "For seven days unleavened bread shall be eaten" (Num. xxviii 17). With the phrasing of the sentences שבעת ימים ... ולא יֵרָאה לך שאור בכל גבולך, "For seven days... and no leaven shall be found with you in all your territory" (Exod. xiii 7), ולא יֵרָאה לך שאור בכל גבולך שבעת ימים, "No leaven shall be found with you in all your territory for seven days" (Deut. xvi 4) compare שבעת ימים ..., תשביתו שאור מבתיכם "Seven days... you shall remove leaven from your houses," שבעת ימים שאור לא ימצא בבתיכם, "For seven days no leaven shall be found in your houses" (Exod. xii 15, 19).

[1] Cf. above, p. 101, n. 1.

yet underlying the text of Deut. xvi 2-3 we find the texture ... וזבחת,
לא ... על(יו) חמץ which corresponds to the wording of the Book
of the Covenant in Exod. xxiii 18 (above, sec. IV).

On the other hand, the version of the second instruction as was
known to D agreed in the main with the wording of Exod. xxxiv 25:
ולא ילין לבקר זבח ..., for in Deut. xvi 4 the phrasing is: ... ולא ילין
תזבח ... לבקר. Furthermore, it appears that the word הפסח mentioned at the end of Exod. xxxiv 25, was also included in the formulation
available to D, for if we continue from the second segment to the
beginning of the following verse, the verbal pattern of the second
instruction is completed to the end: ... ולא ילין ... (תזבח) ... לבקר
לזבח ... הפסח (Deut. xvi 4-5). This means, that the phraseology of the
ancient injunction exerted an associative influence on the author
of D and apparently furnished him with the key words when he
proceeded to voice, in the context of passover, his demand for the
centralization of the cult. Hence it may be posited that the word הפסח
is an original part of Exod. xxxiv 25, and is not to be omitted as an
addition, as a number of scholars think.[1]

Consequently, the text of the directions as they were known to D
and became the basis of his rulings in regard to the passover sacrifice was as follows: לא תזבח על חמץ ... ולא ילין לבקר זבח הפסח,
without the word חג, which is not mentioned in any part of the D
passage. In truth, in such a context the word חג has no place, for we
have already stated that the combination חג הפסח in Exod. xxxiv 25
is improper and has no parallel throughout the Bible, because the
passover is a zebaḥ, not a ḥag. At the same time, the "divided" character
of the formulation known to D—being partly like Exod. xxiii 18 and
partly like Exod. xxxiv 25—confirms the assumption that the author
of D did not extract these instructions from one of those passages, nor
did he copy them from one of them, like a scribe. They reached him
in a form independent of either of the two forms given to them in
Exod. xxiii 18, xxxiv 25, and, as already stated, directly from the
source from which they reached (in an earlier stage) the Books of the
Covenant themselves.

Now although the word חג was apparently not included in the

---

[1] See e.g. WELLHAUSEN, Prolegomena⁶, p. 82 (note); idem, Die Composition des
Hexateuchs⁴, p. 334; BENZINGER, op. cit., coll. 3590, 3593; W. R. ARNOLD, "The
Passover Papyrus from Elephantine," JBL XXXI, 1912, p. 9; H. G. MAY, "The
Passover and the Unleavened Cakes," ibid. LV, 1935, p. 66. To be sure, the phrase
ḥag happesaḥ, "the feast of passover" is impossible in biblical Hebrew, but the
solution is not to remove the word pesaḥ. See further below.

formulation of the injunctions as they were known to D, it would be unduly hasty to erase it from the *text* of Exod. xxxiv 25. True, it is not impossible that it was insinuated there by mistake and is a kind of prolonged dittography of the word זבח preceding it (the ח was duplicated and the ג attached itself to it making it a separate word). However, the analogy with the text of Exod. xxiii 18 suggests the possibility that the word חג plays a more organic role in this context, pointing to one of the two versions that were grafted together in Exod. xxxiv 25: זבח חגי (with the omission of the י) and זבח הפסח. This possibility seems more probable.

The linguistic garb of the ancient directions concerning the passover thus received a number of forms—all of them variant wordings of the same legal rules, whose preservation on the periphery of literature called for inculcation by repetition and declamation. Accordingly, following are the forms of the first direction:

לא תזבח על חמץ דם זבחי   (Exod. xxiii 18; and synthesized in Deut. xvi 2-3).

לא תשחט על חמץ דם זבחי   (Exod. xxxiv 25).

Following are the forms of the second direction:

ולא ילין חלב חגי עד בקר   (Exod. xxiii 18).

ולא ילין לבקר זבח חגי   (incorporated in Exod. xxxiv 25).

ולא ילין לבקר זבח הפסח   (incorporated in Exod. xxxiv 25 and synthesized in Deut. xvi 4-5).

VI. The Passover as the Prelude to the Feast of Unleavened Bread and as a Temple Sacrifice

Our study both of the wording of the verses Exod. xxiii 18, xxxiv 25 and of the nexus between these verses and Deut. xvi 2-5 led us to the inevitable conclusion that the dramatic ceremony of passover, as it is depicted with relative fulness in P (Exod. xii 1-14) and with relative brevity in J (Exod. xii 21-27), is already compressed in a succinct and allusive form in the two ancient instructions in Exod. xxiii 18, xxxiv 25. In the P account, and partly also in J's account, an effort is discernible to expose this ceremony in a concrete, visualized form and to emphasize certain aspects of it (needless to say, the literary formulation

of these accounts is later than that of the Books of the Covenant), but
so long as no explicit contradiction between the testimonies can be
found it would not be fair to assume that they are not fundamentally
in accord.

1

The aforementioned conclusion appears to us important enough in
itself, at least as a key to the correct comprehension of the verses in
the Book of Exodus. But it also leads to two further decisive corol-
laries.

First, that all the biblical sources already recognize the passover
sacrifice as linked to the feast of unleavened bread. This connection
is even explicitly expressed in the directions of Exod. xxiii 18, xxxiv 25,
for they do not permit the passover to be offered up while anything
leavened exists, i.e. it is regarded there as a prelude to the feast of
unleavened bread. In one of the formulations the passover is actually
designated זבח חג, that is to say, the special sacrifice (night sacrifice)
that is attached to the ḥag, the pilgrimage-feast (namely, the feast of
unleavened bread). Consequently, it cannot be argued that the connection of the passover sacrifice with the feast of unleavened bread is an
innovation of D.[1] In the J passage (Exod. xii 21-27) there is no
mention of feast or of unleavened bread only because it intends mainly
to depict the rite of sprinkling the blood of the passover after it has
been slaughtered. This passage says almost nothing of other aspects
of the sacrifice, and no inferences are to be drawn from silence.

Secondly, that in all the biblical pieces of evidence the passover is
regarded as a temple sacrifice, that is to say, a sacrifice that has to be
offered up at one of the "houses of God," not on an isolated altar.
As for D and P it goes without saying that they would not permit the
passover to be sacrificed anywhere but in the one temple, in which,
according to their view, the entire cult is concentrated (see also below).
But even the directions in Exod. xxiii 18, xxxiv 25 are already based
on the temple character of this sacrifice, for they view the passover as
a festal sacrifice and connect it with the feast of unleavened bread, and
it is well established that no ḥag ("feast") can be observed but by a
pilgrimage to one of the temples. Therefore, it is not to be doubted
that the attachment of the passover offering to the temples, just as its

---

[1] Even less reason there is to argue, with DE VAUX (*op. cit.*, p. 386), that the
actual amalgamation of the passover with the feast of unleavened bread is first
discernible in Ezek. xlv 21 and in P.

relation to the feast of unleavened bread, were established in an early
stage of Israel's history, and at any rate this connection preceded the
directions prescribed in the Books of the Covenant.

Scholars who, contrary to WELLHAUSEN, argue in favour of the
passover's antiquity in Israel's life, consider it almost certain that
initially the passover was a family sacrifice, in the sense that it was
offered up on a high place, or on a solitary altar, or even within the
house. Their proofs are derived from the prohibition of D: "You may
not offer the passover sacrifice in any of your cities that the Lord your
God gives you" (Deut. xvi 5), from which one may infer that this was
actually what they used to do with this sacrifice until D transferred it
to the chosen place. Ostensibly these scholars could also find support
in the account of J in Exod. xii 21-27, in which the passover is depicted
as a sacrifice slaughtered in the family circle and its participants, it is
said, do not go out of the door of the house until morning. So, too,
the passover is portrayed even in the priestly account in Exod. xii 1-14,
only that in view of the consensus that P is late, these scholars cannot
set particular store by its testimony.[1]

2

Do those arguments really prove that in biblical times the passover
offering was regarded as a home sacrifice or an oblation of the high
places?

We have already stated that the J passage Exod. xii 21-27 in no way
purports to encompass the whole complex of details connected with
the passover. This passage speaks only of the slaughter (mentioned
here in one word), of a number of rites relating to the sprinkling of
the blood, and of the duty of the participants to remain in the house
till morning. The author found these details deserving of mention and
emphasis in order to exemplify something of the extraordinary character of the passover sacrifice, but they do not by any means exhaust

---

[1] Y. KAUFMANN, too, holds that according to P the passover sacrifice "is offered
up outside the temple and not by a priest"; *inter alia* KAUFMANN endeavours to
base himself on this point in order to prove the absence of the idea of cult centralization in P and that P belongs to "the code of worship of the high places"
(*Toledôt Ha'emûnah Hayyiśre'elît*, I, 122-123). Whereas J. B. SEGAL, relying upon
this point seeks to show the absence of any connection between the passover
sacrifice according to P and the temple, and in all good faith he believes that the
opportunity is here provided to undermine the entire documentary theory (*The
Hebrew Passover*, London 1963, pp. 74-75).

the description of the sacrifice, not even its ceremonial-dramatic aspects alone. The actual eating of the flesh is not even mentioned here.
Yet the author informs us that the passover is *zebaḥ leYahweh*, "a
sacrifice to the Lord" (v. 27), thereby expressing the self-evident premise that the flesh of the passover is destined to be eaten and the pieces
of fat to be burnt on an altar. It is inconceivable that he intended to
tell his readers that the fat should be eaten by the participants, or
burnt within the house, although according to his express statement
it is the participants' duty to keep in doors until morning. Perforce
we must suppose that it is his assumption that before the participants
put the blood on the lintel and the doorposts and proceed to eat the
flesh in the house (staying there until morning), they will have to see
to it that the pieces of fat are burnt and the blood sprinkled on an
altar, as the ritual requires in the case of every properly-offered-up
zebaḥ. With regard to the obligation not to leave the fat of the feast
(festal offering) till morning there is the explicit prohibition in Exod.
xxiii 18, and here, too, it is not to be doubted that the assumption of
the text is that the pieces of fat are not to be burnt in the house but on
an altar. As a matter of fact, just because of the unusual character of
this sacrifice—the fact that it was slaughtered at the beginning of the
evening and consumed in the course of the night without anyone
leaving the house—there was good reason for this injunction, so that
the participants should attend without delay to the separation of the
pieces of fat for the altar before they shut themselves up in their
houses in order to eat the flesh.[1]

However, on which altar is it, according to the premise of the text,
that the fat of the passover has to be burnt at the beginning of the
evening? Is it a high place or one of the provincial altars? Since we
have already concluded that, at all events, there is an indispensable
connection between the passover sacrifice and the near-by altar, the
solitary altar is not, from the outset, preferable in this regard to the
altar adjoining the temple. It is entirely natural that the scene of the
ceremonial drama of the sacrifice should be in the vicinity of the temple
and that the house in which the participants remain for the night
should be one of the chambers in the temple courts. Now the instructions laid down in Exod. xxiii 18, xxxiv 25 clearly attest that the place

---

[1] Note that the priestly law states that the one who brings the peace-offering
must deliver the pieces of fat to the priest with his own hands, while the priest
shall burn them on the altar (Lev. vii 29-31). Cf. also Lev. iii 3-5, 9-11, 14-16: the
owner of the peace-offering presents the pieces of fat and the priest burns them.

of the altar that must hold the fat of the passover, as the place of the sacrifice itself, is none other than that of the *ḥag*, the pilgrimage-feast, namely beside a temple.

Another allusion to the nexus between the passover offering and the temple, according to the view of J himself, is to be found in the special didactic phrasing that marks J's account of this sacrifice, including the direction to explain and teach the nature of the ceremony to the children, when they would ask what it means (Exod. xii 24-27₁). Similar statements appear in E in connection with the eating of un-leavened bread on the feast of the month of Abid (Exob. xiii 5-10) and in regard to the sacrifice of the first-born (ibid. 11-16). In D's style this type of phraseology was elaborated and perfected until it became its distinctive hallmark, but here it still appears in a somewhat restrain-ed form. And although *au fond* this phraseology is common to all the three themes referred to, neverhteless certain differences of nuance are noticeable between J's account of the passover sacrifice and E's account of the feast of unleavened bread and the first-born, that is to say, the difference in the literary identity of the two writers is the cause of the distinction—slight but quite palpable—in their diction and modes of expressions.[1] Now the similar didactic phrasing, which, in this instance, links the three subjects together and interlocks the two sources, bears testimony to common background and circumstances,

---

[1] The citations given below will demonstrate the resemblance in form and motifs between the parallel "proto-Deuteronomic" passages as well as the palpable differences in their expressions.

J on the passover (Exod. xii 24-27₁)

1. ‏ושמרתם את הדבר הזה לחק לך ולבניך‎
‏עד עולם (24)‎
2. ‏והיה כי תבאו אל הארץ אשר יתן יהוה‎
‏לכם כאשר דבר, ושמרתם את העבדה‎
‏הזאת (25)‎

3. ‏והיה כי יאמרו אליכם בניכם מה‎
‏העבדה הזאת לכם, ואמרתם‎

and then the text proceeds to narrate the event of the exodus, which is the aetiological background of the cere-mony (22-27₁)

E on the feast of unleavened bread (Exod. xiii 5-10) *and the first-born* (ibid. 11-16)

‏ושמרת את החקה הזאת למועדה מימים‎
‏ימימה (10)‎
‏והיה כי יביאך יהוה אל ארץ הכנעני‎
‏והחתי והאמרי והחוי והיבוסי אשר נשבע‎
‏לאבתיך לתת לך ... ועבדת את‎
‏העבדה הזאת בחדש הזה (5)‎
‏והיה כי יביאך יהוה אל ארץ הכנעני‎
‏כאשר נשבע לך ולאבותיך ונתנה לך (11)‎
‏והגדת לבנך ביום ההוא לאמר בעבור זה‎
‏עשה יהוה לי בצאתי ממצרים (8)‎
‏והיה כי ישאלך בנך מחר לאמר מה זאת,‎
‏ואמרת אליו‎

and the text proceeds to recount the event as above, the aetiological charac-ter of the passage being noticeable also in the wording of the continuation:

8

because all three cultic scenes are marked by unusual features, all three are interconnected—and most probably all three appertain to the temple precincts. Had the passover been regarded by J as fundamentally a non-temple sacrifice, it is hardly conceivable that he would have enfolded it in the same wrapping as E did with the feast of unleavened bread and the first-born. Indeed, it is difficult to imagine that the passover should be considered of lower status than the sacrifice of the firstlings, which is distinctly a temple sacrifice (the same applies to the tithe, the votive offering, the *ḥerem* sacrifice and other consecrated oblations), and even less than an ordinary free-will sacrifice, which, too, is offered up only in the temple.[1]

The same may be said of the P passage Exod. xii 1-14, which is longer and more detailed than the J passage, but is nevertheless also elliptical in character and likewise does not exhaust the description of the passover ceremony in all its aspects. This passage, too, intends only to treat of certain facets of the ritual and to concretize them particularly. These are: the method of preparing the lamb, the slaughter, the sprinkling of the blood and the rites that embellish the consumption of the sacrifice. Here also it cannot be doubted that in P's own assumption the burning of the fat precedes the eating of the flesh, especially as this order of procedure is accepted even by the non-priestly sources (1 Sam. ii 15). But the burning of the fat is only possible on the one altar beside the tabernacle, which is the sole place of worship in the camp of Israel. If we strip off from P the idea of the centralization of the cult in its specific priestly embodiment, the palpable reality underlying his account will at most be as follows: that the passover was offered up and eaten in temple cities and in order to

---

עַל כֵּן אֲנִי זֹבֵחַ לַיהוה כָּל פֶּטֶר רֶחֶם
הַזְּכָרִים

"*Therefore* I am sacrificing to the Lord every first male issue of the womb" (14-15)

On examining the passages it will be seen that those concerning the feast of unleavened bread and the first-born resemble each other more closely than that which deals with the passover. In the former two there also occurs a similar direction with regard to the sign and frontlet (vv. 9, 16), that does not appear in the passage relating to the passover. Furthermore, the traces that are subsequently due to become—as they are or with slight changes—identification marks of D are much more noticeable in these two passages than in the J passage (because E, not J was lying before D; cf. above, p. 102, n. 2). However, this is not precisely the style of D.

[1] On the firstling and the free-will offering as temple sacrifices cf. my remarks in *Encyc. Miqra'it*, IV, col. 42; V, coll. 324, 784.

present it the families would make a pilgramage to those cities; they did not offer it up on the solitary altars in the provinces. P itself states that as "an ordinance for ever" the Israelites must celebrate the day after passover and observe it as "a *ḥag* to Yahweh" (Exod. xii 14), which implies that the passover was only offered up on pilgramage. P further relates that in the second year after the exodus the Israelites offered up the passover in the camp after the tabernacle had already been erected (Num. ix 1-5), and there he expressly calls it "the Lord's offering" (ibid. 7, 13). It is inconceivable that the Lord's offering should be offered up in the camp without recourse to the altar adjoining the tabernacle and that this oblation should be eaten without its pieces of fat first being burnt on the altar.

But then, both the J and P passages depict the first passover as though it was offered up in Egypt, before the tabernacle itself was erected, or before the Israelites reached Canaan and their temples were established. These accounts entail the appearance of a non-temple sacrifice, even of a home sacrifice, but this is only an optical illusion. It is the endeavour of the biblical tradition to link the passover with the exodus from Egypt that caused certain tension in the portrayal of the model of this offering ("the passover of Egypt"), which was momentarily removed from its real setting and described as it were by itself, without any connection with the temple. This tension was unavoidable on account of the aetiological load resting on the descriptions, which compelled J and P to fit the sacrifice with which they were familiar into anachronistic circumstances, when a temple was not yet in existence.[1] However, there is no difference in principle between these accounts and other biblical narratives in which an anachronistic element is manifest. The narratives of J and P about the manna, for example, state in all innocence, that when the Israelites received their bread from heaven, but had not yet reached Mount Sinai, they were already obliged to keep the Sabbath (Exod. xvi 22-30) and even placed a jar of manna "before the Lord... before the testimony to be kept" (ibid. 32-24), that is, in the Holy of Holies. While the narrative of E portrays the exodus from Egypt in the form of a march with a view to observing a *ḥag*, that is, as a pilgrimage (Exod.

---

[1] Needless to say, according to our conclusion the historical-national motivation of the passover offering, i.e. its connection with the remembrance of the exodus from Egypt, is not the novel idea of D. Such motivation already exists in J (independently it appears also in P). It may be conjectured that E, too, shared their view on this point, only the account of the preparation of the passover according to E has not been preserved.

v 1, x 9).[1] The projection of the regular passover observance, customary and familiar, on the image of "the passover of Egypt," thus
weighed heavily, from several aspects, on the true nature of the sacrifice. Every anachronistic projection is liable to impair the optimal
features of an institution, but the real character of the latter cannot be
decided by its reflection only.

Consequently, of the injunction in Deut. xvi 5 we can only say that
it is directed against the possibility of offering the passover in one of
the temples (as distinct from the solitary altars) outside the chosen
place. Apparently D has this in mind when he employs here his usual
expression "in one of your cities," since in his view all places outside
the chosen place, whether temples or altars only, are to be regarded
as "cities" (literary "gates"). He does not refer, in this context, to
altars unconnected with temples.

---

[1] See my remarks in *S. Yeivin Festschrift* (Hebrew), Jerusalem 1970, pp. 181-184,
and the observations there on Exod. iii 21-22, xi 2-3, xii 35-36.

DAS GOTTESBILD
DER ÄLTEREN WEISHEIT ISRAELS

VON

HORST DIETRICH PREUSS
Göttingen

Unter älterer Weisheit[1] Israels sollen hier die jetzt in Prov. x-xxix vereinten Sammlungen verstanden werden, d.h. die sog. Sammlung II (x 1-xxii 16), Sammlung III (xxii 17-xxiv 22), IV (xxiv 23-34), V (xxv-xxvii) und VI (xxviii-xxix), wobei Sammlung II noch zu unterteilen ist in IIA (x-xv) und IIB (xvi-xxii 16) und auch Sammlung III noch Untersammlungen in sich birgt. Ein kurzer Seitenblick nur soll auf die in Kap. xxxf. vereinigten Sammlungen[2] (xxx; xxxi 1-9, 10-31) geworfen werden.

Diese Aufteilung des Proverbienbuchs in Untersammlungen erfolgt nicht nur wegen eines gewissen common sense heutiger Forschung, sondern auch wegen der Tatsache, daß diese Untersammlungen sich auch deutlich im Blick auf die Erwähnungen Jahwes bzw. Gottes und die Nennungen religiöser Sachverhalte unterscheiden. Innerhalb der Sammlung III etwa müssen xxii 17-xxiii 11(14) im Vergleich zur ägyptischen Weisheitslehre des Amenemope interpretiert werden. xxiii 29-35 können als weitere kleine Untersammlung aus den folgenden Untersuchungen ausscheiden, da sich in ihr—im Unterschied wieder zu xxiv 1-22 und xxiii 15-28—keinerlei Jahwesprüche oder ähnliches Gut finden, was auch für die Untersammlung xxiv 23-34 zu-

---

[1] Zu dem, was „Weisheit" ist, vgl. die knappe Beschreibung durch H. H. SCHMID (*WuD* NF 10, 1969, 98): „Dann ist Weisheit, in aller Kürze ausgedrückt, die sich (mündlich oder schriftlich) äußernde Bemühung des Menschen, bestimmte Erfahrungen und Erlebnisse zu formulieren, zu sammeln und zu ordnen, um so ein Stück weit die Regeln und Ordnungen der Welt zu erkennen, um sich nach Möglichkeit ihnen entsprechend zu verhalten und so die Ordnung der Welt zu erhalten bzw. immer wieder neu zu konstituieren". Vgl. auch W. ZIMMERLI, *Der Mensch und seine Hoffnung im Alten Testament*, Göttingen 1968, 19f.; G. VON RAD, *Weisheit in Israel*, Neukirchen 1970, 13ff.

[2] Zu xxx 1-14 und den Aussagen über Gott darin vgl. J. FICHTNER, *Die altorientalische Weisheit in ihrer israelitisch-jüdischen Ausprägung*, Gießen 1933 (BZAW 67), 98; zu Kap. xxx insgesamt siehe G. SAUER, *Die Sprüche Agurs*, Stuttgart 1963 (BWANT 84), 92ff. 114-116.

trifft.[1] In der wohl ältesten Sammlung V ist von Gott bzw. Jahwe nur zweimal die Rede (xxv 2.21f.), wobei FICHTNER [2] auch diese Stellen für nicht ursprünglich hält, den Beweis dafür jedoch schuldig bleibt. Die bereits hier erkennbare unterschiedliche Streuung jahwebezogener Aussagen im Proverbienbuch—in Kap. xv ist z.B. besonders häufig von Jahwe die Rede—wird bei näherer Betrachtung der Belege noch deutlicher werden.[3]

I

Wenn nach dem Gottesbild der älteren Weisheit Israels gefragt werden soll,[4] legt ein kurzer Blick auf die einschlägigen Texte es nahe, eine Gliederung des Materials nach den wichtigsten Themenbereichen zu versuchen. In den Proverbien wird nun von Jahwe (bzw. von Gott) hauptsächlich als von dem Stifter und Erhalter des Tun-Ergehen-Zusammenhangs gesprochen (II). Diesen Aussagen zugeordnet sind die Texte, welche von Jahwe als dem Schöpfer der Menschen, dem Schöpfer und Beschützer der Armen und Geringen (III) wie von der Vorherbestimmung durch Jahwe (IV) sprechen. Jahwe hegt ferner Wohlgefallen oder Abscheu gegenüber bestimmten Dingen oder Verhaltensweisen (V). Geht es umgekehrt um das in den älteren Weisheitstexten angesprochene Verhalten des Menschen gegenüber

---

[1] Auch die ägyptischen Weisheitslehren zeigen einen unterschiedlichen Gebrauch in der Nennung der Gottheit(en). So wird z.B. keine Gottheit erwähnt in der Lehre des Amenemhet oder im Pap. Lansing; bei Kagemni nur in II 2f. Zur Sache A. SCHARFF, *ZÄS* 77, 1942, 15, Anm. 2.

[2] a.a.O., 62, Anm. 3 und S. 97.

[3] Auch in Texten der jüngeren Weisheit wird von Jahwe in unterschiedlicher Streuung gesprochen: In Prov. iii 1-12 konzentriert; gar nicht dagegen in iv 1-V 20 und vi 20-vii 27.—Daß in Prov. i-ix bei aller formgeschichtlichen Ähnlichkeit zur alten weisheitlichen Lehrrede vor allem Ägyptens doch jüngere Texte vorliegen, kann hier nicht erörtert werden; zu diesen Fragen jetzt. CHR. KAYATZ, *Studien zu Proverbien 1-9* (WMANT 22), Neukirchen 1966 und B. LANG, *Die weisheitliche Lehrrede* (SBS 54), Stuttgart 1972.

[4] Frühere allgemeine Untersuchungen zum Thema: J. MEINHOLD, *Die Weisheit Israels*, Leipzig 1908, 29-68; J. FICHTNER, o.c., 97-123; A. ROBERT, „Le Yahvisme de Prov. X 1-XII 16; XXV-XXIX", in: *Mémorial Lagrange*, Paris 1940, 163-182; J. C. RYLAARSDAM, *Revelation in Jewish Wisdom Literature*, Chicago 1946; G. SPRONDEL, *Untersuchungen zum Selbstverständnis und zur Frömmigkeit der alten Weisheit Israels*, Diss. Göttingen (maschinenschr.) 1962, 45-58.—Allgemeiner Überblick bei R. B. Y. SCOTT, *Proverbs-Ecclesiastes* (Anchor Bible 18), New York 1965, 22ff.; ders., „The Study of the Wisdom Literature, *Interpretation* 24, 1970 (H.1), 20-45; W. MCKANE, *Proverbs*, London 1970, S. 1-208; vieles auch bei H. H. SCHMID, *Wesen und Geschichte der Weisheit* (BZAW 101), Berlin 1966.—Eine erneute Untersuchung ist infolge veränderter Fragestellung (siehe dazu Teil VII) und der sich ausweitenden Fülle altorientalischen Vergleichsmaterials notwendig.

Jahwe, so wird vornehmlich von Jahwefurcht (VI) und etwas auch von Vertrauen auf Jahwe gesprochen, womit der Gang der Untersuchung markiert ist.

Diese Untersuchung geschieht nun allerdings nicht nur um der Zusammenstellung eben dieses Materials willen, sondern es soll vielmehr gefragt werden, ob in den genannten Themenbereichen der Jahweglaube Israels innerhalb der älteren Weisheit sich wirklich in seiner Eigenheit zu Worte meldet und zur Sprache kommt. Wenn früher behauptet wurde, daß die Weisheitsliteratur keineswegs den Jahweglauben in dessen voller Eigenart sozusagen im Rücken habe und von ihr her lebe,[1] die Weisheitsliteratur vielmehr dem „eigentlichen" Alten Testament sich theologisch nicht recht zuordnen läßt,—was kritisiert wurde, jedoch nicht an der Theologie, wohl aber an der Weisheitsliteratur liegt und zur Kenntnis genommen, nicht aber gewaltsam theologisch überspielt werden sollte,—dann muß nachgewiesen werden können daß die Weisheitsliteratur in ihrem Reden von Jahwe nicht die dem sonstigen Alten Testament wesentlichen Aussagen über Jahwes Art und Tun aufnimmt,[2] daß vielmehr die Art, wie die ältere Weisheit Israels—und nur sie ist vorerst hier zu untersuchen—von Jahwe spricht, sich in nichts von der Art unterscheidet, wie die Weisheitsliteratur des Alten Orient von Gott oder den Göttern spricht. Folglich wird jeder Teil dieser Studie entsprechendes Textmaterial der Umwelt Israels heranzuziehen haben.

Israel hat im weiteren Verlauf seiner Geschichte versucht, diese „Weisheit" seinem Jahweglauben fortschreitend zu integrieren (Prov. i-ix; Jes. Sir.; Sap.; Pirqe Abot u.a.). Dieser Versuch ist aber einerseits gescheitert (Hiob, Qohelet), andererseits hat er zu verschiedenen Umprägungen des Jahweglaubens wie der Weisheit geführt. All dies ist

---

[1] „Erwägungen zum theologischen Ort alttestamentlicher Weisheitsliteratur", *EvTh* 30, 1970, 393-417, dort 414; vgl. jetzt die ähnlichen Fragen von J. L. CRENSHAW, *ZAW* 82, 1970, 395 und Ders., *Prophetic Conflict* (BZAW 124), Berlin-New York 1971, 116-123 (Die Flucht zur Weisheit heute sei vergleichbar der Flucht Jonas—so 121—; man soll und kann aber nicht zur Weisheitsliteratur fliehen, um der Offenbarungskrise zu entgehen—so 123; siehe neuerdings auch die Fragen von O. KAISER in: *Der Gott, der mitgeht*, Gütersloh 1972, 32f.

[2] Es wird in der alttestamentlichen Weisheitsliteratur geschwiegen von: Erwählung und Bund, Verpflichtung und Gebot Jahwes, Väterverheißung Landverheißung, Davidverheißung, Zion, Tempel, Gottesstadt, Geschichte als zielgerichteter Ganzheit, Eschatologie, Gottesvolk usw.—Zum Thema Geschichte s. H.-J. HERMISSON, „Weisheit und Geschichte", in: *Probleme biblischer Theologie*, München 1971, 136-154 (dort auch auf S. 136 wichtiges zur Auffassung der Geschichte in der Weisheitsliteratur bei H. H. SCHMID, o.c.; zum Thema Gottesvolk und Weisheitsliteratur s. N. LOHFINK in: *Probleme biblischer Theologie...*, 279.

hier nicht mehr zu untersuchen. Gefragt aber soll werden, ob sich schon in der älteren Weisheit ein (um-?) prägender Einfluß des Jahweglaubens aufzeigen läßt, ob man davon sprechen kann, daß der Jahweglaube auch diese Literaturgruppe und die sich darin zeigende Welt- und Lebensanschauung bestimmt habe. Diese Frage ist keine nebensächliche. Zielt sie doch erneut [1] auf das Problem, welcher Ort der Weisheitsliteratur innerhalb des Alten Testaments zuerkannt werden kann und wie sie zu werten ist. GERHARD VON RAD als Meister des Hörens und Lesens hat in seinem Buch über die Weisheit Israels [2] einen erneuten Beweis seines Willens zum Verstehen geliefert. Dieser Wille zum Verstehen muß aber ergänzt werden durch das Fragen nach Wertung und Geltung des so Erhobenen.[3] In dieser Richtung soll daher (in Teil VII) diese Studie weitergetrieben werden.

Dabei wird sicher VON RAD's warnender Hinweis nicht überhört werden dürfen, daß jede Sentenz der Weisheitsliteratur für sich ernst genommen werden sollte und möchte, nicht aber gleich mit anderen kombiniert zu werden wünscht.[4] Aber es steht eben doch—wie VON RAD's Buch selber deutlich zeigt—hinter der Weisheit auch insgesamt eine bestimmte Art zu denken und zu glauben („so merkwürdig aufs Messers Schneide zwischen Wissen und Glauben" [5]), daß es doch legitim und notwendig ist, nach diesem Verbindenden, Grundlegenden zu suchen. Die Beschränkung auf die ältere Weisheit kann darüberhinaus vor vorschneller Pauschalisierung und zu weit gefaßtem Fragen bewahren. Außerdem geben die didaktischen Texte, soweit sie von Jahwe sprechen, damit dieser Untersuchung selbst das Thema, wie VON RAD es mit Recht forderte.[6]

II

Wenn vom Gottesbild der älteren Weisheit Israels die Rede sein soll, muß aus statistischen wie inhaltlichen Gründen zuerst davon gehandelt werden, daß diese Texte von Jahwe [7] vornehmlich als von

---

[1] Vgl. meinen auf S. 119 Anm. 1 genannten Aufsatz mit seiner Zielrichtung auf die Frage nach der Prädikabilität weisheitlicher Texte.

[2] G. VON RAD, *Weisheit in Israel*, Neukirchen 1970.

[3] Einige Fragen schon bei W. ZIMMERLI, „Die Weisheit Israels", *EvTh* 31, 1971, 680-695, einer Würdigung des VON RAD' schen Buchs.

[4] o.c., 16f.

[5] o.c., 16; vgl. 86.

[6] o.c., 23.

[7] „Jahwe" in Prov. x-xv 20 mal; in xvi 1-xxii 16: 33 mal; in xxv-xxviii nur xxv 22; in xxviii-xxiv: 5 mal.—אלהים nur in xxv 2.

dem Stifter und Garanten der kosmisch-sittlichen Weltordnung,[1] des Tun-Ergehen-Zusammenhangs (der schicksalwirkenden Tatsphäre, des Zusammenhangs von Haltung und Schicksal) sprechen,[2] damit von der Auffassung der Welt als Ordnung,[3] welche für die Weisheit typisch ist (vgl. etwa Prov. xx 6, 9, 24, 30; xi 8, 11, 17, 18, 19, 21, 25, 31;[4] xii 2 u.ö.; in xxv 23 und xxvi 20 beachte man die Natur-bilder). Dieser Zusammenhang von Tat und Tatfolge ist dem richter-lichen Walten Jahwes eingeordnet.[5] Jahwe setzt diese Ordnung (xii 2), wirkt in ihr und durch sie, erhält sie, ist ihr Garant, hält sie und da-durch die Welt in Gang (x 3, 22; xv 25; xvi 1, 9; xx 24; xxi 1, 31; auch xx 22).[6] Daher versucht der Weise auf diese Ordnung zu hören (xv 31; xxv 12). Kernfrage der älteren Weisheit ist daher: „Wie er-kennt der Mensch die von Jahwe gesetzte und garantierte Ordnung der Welt und wie wird er ihr im Alltagsleben gerecht—in der Verant-wortung für die Gemeinschaft wie für sein eigenes Schicksal?"[7] Wenn in Begründungen älterer weisheitlicher Mahnsprüche Jahwe genannt wird, so geschieht dieses ausschließlich im Zusammenhang des Tat-und Tatfolge-Denkens, der „Vergeltung" (xxii 23; xxiii 11; xxiv 12, 18, 22; xxv 22). Somit wird Jahwe hauptsächlich (weder Prov. xiii 12 noch xix 16 meinen das Gebot Jahwes[8]) als der gesehen, welcher durch diese

---

[1] G. von RAD, „Die ältere Weisheit Israels," *KuD* 2, 1956, 54-72 (dort 60 f.); H. H. SCHMID, *Gerechtigkeit als Weltordnung*, Tübingen 1968, besonders S. 96 ff., 157 ff.; G. von RAD, *Weisheit in Israel*, 127-129, 165 ff.

[2] Zur Sache schon die in Anm. 1 genannte Literatur; dazu H. GESE, *Lehre und Wirklichkeit in der alten Weisheit*, Tübingen 1968; U. SKLADNY, *Die ältesten Spruchsammlungen in Israel*, Göttingen 1962, 71-76; CHR. BAUER-KAYATZ, *Einfüh-rung in die alttestamentliche Weisheit* (BSt 55), Neukirchen 1969, 28-30.—Das bedeutet aber nicht, daß Gott damit den menschlichen Wünschen widerfahre (so früher W. ZIMMERLI, „Zur Struktur der alttestamentlichen Weisheit," *ZAW* 51, 1933, 177-204, dort 189; dagegen besonders B. GEMSER, „The Spiritual Structure of Biblical Aphoristic Wisdom," in; *Adhuc loquitur*, Leiden 1968, 138-149).—Ob man im altorientalischen Denken zwischen Tat-Ergehen- und Haltung-Schicksal-Zusammenhang unterscheiden kann, wie H. H. SCHMID es tut (*Wesen und Ge-schichte..*, 157 und 163 mit SKLADNY), erscheint mir zweifelhaft.

[3] Vgl. *EvTh* 30, 1970, 393-417.

[4] Zur Auslegung von Prov. XI s. jetzt O. PLÖGER „Zur Auslegung der Senten-zensammlungen des Proverbienbuches, in: *Probleme biblischer Theologie..*, 402-416.

[5] Dazu A. DÜNNER, *Die Gerechtigkeit nach dem Alten Testament*, Bonn 1963, 19 ff. (zu K. KOCH, *ZThK* 52, 1955, 1-42); R. KNIERIM, *Die Hauptbegriffe für Sünde im Alten Testament*, Gütersloh 1965, 73 ff.

[6] Zur—hier nicht zu erörternden—Rolle des Königs in dieser Ordnung vgl. xiv 35; xvi 10, 12, 13. 14, 15; xix 12; xx 2, 8, 26, 28; xxi 1.

[7] SKLADNY, o.c., 93.

[8] „Gotteswort" meint auch in ägypt. Texten die Lehre der Weisen: vgl. A. ERMAN, *Die Literatur der Ägypter*, Leipzig 1923, 247, 279; vgl. auch J. J. VAN DIJK, *La sagesse suméro-accadienne*, Leiden 1953, 105.

von ihm gesetzte und garantierte Ordnung Gutes belohnt und Böses bestraft und beides darin zur Vollendung (שלם) bringt [1] (vgl. x 29; xi 31; xii 2; xiv 27; xv 25; xvi 5; xviii 10; xix 17; xx 22; xxii 4, 23; xxiv 12; xxv 21 f.; xxix 25). Er ist fern den Frevlern, aber erhört das Gebet des Gerechten (xv 29). Er belohnt die Feindesliebe (xxv 21 f.). Er läßt nicht ungestillt den Hunger des Gerechten, aber die Gier der Frevler stößt er zurück (x 3). Er reißt das Haus des Stolzen ein (xv 25). Er ist eine Schutzwehr dem, der lauter wandelt, aber Verderben den Übeltätern (x 29, vgl. aber x 9 ohne Nennung Jahwes). So wird „vergolten", und zwar auf Erden (xi 31). Das Problem dieser Sicht bleibt hier noch außerhalb des Blickfeldes. Dem Weisen wird von seinesgleichen dieser Tatbestand nur vor Augen gehalten. Er soll und wird daraus die Folgen ziehen: Tue Gutes, und es wird dir (d.h. Jahwe läßt es dir) gut gehen gemäß dieser der Welt innewohnenden, ihr eingestifteten Ordnung (x 2, 4, 15, 30; xi 11, 21; xii 11, 14, 21; xiii 21, 25; xiv 14, 22; xv 6, 32; xviii 7; xxvi 20; xxix 6, 18 u.ö.). So errettet Gerechtigkeit vom (zu frühen) Tode, während Vermögen am Tage des Zornes (Jahwes) nichts nützt (xi 4) [2]. Jahwes Augen bewahren und behüten Erkenntnis (d.h. den Weisen), die Worte des Treulosen aber bringt er zu Fall (xxi 13). Und wem Jahwe zürnt, der fällt in eine tiefe Grube, den der Mund einer fremden Frau darstellt (xxii 14). Dem, was Jahwe gibt, kann daher auch menschliche Mühe nichts hinzufügen (x 22). Niemand soll aber Jahwe die Schuld geben, wenn nur eigene Dummheit vorliegt (xix 3). Folglich soll der Mensch auch Jahwe die Vergeltung überlassen (xx 27). Auch die Texte, welche nicht direkt von Jahwe reden, wohl aber sein Tun beschreiben, ordnen sich hier ein (x 6, 8, 9; xi 4, 18, 31 u.ö.).

So will und kann der Weise gemäß der Ordnung leben, Glück und Hoffnung [3] in ihr und durch sie haben, und er fragt dann daher auch nach der Gottheit, denn nur sie schenkt den Erfolg (xxi 31; in Kap. xxi wirken V. 1 f. und 30 f. geradezu als thematischer Rahmen). Dahinter steht der Glaube an Jahwe als den Weltregenten [4] (so besonders oft in xvi 1-xxii 16; vgl. nur xvi 1-9). „Das also war Weisheit: zu wissen, daß auf dem Grund der Dinge eine Ordnung waltet, die

---

[1] Kritisch dazu E. Würthwein, *Die Weisheit Ägyptens und das Alte Testament*, Marburg 1960, 10: Segen Gottes außerhalb des Bundes erlangen zu wollen „das war vielleicht ägyptisch, jedenfalls nicht genuin israelitisch gedacht".

[2] Zur Stelle jetzt besonders O. Plöger, o.c., 407f.

[3] Zu den Hoffnungsaussagen des Proverbienbuchs vgl. W. Zimmerli, *Der Mensch und seine Hoffnung...*, 19-23.

[4] Dazu Fichtner, o.c., 114-117.

still und oft kaum merklich auf einen Ausgleich hinwirkt." [1] Jahwe steht hinter all diesem irdischen Geschehen (x 3, 22, 27, 29 usw.), ist der Urgrund aller Dinge (xvi 1 ff.). Er belohnt den Gerechten, straft den Gottlosen, macht reich durch seinen Segen, macht satt den Hunger des Gerechten. Hierbei geht es in den Proverbien vorwiegend um das Geschick und Leben des einzelnen. Daß Jahwe etwa der Bundesgott seines Volkes ist, kommt nicht in den Blick.

Nun wird man kaum sagen können, daß das Alte Testament angesichts dieser „Gerechtigkeit als Weltordnung" von den entsprechenden Texten seiner Umwelt (etwa denen Ägyptens) „tief geschieden" [2] sei. Gott als der, welcher die strafende oder belohnende Ordnung setzte, sie bewahrt und sich vollziehen läßt, ist für die altorientalische Weisheit (und nicht nur dort, aber eben dort besonders) typisch.[3] „Befiehl Jahwe deine Werke, so werden deine Pläne sich verwirklichen" (xvi 3) ist sozusagen Motto (vgl. xx 22b). Es ist angesichts von Hiob und Qohelet wohl nicht nur der moderne Ausleger,[4] den hier ein Unbehagen befällt.

So sind es zahlreiche Texte, welche in der Weisheitsliteratur der Umwelt Israels von dieser Gerechtigkeit als Weltordnung reden und von der Gottheit,[5] welche diese gestiftet hat, sie garantiert und selbst in ihr und nach ihr handelt. Den schlechten, unwissenden Ratgeber soll man sich selber überlassen, „so bestraft er sich selbst." [6] Besitz ist Lohn der Gottheit.[7] „Zeige dich deiner Stadt gütig, so dankt dir Gott,

---

[1] G. VON RAD, *KuD* 2, 1956, 62 (nicht: Wie sichere ich als Mensch mein Dasein?, so früher W. ZIMMERLI, *ZAW* 51, 1933, 194).

[2] G. VON RAD, *Weisheit in Israel*, 100.

[3] FICHTNER, o.c., 105: „Das Gottesbild der isr.-jüd. und der übrigen altorient. Wsht trägt weithin die gleichen Züge... Gott ist für den Weisen in erster Linie der vergeltende Gott, der Bürge für die Durchführung der Vergeltung, an die er glaubt." Vgl. weiter R. LAPOINTE, „Foi et vérifiabilité dans la language sapiental de rétribution", *Bibl* 51, 1970, 349-368.

[4] G. VON RAD, *Weisheit in Israel*, 97.

[5] Zur Rede von Gott in ägyptischen Weisheitstexten siehe J. VERGOTE, „La notion de Dieu dans les livres de sagesse égyptiens", in: *Les sagesses du proche-orient ancien*, Paris 1963, 159-190, dort 170ff. auch Texte; H. H. SCHMID, *Wesen und Geschichte...*, 59f., 61ff., 68f. zu Ägypten u.ö.; E. HORNUNG, *Der Eine und die Vielen*, Darmstadt, 1971, 32, 38ff., 190f. (dort zu *Vergote*); auch FICHTNER, o.c., 103f. zum A.T.

[6] FR. W. FREIHERR VON BISSING, *Altägyptische Lebensweisheit*, Zürich 1955, 45 aus Ptahhotep; vgl. ERMAN, *Literatur...*, 89. Zu den ägyptischen Texten siehe auch J. SPIEGEL, *Das Werden der altägyptischen Hochkultur*, Heidelberg 1953, 455ff. und H. BRUNNER, *Altägyptische Erziehung*, Wiesbaden 1957; wichtige formkritische Beobachtungen bei CHR. KAYATZ, *Studien zu Proverbien 1-9*, 17-75 (mit Texten).

[7] VON BISSING, o.c., 49; ERMAN, o.c., 90f.; KAYATZ, o.c., 28.

und man preist deine Güte und betet für deine Gesundheit." [1] Gott vergilt, was man für ihn tut. [2] Mit einem Opfer an die Gottheit sorgt man am besten für sich selbst.[3] Heil und Gesundheit gibt Gott (Re) auf ein Gebet hin und befreit so von Sorge. Die Macht Gottes sichert den Menschen.[4] „Vertrau dich dem Arme Gottes, so wirst du in Ruhe deine Gegner niederwerfen." [5] Gott hilft dem weisen Mann, der ihm dient.[6] Der Gott verläßt seine Stadt während der Regierung eines schlechten Herrn.[7] Gott läßt Reichtum entstehen, weil man das Gute tut,[8] gibt dem weisen Mann Freude in dem Jahr der Not und ist die Festung des Frommen in dieser Zeit.[9] Wer Gottes Namen im Munde führt während des Unglücks, wird daraus errettet; [10] wo Gott gnädig ist, gibt es weder Unglück noch Sorge.[11] „Fortdauert ein Mann, der der Maat entspricht." [12] Vergeltung soll man Gott überlassen.[13] Wenn Re zürnt, hören Recht, Maat, Werte auf.[14] Gott kehrt den Mund des Verbrechers um und reißt aus seine Zunge.[15] Auch sumerische Proverbien sprechen von der Gottheit.[16] Schamasch wird als Vergelter ge-

---

[1] VON BISSING, o.c., 54 (Merikare).—Historische Aufgliederung bei SCHMID, *Weisheit*.

[2] o.c., 56 (Merikare x 67; xix 130); ERMAN, o.c., 114, 118.

[3] VON BISSING, 73 (Anii); ERMAN, 295; Vgl. auch Merikare 119-123 (*AOT*², 35); dazu H. BRUNNER, in: *Les sagesses du proche-orient ancien*, Paris 1963, 104f.—Die genauere historische Differenzierung der Texte ist auch deswegen hier unnötig, weil sowieso die meisten ägyptischen (und auch mesopotamischen) Texte dieser Art älter als die entsprechenden israelitischen sind. Eindeutig jüngere Texte—wie etwa Pap. Insinger—führen früheres weithin nur ausführlicher aus.

[4] Beides Von BISSING, o.c., 83 (Amenemope); vgl. 104 (Pap. Ins.); siehe auch bei VERGOTE, o.c., 179ff.

[5] VON BISSING, o.c., 88f.

[6] o.c., 99 (Pap. Ins.).

[7] o.c., 10.

[8] o.c., 105.

[9] o.c., 107; vgl. 116; siehe aber (107) kurz dahinter: „Ein Weiser kommt nicht in Not, der seinen Verstand zum Genossen nimmt." (108).

[10] o.c., 115.

[11] o.c., 119 (dort 119f. über Vergeltung durch Gott); zum Zerbrechen dieser Ordnung vgl. die Mahnworte des Ipuwer (VON BISSING, 129ff. und *AOT*², 51ff.; dazu jetzt G. FECHT, *Der Vorwurf an Gott in den Mahnworten dew Ipuwer*, Heidelberg 1972.

[12] Ptahhotep 19 (KAYATZ, *Proverbien 1-9*, 31).

[13] Anii viii 14-16 (o.c., 34); vgl. Amenemope xxii 5-8; xxiii 8-21; auch xi (o.c., 39 und *AOT*², 44); weitere ägypt. Texte zur Sache bei VOLTEN, *Les sagesses...*, 78ff.

[14] Anch-Scheschonqj; zitiert bei H. BRUNNER, *Les sagesses...*, 112f.

[15] Aḥiqar 156 (*AOT*², 461).

[16] Z.B. Inanna; vgl. E. I. GORDON, *BiOr* 17, 1960, 131 Nr. 9; betr. Enlil o.c., 133, Nr. 3. 27. Vgl. E. I. GORDON, *JAOS* 77, 1957, 69 Nr. 4. 2.; ders., *Sumerian Proverbs*, Philadelphia 1959, 306 f.

nannt [1] oder Ea.[2] Ein assyrisches Sprichwort sagt: „Wenn du dich anstrengst, ist dein Gott auf deiner Seite,"[3] d.h. du hast Erfolg durch und mit Gott. Da die israelitische Weisheitsliteratur von einem Totengericht nichts weiß, ist hier auf die damit gestellte Problematik (d.h. Totengericht, Weisheit und Gottesglaube) nicht einzugehen.[4]

Nun hat GESE behauptet,[5] daß durch das Wissen um Jahwe diese Lehre vom Tun-Ergehen-Zusammengang in Israel „durchbrochen" worden sei, da einige Texte die Unabhängigkeit Jahwes von dieser Ordnung bezeugen würden. Er verweist in diesem Zusammenhang auf Prov. x 12; xvi 1, 9; xx 24 und xxi 21 [6] (vgl. xix 21; xvi 33). Schaut man näher auf diese Texte, so sprechen sie aber nicht davon, daß Jahwe diesem Tun-Ergehen-Zusammengang entgegen handelt, sondern davon, daß dieser—und damit der ihm zugrunde liegende Plan der Weltordnung—dem Menschen nicht einsichtig ist (xxi 30; vgl. xiv 12; xvi 33; xx 9; xxi 1). Darüberhinaus ist zu fragen, wie das Alte Testament am historischen Ort dieser Texte ein Handeln Jahwes abgesehen von menschlichem Tun (so in xvi 33 und xx 1 nach GESE [7]) bezeugt oder genauer inwiefern die obengenannten Texte wirklich von der frei waltenden Gnade Gottes sprechen.[8] Von der erwähnten Durchbrechung kann doch wohl erst bei Qohelet und Hiob die Rede sein, noch nicht aber in den älteren Teilen des Proverbienbuchs. Nur xxviii 13 redet in den Proverbien von Barmherzigkeit; und man kann hier fragen, ob wirklich diejenige Gottes gemeint und der Vers nicht außerdem noch ein Zusatz ist.[9] Die Frage ist ferner, ob z.B. in xvi 9 wirklich ein Gegensatz ausgesagt werden soll,[10] da Jahwe eben lenkt, wie es der Ordnung entspricht (xvi 33!). xxi 30 („Es gibt keine Weisheit, keine Einsicht und keinen Rat Jahwe gegenüber") ist nicht Selbstaufgabe der Weisheit vor Jahwe, sondern Demutsaussage (vgl.

---

[1] W. G. LAMBERT, *Babylonian Wisdom Literature*, Oxford 1960, 105, Z. 129f. (Bab. Precepts and Admonitions).

[2] o.c., 113.

[3] o.c., 230f.; vgl. 231, Nr. II 29f. 31f.

[4] Vgl. H. H. SCHMID, *Wesen und Geschichte der Weisheit, 64ff.*

[5] H. GESE, *Lehre und Wirklichkeit in der alten Weisheit*, Tübingen 1958, 45-50 (50).

[6] Daß diese Stellen auch anders interpretiert werden können, meint auch E. WÜRTHWEIN, o.c., 11, Anm. 17; vgl. auch SKLADNY, o.c., 27f. 42, 73-75.—Wie GESE wieder H.-J. HERMISSON, *Studien zur israelitischen Spruchweisheit* (WMANT 28), Neukirchen 1968, 69, aber kaum zutreffend.

[7] o.c., 48.

[8] o.c., 50.

[9] FICHTNER, o.c., 109.

[10] Vgl. schon *EvTh* 30, 1970, 398; auch SPRONDEL, o.c., 50.

xxi 31).[1] Gott ist unerforschlich (xxv 2) [2]; es ist seine Ehre, etwas zu verbergen.

Von Rad meinte nun,[3] daß die hier aufbrechende Grenze der Weisheit „in letzten Grundüberzeugungen des Jahweglaubens" wurzele.[4] Ob es zu diesen Aussagen der Proverbien dagegen nicht nur handfester Empirie bedarf, darf zumindest als Frage angemeldet werden. Hinzukommt, daß die Weisheitsliteratur der Umwelt Israels auch hier ähnliche Aussagen kennt, so daß von einer Verwurzelung dieser Einsichten in die letzte Unverständlichkeit des Handelns der Gottheit allein im Jahweglauben keine Rede sein kann.[5] Die Erkenntnis, daß der Mensch mit seinem Denken die Pläne Gottes und seine Absichten weder erkennen noch gar begreifen kann, ist nichts für die Weisheit des Alten Testaments Spezifisches, sondern sie findet sich auch innerhalb der Weisheit Ägyptens wie Mesopotamiens. Schon 1925 hat K. Sethe im Zusammenhang mit Prov. xvi 9 (vgl. xix 21; xx 24; xxi 30) auf Amenemope 18 verwiesen [6]—wozu man Am. XIX 16 (ANET[2] 423) nehmen kann—und dort übersetzt: „Anders [7] sind die Worte, die die Menschen sagen; anders ist das, was der Gott tut". Zahlreiche weitere Texte lassen sich hinzuziehen, die ebenfalls von der Grenze menschlicher Weisheit und Erkenntnis angesichts des Waltens der Gottheit sprechen.

Nicht was Menschen sagen, nur was Gott befiehlt geschieht.[8] Gott ist es, der den vorderen Platz verleiht, mit dem Ellenbogen erreicht man nichts.[9] „Der Mensch weiß nicht, wie der Morgen sein wird. Gott

---

[1] Sprondel, o.c., 52f.; vgl. Zimmerli, ZAW 51, 1933, 191.

[2] Aus der Tatsache, daß hier keine alltägliche Erfahrung vorliegt, sondern eine im Verlauf einer langen Tradition des Denkens gewonnene Einsicht, folgert Hermisson (o.c., 69), daß es sich nicht um Volkssprichwörter, sondern um lehrhafte Schulsprüche handeln müsse. Bei aller Anerkennung der formkritischen Erwägungen muß gefragt werden, ob aber nicht schon normale Empirie diese Erfahrung machen kann.

[3] Weisheit in Israel, 138, vgl. 141.

[4] Gott als großer Vergelter in der Geschichte ist im Alten Testament auch sonst problematisch und nicht aufrechenbar. Ob sich jedoch die Weisheit gerade um diese Eigenart alttestamentlicher Offenbarung müht (so H. Gross, TThZ 80, 1971, 218, Anm. 15), erscheint zweifelhaft.

[5] Israel spricht, wenn es in der Weisheitsliteratur von der Verborgenheit Gottes handelt, ja gerade nicht „proprie" (so mit Recht L. Perlitt, „Die Verborgenheit Gottes", in: Probleme biblischer Theologie, München 1971, 367-382 (373f. Anm. 13)).

[6] K. Sethe, „Der Mensch denkt und Gott lenkt bei den alten Ägyptern", in: NGWG, Phil.—hist. Kl., 1925, 141-147; vgl. jetzt H. Brunner, in: Les sagesses..., 104.

[7] Nicht „schwinden dahin" oder „verscheuche".

[8] Von Bissing, o.c., 46 (Ptahhotep); Erman, o.c., 89.

[9] o.c., 47; Erman, o.c., 91.

ist immer trefflich, aber der Mensch bleibt mangelhaft." [1] Gott verleiht Gerechtigkeit wem er will, und seine Gedanken kennt man nicht.[2] Jeder größere Abschnitt der Lehren des Pap. Insinger schließt mit dem Satz: „Das Glück und das Schicksal, das kommt, wird von Gott bestimmt" bzw. „Glück und Schicksal kommen, wie er es ihnen befiehlt" (oder ähnlich).[3] Es gibt folglich keinen wahren Schutz, ohne daß er Gottes Werk wäre, denn der Starke wie der Schwache sind vor Gott ein Spielzeug.[4] Das Tun eines unter Millionen segnet Gott, indem das Schicksal ihm gnädig ist. Weder der Gottlose noch der Fromme kennen die Länge der Lebenszeit, die ihnen aufgeschrieben ist.[5] „Man erkennt die Absichten Gottes nicht, bis das eingetroffen ist, was er befohlen hat." [6] „Der Gott ist in seiner Vortrefflichkeit, und der Mensch ist in seiner Mangelhaftigkeit." [7] Die Gedanken Gottes kennt man nicht und man weiß nicht, was er tun wird, wenn er straft.[8] Zu Prov. xx 30 f. ist hinzuweisen auf Anii xiv 15 f.; Amenemope xxiv 15 ff.; Achiqar 122 (Es steht nicht in der Macht der Menschen, ihre Füße aufzuheben und niederzusetzen ohne den Willen der Götter; [9] weiter auch Anii vi 7 ff.; Anch-Scheschonqj xi 21-23; Pap. Insinger xvii 6 f.; xix 4; xxi 3 f.). „Der Wille eines Gottes kann nicht verstanden werden, der Weg eines Gottes kann nicht erkannt werden. Alles von einem Gott (ist schwierig) herauszufinden." [10] Weitere Texte dieser Art erwähnt und bespricht A. VOLTEN [11]. Abschließend für die Texte aus Ägypten sei aus der Lehre des Anii (viii 9 f.) festgehalten: „Geht es so nicht auch den Menschen? Eines ist ihr Planen, etwas ganz anderes ist der Herr des Lebens." [12] Auch hier wird somit die Maat menschlicher Erkenntnis nicht voll zugänglich.[13] Ein

[1] VON BISSING, 87 (Amenemope; vgl. *AOT*², 43); dazu H. BRUNNER, in: *Les sagesses...*, 111: „Bei Amenemope wird also durch den Einbruch des Gedankens von Gottes freier Wahl nach unberechenbarer Liebe der Tun-Ergehen-Zusammenhang wesentlich aufgelockert."

[2] VON BISSING, o.c., 88; *AOT*², 44 und 45 (Amenemope xx, xxi und xxii).

[3] VON BISSING, o.c., 91ff.; vgl. Prov. xv 30f.

[4] o.c., 100 (Pap. Ins.).

[5] o.c., 106.

[6] o.c., 117.

[7] Amenemope xix 14 (*AOT*², 43); vgl. Prov. XIX 27.

[8] Amenemope xxii 5; xxiii 8 (vgl. H. H. SCHMID, *Wesen und Geschichte der Weisheit*, 219f.); siehe auch Kagemni ii 2 (A. SCHARFF, *ZÄS* 77, 1942, 17f.).

[9] *AOT*², 459; vgl. auch Aḥiqar 194f.

[10] LAMBERT, *BWL*, 266 (Bilingue).

[11] In: *Les sagesses...*, 76.

[12] Zit. bei VOLTEN in: *Les sagesses...*, 176.

[13] Zur Sache vgl. H. BRUNNER, „Der freie Wille Gottes in der ägyptischen Weisheit", in: *Les sagesses...*, 103-120.

sumerisch-akkadischer Spruch aus Ugarit [1] lautet: „Die Menschen, was sie machen, wissen sie selbst nicht; der Sinn ihrer Tage und Nächte liegt bei den Göttern." Folglich ist auch dieser Aspekt, nach dem das Walten und Planen der Gottheit(en) dem Menschen nicht einsichtig ist, nicht nur dem Jahweglauben arteigen [2] und kann folglich nicht als eine Auswirkung dieses Glaubens oder eine durch seine Eigenart bedingte typisch israelitische Erkenntnis verstanden werden.

III

Dem Ordnungsdenken zugeordnet sind dann auch die Aussagen über Jahwe als den Schöpfer [3] (Prov. xiv 31; xvi 4; xvii 5; xix 17; xx 12; vgl. xvi 11; xxii 2; xix 13), eben weil er als Schöpfer auch und vornehmlich der Schöpfer dieser Weltordnung ist, nach welcher es z.B. Arme wie Reiche gibt (xix 13), ohne daß daraus immer soziale Folgerungen gezogen würden (xiv 31; xv 25; xx 2; weiter xv 11; xvi 1; xx 12; dann xxii 9, 22; xxiii 10). So ist Jahwe der Schöpfer des Armen (xvii 5), des Reichen (xxii 7), des Gerechten (xx 12) und des Frevlers (xvi 4; vgl. noch xvi 11). „Wer den Geringen bedrückt, schmäht dessen Schöpfer, aber ihn ehrt, wer sich des Armen erbarmt" (xiv 31). „Wer den Armen verletzt, lästert seinen Schöpfer; wer sich über ein Unglück freut, bleibt nicht ungestraft" (xvii 5). Daher leiht letztlich an Jahwe, wer sich des Armen erbarmt (xix 17), —und Jahwe vergilt ihm diese Guttat! xxii 22 f. sprechen von Jahwe als dem Schutz der Schwachen, wozu man schon—weiteres siehe unten—auf Amenemope 2 (*AOT*², 40) verweisen kann; das Plus des Alten Testaments ist hier nur die Wendung „im Tor". xxiii 10 f. reden ähnlich, aber ohne Nennung des Gottesnamens,—weil im entsprechenden Text Amenemope 6 (*AOT*², 40) der Mondgott genannt wird? Für Prov. xix 13 ist auch noch auf Amenemope 25 (*AOT*², 45) zu verweisen, wonach Gott tausend Geringe wie tausend Aufseher nach seinem Belieben schafft. Die Aussagen über den Schöpfer Jahwe sind

---

[1] Ugaritica V Nr. 164.—Zur Sache auch H. CAZELLES in Ugaritica VI, 1969, 36-40.

[2] Anders auch (z.B. mit Verweis auf GESE; so auf S. 65) M. V. Fox, „Aspects of the Religion of the Book of Proverbs", *HUCA* 39, 1968, 55-69; dort 57 und 64-67 unter „The Yahwistic stage; er sieht aber auch, daß die Mehrzahl der Proverbien in der Weise des Alten Orients denkt und glaubt, zieht für seine These dann aber wiederum Prov. xvi 9 und xxi 31 vor allem heran.

[3] Zum Schöpfungsdenken der Weisheit s. FICHTNER, o.c., 111-113; HERMISSON, *Studien*, 70f.; O. S. RANKIN, *Israels Wisdom Literature*, Edinburgh 1936 (Repr. 1964), 9-15.

in der älteren Weisheit dem Glauben an den Gott der Weltordnung folglich eng zugeordnet (Prov. xvii 5!), und sie erfahren damit gegenüber anderen Schöpfungsaussagen des Alten Testaments eine wesentliche Umakzentuierung wie Engführung.

Nur selten kommt die ältere Weisheit darauf zu sprechen, daß die Weisheit selber (vgl. dagegen Prov. ii 6 f.; iii 5, 7, 19 f. u.ö.) eine Gabe Gottes sei (so wohl in xx 12). FICHTNER [1] meinte noch, daß in Texten des Alten Orients sich kaum dergleichen Aussagen fänden, aber auch hier wandelt sich das Bild. Akkadische, in Ugarit aufgefundene Sprüche des Schube 'awilum nennen diesen Mann, „welchem seinen Verstand der Gott Enlilbanda schenkte," [2] und auch in Sumer war klar, daß die ME wie die Weisheit von den Göttern stammte.[3]

Häufig findet sich in den Proverbien die Aussage, daß Jahwe als Schöpfer sich besonders der Witwen, Waisen und Armen annehme [4] (xiv 31; xv 25; xxii 22 f.; xxiii 10 f.; xxviii 8). Man ist geneigt, hier etwas allein für Israel Typisches,[5] ein Proprium des Jahweglaubens zu finden (xxii 23 ist gegenüber xxii 22 ohne Parallele bei Amenemope 4; vgl. AOT², 39), zumal auch in den Gesetzen des Alten Testaments dergleichen Hinweise nicht selten sind (Ex. xxii 21-24; xxiii 3, 6; Deut. x. 18; xiv 28 f.; xix 14; xxvii 19; xxix 14 f., 17-22; Num. xxxv 12; vgl. weiter die Propheten).[6] Aber xv 25 wie xix 17 zeigen auch hier deutlich die Verzahnung mit dem Tun-Ergehen-Zusammenhang: „Das Haus des Stolzen reißt Jahwe ein, aber die Grenze der Witwe stellt er fest" (vgl. auch xvi 4 und wohl auch xxii 28, wo ein אלמנה statt עולם wahrscheinlich ist).[7] Jahwe erbarmt sich des Armen, daher fällt unrecht erworbenes Gut oder unrecht vermehrtes Vermögen letzlich ihm zu (xxviii 8). Jedem wird somit von Jahwe sein Recht zuteil (xxix 26).

Auch hier muß nun daran erinnert werden, daß sowohl in Gesetzestexten und Königsinschriften des Alten Orients wie auch ebenfalls in

---

[1] o.c., 120; auch im Alten Testament erst in späteren Texten: VON RAD, *Weisheit in Israel*, 72f.

[2] Ugaritica V, Nr. 163 (S. 273ff.).

[3] J. J. A. VAN DIJK, *La sagesse suméro-accadienne*, Leiden 1953, 17ff.; weitere Texte und Erwägungen zur Weisheit als Eingebung der Gottheit siehe bei B. LANG, *Die weisheitliche Lehrrede*, 79f. Anm. 12.

[4] Zu den Bezeichnungen genauer bei W. RICHTER, *Recht und Ethos*, München 1966, 147-162.

[5] So noch H. BRUPPACHER, *Die Bedeutung der Armut im Alten Testament*, Zürich 1924, 16.

[6] Vgl. zur Sache auch BOTTERWECK, s.v. אביון, *ThWAT* I, 35-37 (zur Weish.— Lit.; vgl. GERSTENBERGER, *THAT* I, 23-25); HOFFNER, s.v. אלמנה, *ThWAT* I, 308-313, vgl. KÜHLEWEIN, *THAT* I, 169-173.

[7] Vgl. die Kommentare.

altorientalischer Weisheitsliteratur—beide Textgruppen folglich auch
hier sich nahestehend—dergleichen Erwähnungen sich recht häufig
finden,[1] und zwar früher als es in Israel möglich war.

RE ist auch Schöpfer der Wahrheit; [2] er macht auch das Licht wie
Himmel und Erde nach der Menschen Wunsch (!).[3] Gott hat dem
Menschen seine Mutter geschenkt [4]; aber der Mensch ist auch ein
Nichts, der eine reich, der andere arm.[5] Rechtes Verhalten gegenüber
der Witwe, dem Waisen, den Armen, den Gewichten, den Ackergren-
zen wird erwähnt oder gefordert, und zwar einerseits ohne Rückgriff
auf den Willen eines Gottes (so z.B. bei Amenemope [6] vii 12, 15;
viii 9, 11 f.; Amenemhet I 6-9; Merikare xlvi ff.; Pap. Ins. xxxi 3-5),
andererseits mit Rückgriff auf die Gottheit (vgl. etwa Amenemope
xvi und xvii—Gott liebt den, der den Geringen erfreut—, dann auch
Amenemope vi mit Bezug auf den Mondgott,[7] vgl. dazu Prov. xxiii
10 f.; zu Prov. xxii 2—Arm und reich begegnen sich, der sie alle schuf
ist Jahwe—vgl. auch Amenemope xxiv 9-14). Der Mensch ist Lehm
und Stroh und Gott sein Baumeister, der Geringe oder Aufseher nach
seinem Belieben schafft.[8] Die Herausstellung der Schöpfung durch die
Gottheit steht hier im Dienst der Aussage von einer Vorherbestimmung durch diese. Gott gibt Reichtum, der kluge Mann bewahrt ihn.[9]
Gott gibt Reichtum in einen Speicher ohne Einnahmen, er schafft
aber auch Armut in einer Börse ohne übertriebenen Aufwand.[10] „Wer
vor dem Herzen Gottes würdig ist, erhält eine anständige Frau." [11]
Gott gibt Reichtum und Armut, wie er es befiehlt.[12] Er liebt den Gast-

---

[1] Einiges schon bei F. C. FENSHAM, „Widow, Orphan, and the Poor in Ancient
Near Eastern Legal and Wisdom Literature", *JNES* 21, 1962, 129-139.

[2] VON BISSING, o.c., 47 (Ptahhotep); ERMAN, o.c., 89.

[3] VON BISSING, o.c., 56 (Merikare XX, 134; vgl. überhaupt dort XX, 130ff.;
weiter AOT², 35f.; ERMAN, o.c., 119).

[4] VON BISSING, o.c., 76 (Anii).

[5] ebd., 76 (Anii VIII 3-5).

[6] VON BISSING, o.c., 82, 86; vgl. Amen. ii (*AOT²*, 39) und Prov. xxii 23f.;
weiter VON BISSING, 97.

[7] Vgl. VON BISSING, o.c., 61.

[8] Vgl. VON BISSING, o.c., 82 (Amenemope) und 90 (auch AOT², 43 und 40).—
VON BISSING, 89 (Amenemope xxv; *AOT²*, 45; öfter zitiert als xxiv 9-14, s. H.
BRUNNER, in: *Les sagesses...*, 107f.—Zur Stelle auch S. MORENZ, *Untersuchungen zur
Rolle des Schicksals in der ägyptischen Religion*, Berlin 1960, 10f.—Zu den im Pap.
Insing. häufigen Aussagen über die Gottheit als Schöpfer vgl. VERGOTE, in: *Les
sagesses...*, *184f.*

[9] VON BISSING, o.c., 94 (Pap. Ins.).

[10] o.c., 96.

[11] o.c., 97.

[12] o.c., 105 (Pap. Ins.).

freien, der den Armen bewirtet, und was man dem Armen gibt, gibt man Gott.[1] Re ist Beschützer der Armen oder auch Ptah.[2] Gott liebt den, der den Geringen erfreut und die Witwe nicht ungerecht behandelt.[3] Auch nicht der Weise allein, sondern alle Menschen sind Gottes Ebenbild.[4]

Die Gottheit als Schöpfer wird auch genannt in der sog. babylonischen Theodizee und anderswo in babylonischen Weisheitstexten.[5] Soziales Verhalten wird in einer Hymne an Ninurta angesprochen.[6] Zweierlei Gewichte werden in der Schamasch-Hymne erwähnt; wer es gebraucht, verliert sein Kapital.[7]

„Der Gott der Weisheit entspricht dem Urheber", schreibt H. H. Schmid.[8] Diese Charakterisierung findet besonders in den hier verhandelten Eigenschaften und Taten der Gottheit ihre Rechtfertigung.

IV

Als Schöpfer und Erhalter der Weltordnung ist Jahwe selbstverständlich auch der, welcher alles vorherbestimmt (hat). Er ist Lenker und Leiter des menschlichen Lebens, was wiederum heißt, daß er „der Ordnung gemäß" lenkt (Prov. xviii 22; xix 14; xxi 31). Viele Pläne sind im Herzen des Menschen, aber der Rat Jahwes besteht (xix 21; vgl. xvi 1, 9). Da Jahwe alle Schritte des Mannes leitet, kann der Mensch seinen Weg auch nicht verfehlen (xx 24; vgl. xvi 1, 9; xix 21). So wacht (xx 27 *BH*[3]) Jahwe auch über den Geist des Menschen und durchforscht alle Kammern des Leibes. Er lenkt das Herz des Königs wohin er will (xxi 1). Göttliche Führung und Allmacht werden besonders in Prov. xvi betont, wo sich aber auch zeigt, wie sehr sie im Dienst des Tun-Ergehen-Zusammenhanges stehen (xvi 4, 7, 9, 33) und dazu herausstellen, daß Jahwes Handeln in ihnen zwar geglaubt wird, nicht aber einsichtig (zu machen) ist.

In diesen Zusammenhang gehören auch die Aussagen darüber, daß Jahwe alles sieht (xv 3, 11; vgl. xx 27), die Bösen wie die Guten, das

---

[1] Vgl. Pap. Ins. XV 10f.; XVI 4, 11ff.; XVII 1 und dazu Volten, in: *Les sagesses...*, 75.

[2] Fensham, o.c., 133 mit Belegen.

[3] Amenemope XXVIII (*AOT*[2], 46).

[3] So polemisch bei Anii; dazu Brunner, *Erziehung*, 167; weiter dort 137f.

[5] Vgl. bei Lambert, *BWL*, 86f. 109.

[6] o.c., 119.

[7] o.c., 133; vgl. auch die Texte bei Schmid, *Weisheit*, 109ff.

[8] o.c., 27; dort auch 54ff. zur Verwandschaft mit den biographischen Schriften betr. des sozialen Gedenkens an Witwen usw.

Totenreich wie die Herzen der Menschen. „Anlaß zu diesen Aussagen ist jedoch nicht ein theologisches Interesse am Wesen Jahwes, sondern ihre Beziehung zum Haltung-Schicksal-Zusammenhang." [1] Gott weiß alles (xxiv 12),—folglich entgeht niemand seiner Strafe! Daher freue man sich nicht zu sehr, wenn es dem Feind schlecht geht, „damit nicht Jahwe es sehe und mißbillige und seinen Zorn von ihm abwende" (xxiv 17 f.). Schadenfreude zahlt sich also nicht aus, da Jahwe es dem anderen „zur Strafe" dafür wieder gutgehen lassen könnte.[2]

Kann zum „Sehen" Jahwes schon auf ähnliche Aussagen außer-israelitischer Weisheitsliteratur verwiesen werden,[3] so ist bei der Wendung „Jahwe, der die Herzen prüft (xvi 2; xvii 3; xxi 2; auch xv 3, 11; xxiv 12 [4]) die Herkunft des Bildes aus Ägypten (dort mit der „Waage") mehr als wahrscheinlich,[5] so daß von hier aus sich der Übergang zu den Texten der Umwelt ungezwungen ergibt. Jahwe prüft dabei aber auch anders, als der Mensch es oft denkt (xvi 2; xxi 2). Mit allem wird auch hier offenkundig, wie sehr der Gedanke einer „Vergeltung" durch die Gottheit der Weisheitsliteratur wesentlich ist.

Daß über die Gottheit und die Vorherbestimmung durch sie auch in der Weisheitsliteratur des Alten Orients sich Aussagen finden, dürfte nach allem nicht mehr überraschen. Es ist eben keineswegs so, daß in der so(!) gefaßten Geschichtslenkung das Proprium Jahwes liegt.

„Ein von Gott Geliebter ist der, welcher hört; wen aber Gott verabscheut, der hört nicht." [6] „Gott kennt den, der etwas für ihn tut"; er kennt daher auch die Widerspenstigen—und straft sie! Er kennt das Wesen der Menschen, hält sich aber verborgen,[7] er kennt

---

[1] SKLADNY, o.c., 16, vgl. 23.

[2] Wieso bei diesem Spruch von einer besonderen „ethischen Höhe" gesprochen werden kann (so RICHTER, *Recht und Ethos*, 167), ist schwer einsehbar.

[3] Vgl. schon FICHTNER, o.c., 116; GORDON, *Sumerian Proverbs*, S. 307.

[4] Über die Rolle des Urteils Jahwes in Prov. xvi-xxii 16 vgl. SKLADNY, o.c., 25f.; s. auch VON RAD, *KuD* 2, 1956, 69.

[5] S. MORENZ, *Ägyptische Religion*, Stuttgart 1960, 134; H. BONNET, *Reallexikon der ägypt. Religionsgeschichte*, Berlin 1952, 296f. 339; J. SPIEGEL, *Die Idee vom Toten-gericht in der ägypt. Religion*, Glückstadt und Hamburg 1935, 64ff.; R. GRIESHAM-MER, *Das Jenseitsgericht in den Sargtexten*, Wiesbaden 1970, 46ff.—Weitere Hinweise und Lit. bei F. STOLZ, *THAT* I, 863.

[6] VON BISSING, o.c., 50 (Ptahhotep); ERMAN, o.c., 97.—Zur göttlichen Fügung durch Ptah s. SPIEGEL, *Hochkultur*, 477f.; auch MORENZ, *Schicksal*, 8f. 15f.; vgl. dazu Ptahhotep 12 bei KAYATZ, *Prov. 1-9*, 29; kurz auch *AOT²*, 33; weiter Ptahhotep 206ff., 217ff., 545f.

[7] VON BISSING, o.c., 55 (Merikare), auch 56; *AOT²*, 35; zum „Gott, der den Wandel kennt" siehe KAYATZ, o.c., 69f.

jeden Namen.[1] Gott ist es, der dem Vogelfänger keinen Erfolg zukommen läßt, wenn dieser über seinen Mißerfolg klagt,[2] und umgekehrt ist es die Göttin, welche einen Schreiber an die Spitze der Verwaltung bringt.[3] Reichtum ist Gabe der Gottheit, sagt Amenemope.[4] „Die Zunge des Menschen ist zwar das Steuerruder des Schiffes, doch der Allherrscher ist sein Steuermann." [5] „Es gibt auf Erden unter den Frauen gute und schlechte; die anständige und die schlechte Frau wird vom Befehl Gottes bestimmt;" [6] so gibt Gott auch das Herz, das Kind und den guten Charakter wie den Reichtum.[7] Vergeltung soll man Gott überlassen, nicht aber selbst sie üben.[8] Gott kennt die Antwort der Zunge noch ehe Fragen gestellt sind,[9] und wie Gott befiehlt, geschieht es.[10] Auf die ähnlichen Sätze am Ende jedes größeren Abschnitts der Lehre das Pap. Insinger wurde bereits verwiesen („Das Glück und das Schicksal, das kommt, wird von Gott bestimmt" o.ä.). Man beachte noch: „Wer geht, indem er sagt: ‚Ich werde zurückkommen', wird (nur) durch die Hand Gottes zurückgesandt." [11] „Der Pavian (Tier des Thot) sitzt (in) Hermopolis, aber sein Auge durcheilt die beiden Lande." [12] Von der Vorherbestimmung [13] spricht auch die Sentenz aus Ptahhotep: „Wen Gott liebt, der kann hören, aber nicht kann hören, wen Gott haßt"; über „Führung" durch die Gottheit Thot handelt ausführlich Pap. Anastasi V[14], über Vorherbestimmung des Menschen durch die Gottheit auch Pap. Chester Beatty.[15] Eine genauere Untersuchung zum Themenbereich Vorherwissen, Vorherbestimmung und Schicksal liegt für den Bereich der ägyptischen Reli-

---

[1] VON BISSING, o.c., 56; AOT², 36; ERMAN, o.c., 119.

[2] VON BISSING, o.c., 59 (Cheti; BISSING übersetzt aber „kein Netz"); anders (s. Text) ERMAN, o.c., 104 und vor allem jetzt W. HELCK, *Die Lehre des Dw', -Htjj*, 2 Teile, Wiesbaden 1970, S. 114.

[3] VON BISSING, o.c., 60 (Cheti); HELCK, o.c., 150f.

[4] AOT², 40; VON BISSING, o.c., 83.

[5] Amenemope XX 3-6; dazu H. BRUNNER, in: *Les sagesses...*, *110;* Text bei *AOT²*, 44; VON BISSING, o.c., 87.

[6] Pap. Ins. VIII 13-19; VON BISSING, o.c., 97.—Zur Vorherbestimmung durch Gott und zur Allwissenheit Gottes nach Pap.Ins. siehe VERGOTE, o.c., 185f. (vgl. Pap. Ins. iv 18; v 15; xvii 17; ix 19).

[7] VON BISSING, o.c., 98; vgl. BRUNNER, *Erziehung*, 186.

[8] VON BISSING, o.c., 116 (Pap. Ins.).

[9] o.c., 117 (dort 117f. vieles betr. „Lenkung" durch Gott).

[10] o.c., 121 (Sprichwort aus dem beredten Bauern).

[11] Bei VERGOTE, o.c., 182.

[12] Amenemope XV; *AOT²*, 42f.

[13] Siehe H. BRUNNER, *Erziehung*, 113 (vgl. dort 156 zum folgenden Text).

[14] o.c., 172f.

[15] o.c., 178.

gion von S. Morenz vor.[1] Auf sie und die in ihr verarbeiteten Belege
(auch aus der Weisheitsliteratur) sei hier nur verwiesen. Auch die
Texte, die davon handeln, ob die Gottheit einen Menschen „liebt"
oder „haßt", sind dort genannt. So gilt: „Nothing happened except
what God ordains." [2] Wenn die Götter jemanden lieben, legen sie
ihm Gutes zu sagen in den Mund; aber es steht nicht in der Macht
der Menschen, ihre Füße aufzuheben und niederzusetzen ohne den
Willen der Götter.[3] Schamasch kennt die Taten des Übeltäters.[4]
„Wohin kann der Fuchs gehen vor Schamasch?" [5]

Auch in diesem Bereich gehen die Aussagen über Jahwe in der
älteren israelitischen Weisheit über die analogen Aussagen der Texte
aus der Umwelt nicht hinaus.

V

Man ist geneigt, wenigstens bei רצון und תועבה und deren Bindung
an Jahwe an kultischen Ursprung zu denken und dann auf „genuin
Israelitisches" zu hoffen. Von daher mag schon die Häufigkeit dieser
Wörter auch im Proverbienbuch überraschen.[6] Jahwes Wohlgefallen
wird innerhalb älterer Texte des Proverbienbuchs erwähnt in xi 1, 20;
xii 22; xv 8; xvi 7 (vgl. xv 9 und xxii 12 betr. Jahwes Liebe). Volles
Gewicht steht unter Jahwes Wohlgefallen (xi 1). Wenn jemandes Verhalten Jahwe wohlgefällt, söhnt er sogar dessen Feinde mit ihm aus
(xvi 7). Auch hier zeigt sich wieder die Verbindung zum Tun-Ergehen-
Zusammenhang, zum Ordnungsdenken und der damit zusammen-
hängenden „Vergeltung". Die Kombination von רצון und תועבה im
antithetischen Parallelismus findet sich nicht in kultischen Texten, und
selbst im Proverbienbuch ist sie auf die Sammlung Kap. x-xv (in
xi 1, 20; xii 22; xv 8) beschränkt.[7] Ein Guter erlangt Wohlgefallen vor
Jahwe (xii 2) oder wer Wahrhaftigkeit übt (xii 22; vgl. xvi 1). Wer eine

---

[1] Vgl. S. 130 Anm. 8.

[2] Anch-Scheschonqj xxii 25 (bei Kayatz, Prov. 1-9, 23).

[3] Aḥiqar 115 (AOT², 459).—Vgl. das „allerorten sind ihre Augen" bei Aḥiqar
96f., wobei allerdings unklar ist, ob die Augen der Lauscher oder die der Götter
gemeint sind (ANET², 428 denkt an Menschen).

[4] Lambert, BWL, 219, Z. 10.

[5] o.c., 282.

[6] Dazu Gemser, HAT 16², 65; weiter auch P. Humbert, ZAW 72, 1960, 217-
237.

[7] Was u.a. der Ablösung der Kap. X-XV als ursprünglich selbständiger Teil-
sammlung entgegenkommt (Zimmerli, ZAW 51, 1933, 90, Anm. 1 mit Verweis
auf Fichtner).—Zu XI 1 siehe besonders Plöger, o.c., 405f.

gute Frau gefunden hat, kann darin ein Zeugnis dafür sehen, daß Jahwe Wohlgefallen an ihm hat (xviii 22; vgl. xix 14).

Ein „Greuel für Jahwe" (xi 1; xv 8, 9, 26; xvi 5; xvii 15; xx 10, 23; xxi 27; xxviii 9) ist z.B. falsche Waage oder zweierlei Gewichte (xi 1; xx 10; vgl. Lev. xix 35 f.; Deut. xxv 13-16; die Begründung in Prov. xvi 11 weist darauf hin, daß Jahwe Maß und Gewicht geschaffen habe!). Falschherzige sind Jahwe ein Greuel (xi 20), jeder Hochmütige (xvi 5), boshafte Anschläge (xv 26), Lügenlippen (xii 22), der Wandel des Gottlosen (xv 9) wie sein Opfer (xv 8; vgl. xvii 1; xxi 3, 27) oder auch sein Gebet (xxviii 9). Wer den Unschuldigen verurteilt, den Schuldigen aber freispricht (xvii 15), beide sind Jahwe ein Greuel, weil sie die Weltordnung mißachten wie zerstören. Daher sind auch zweierlei Maß und Gewicht Jahwe ein Greuel (xx 10; vgl. xi 1; xvi 11; xx 23). Hierbei finden sich in Prov. xx 10 und xxiv 28 zwar Anklänge an Ex. xx 16 und Deut. xxv 13 ff., aber die Verschiebung vom Jahwegebot hin zur Sachaussage des Weisen ist nicht ohne Belang. Wohlgefallen einerseits und Abscheu andererseits sind dabei aber nun nicht nur Empfindungen eines Gottes, der zusieht, sondern sie äußern sich als Taten (xvi 7),[1] sind Ausdrücke für den Tun-Ergehen-Zusammenhang (vgl. xvi 5!). Daher kann man nicht nur sagen, daß Jahwes Wohlgefallen hier anthropozentrisch, nicht aber theozentrisch verstanden sei.[2]

Auch die Weisheitsliteratur der Umwelt des alten Israel kennt nun den „Abscheu" der Gottheit gegenüber bestimmten Sachverhalten oder Personen.[3] So ist „Abscheu" in der ägyptischen Weisheit kein seltenes Wort.[4] Wen Gott verabscheut, der hört nicht.[5] Die Tugend des Rechtschaffenen nimmt Gott lieber entgegen als den Ochsen dessen, der Unrecht tut.[6] Lautes Wesen und Geschrei sind ein Greuel für das Haus des Gottes.[7] „Opfere deinem Gott, aber hüte dich vor dem, was er verabscheut!"[8] „Rede nicht heuchlerisch mit einem Mann, das ist dem Gott ein Greuel", steht bei Amenenope,[9] in dessen Lehre sich überhaupt der Hinweis auf den „Greuel" für die Gottheit häufiger

---

[1] SKLADNY, o.c., 14 mit K. KOCH.
[2] ZIMMERLI, *ZAW* 51, 1933, 190; in XI 27 sei „Wohlgefallen" schon „ganz von Gott abgelöst".
[3] Dazu SPRONDEL, o.c., 107.
[4] Vgl. VON BISSING, o.c., 46 (Ptahhotep).
[5] o.c., 50.
[6] o.c., 56 (Merikare); ERMAN, o.c., 118.
[7] VON BISSING, o.c., 74 (Anii); *AOT²*, 37.
[8] Anii vii 12; so bei VERGOTE, o.c., 175; anders VON BISSING, o.c., 76.
[9] Am. x (*AOT²*, 41 und 42); vgl. xiii (*AOT²*, 42).

findet (betr. des Doppelzüngigen, des Betrugs bei Steuerlisten usw.;
vgl. Am. xiii 15; xiv 2 f.; xv 20; xiv 1; xxiv 20).[1] Einer der groß ist
in Kleinigkeiten ist ein Abscheu des KA.[2] Abscheu des Re ist der,
welcher vom Scheffelmaß fortnimmt.[3] Auch vom Abscheu des Marduk ist die Rede oder vom Gefallen bei Schamasch,[4] welcher z.B.
einem das Leben verlängert, weil dieser keine Bestechung annimmt
und für den Schwachen Fürsprache einlegt oder ein ehrlicher Gläubiger
ist.[5] Auch Baal haßt schließlich bestimmte Dinge (und zwar z.B.
sechs!,—vgl. Prov. vi 16; xxx 11-14), allerdings kultischer, nicht
sittlicher Art.[6] Selbst Wohlgefallen oder Abscheu Gottes sind somit
keine nur Jahwe eigenen Empfindungen und Verhaltensweisen.

VI

War bisher vom Handeln der Gottheit nach dem Zeugnis der älteren Weisheit Israels und seiner Umwelt die Rede, so ist nun umgekehrt auf das Verhalten des Menschen gegenüber der Gottheit, wie es
diese Texte zeichnen, einzugehen, da auch hier sich wesentliches vom
Gottesbild zeigt. In einer Gruppe von Sprüchen findet sich die Wendung „Furcht Jahwes"[7] (x 27; xiv 26 f.; xv 16, 23; xvi 6; xix 23;
xxii 4; xxiii 17 f.; xxiv 21 f; xxviii 14; xxxi 30; adjektivisch in xiv 2;
immer „Furcht Jahwes", niemals „Furcht Gottes",—also besonders
für den Jahweglauben typisch bzw. durch ihn geprägt?), wobei hier
wieder nur die Texte der älteren Weisheit zur Diskussion stehen.[8] Es
handelt sich dabei fast ausschließlich (anders nur xxiii 17 f.; xxiv 21 f.)
um Einzeiler, die konstatierend eine Aussage machen. Die beiden
zuletzt erwähnten Texte hingegen[9] sind Mahnworte und finden sich

---

[1] bw.t bezeichnet im Ägyptischen allerdings sonst meist Verstöße gegen Kult-
vorschriften (SPIEGEL, *Hochkultur* 674).—Zur Textzählung bei Amenemope vgl.
ANET[2], 421ff.; die Texte auch bei VERGOTE, o.c., 177f.

[2] SPIEGEL, o.c., 475 (Ptahhotep); dazu auch o.c., 678.

[3] Amenemope xvii (*AOT*[2], 43); vgl. auch xxix (*AOT*[2], 46).

[4] LAMBERT, *BWL*, 100, Z. 47f.; 103, Z. 64; vgl. *ANET*[2], 595; vgl. auch *AOT*[2],
292, Z. 33f. 38 (ethisches Verhalten gefällt Schamasch).

[5] LAMBERT, o.c., 133 (mehrfach); vgl. 215, Z. 15f.

[6] UT 51: III: 17-22 und dazu SAUER, *Sprüche Agurs*, 114-116.

[7] Zur Sache: W. ZIMMERLI, *ZAW* 51, 1933, 190f.; A. ROBERT, in: *Mémorial
Lagrange* 1940, 175-178; SPRONDEL, o.c., 53ff.; S. PLATH, *Furcht Gottes*, Berlin 1963,
54-84 (dort wird xiv 2 übersehen); J. BECKER, *Gottesfurcht im Alten Testament*
(AnBibl 25), Rom 1965 (210-241, mit Einzelanalyse der Belege); J. DEROUSSEAUX,
La crainte de Dieu dans l'A.T., Paris 1970, 301-357; G. VON RAD, *Weisheit in Israel*,
Neukirchen 1970, 91ff.; H.-P. STÄHLI, *THAT I*, 765-778 s.v. ירא.

[8] Auch „Furcht Gottes" zeigt in Prov. i-ix einen veränderten Gehalt.

[9] Zu den Sprüchen als Aussagesätzen und den Übergangsformen zum Mahn-

in den stark religiös geprägten Untersammlungen xxiii 15-28 und xxiv 1-22. Was wird von der Furcht Jahwes ausgesagt? Sie verlängert die Lebenstage (x 27). In ihr ist starke Sicherheit, ist Zuflucht (xiv 26). Sie ist (xiv 27) eine Quelle des Lebens,[1] um die Fallen des Todes zu meiden (xiii 14 sagt eben dieses vom Rat des Weisen [2]; vgl. auch xvi 22 und xxx 3). Sie ist daher Zucht zur Weisheit und verschafft diese (xv 33). Folglich wandelt in Geradheit, wer Jahwe fürchtet (xiv 2).[3] Durch Jahwefurcht—wie durch Weisheit—entgeht man dem Unheil (xvi 6; vgl. viii 13). Durch sie hat man eine positive Zukunft (vgl. xxiv 14 wieder analog über die Weisheit), erkennt man, daß wenig mit Jahwefurcht besser ist als reiche Schätze und Unruhe dabei. Jahwefurcht befreit von Unruhe wie von Sorge (xv 16; V.17 führt diesen Satz in bezeichnender Weise weiter). Furcht Jahwes gereicht somit zum „Leben" im Vollsinn (x 27; xiv 27; xix 23), und man nächtigt satt (!), wird nicht heimgesucht von Unheil (xix 23). Der Lohn der (Demut und der) Jahwefurcht ist eben Reichtum, Ehre, Leben (xxii 4)[4], da sie vom Bösen fernhält und somit dem Unheil entgehen hilft (xvi 6; vgl. Job xxviii 28). So soll das Herz des Weisen sich nicht betreffs der Sünder ereifern, wohl aber betreffs der Furcht Jahwes, „dann gibt es (für dich) sicherlich noch eine (gute) Zukunft, und deine Hoffnung wird nicht zuschanden" (xxiii 17 f.; vgl. wieder analog über die Weisheit in xxiv 14). Jahwefurcht beschert Erfolg, bewahrt vor Unglück (xxviii 14 ist wohl auch Jahwefurcht gemeint; vgl. auch xxix 25). Man fürchtet Jahwe (Gott) und den König (so oft auch in ägyptischen Texten), läßt sich daher mit Aufrührern (? Leuten von hohem Stand?) nicht ein, denn plötzlich kommt ihr Unheil und unvermutet ihr Untergang, da Jahwe wie der König alles Unrecht bestrafen (xxiv 21 f.)

Jahwefurcht begegnet hier folglich in ganz bestimmter, eben in weisheitlicher Prägung. Sie ist mit der Lehre der Weisen identisch, sie ist Weisheit (vgl. xxiii 17 f. mit xxiv 14). Sie schafft vieles Gute, kurz, sie lohnt sich. Jahwefurcht und Tun-Ergehen-Zusammenhang sind selbstverständlich gekoppelt (x 27; xiv 26; xv 16; xvi 6; xix 23; xxii 4).

wort siehe H.-J. HERMISSON, *Studien...*, 141ff., 160ff.; dort S. 71 auch kurz zur „Furcht Jahwes".—Zu den Mahnworten und ihrer Streuung siehe W. RICHTER, *Recht und Ethos*, passim.

[1] Mit „Leben" kann hier nie „Unsterblichkeit" gemeint sein; gegen M. DAHOOD, *Bibl* 41, 1960, 176-181; ders., *Proverbs and Northwest Semitic Philology*, Rom 1963, 25, 29, 48.

[2] Zum Verhältnis beider Texte siehe J. BECKER, o.c., 225: xiv 27 gegenüber xiii 14 sekundär!

[3] Übersetzung mit BECKER, o.c., 229.

[4] Anders z.St. DAHOOD, *Proverbs*, 23f.

Der Weise ist beinahe mit einer gewissen Selbstverständlichkeit auch jahwefürchtig, wobei dieses Prädikat hier aber nicht in seiner ganzen Fülle verstanden wird und werden darf, sondern nur in der durch diese Texte vollzogenen und vollziehbaren Füllung. Es genügt nicht, das Vorhandensein der Wendung „Furcht Jahwes" auch in der Weisheit zu konstatieren, vielmehr ist zu fragen, was durch sie dort ausgesagt, wie sie gefüllt wird und welche Funktion sie hat. Man könnte allgemein schlicht „Frömmigkeit" dafür sagen, wenn deutlich ist, daß diese Frömmigkeit in keiner Weise hier durch die besondere Art Jahwes gefüllt und bestimmt ist, wie sie Propheten und Geschichtsbücher des Alten Testaments bezeugen. Man kann noch nicht einmal einseitig sagen, daß Jahwefurcht hier vorwiegend eine Haltung von Ehrfurcht und Gehorsam, der der Majestät Gottes gehört, umschließt,[1] schon gar nicht eine Furcht vor dem Numinosen, aber auch nicht (höchstens etwas in xiv 2) eine ganz persönliche Gottesbeziehung. Will man vielmehr alles über die Furcht Jahwes Ausgeführte auf einen kurzen Nenner bringen, so bleibt nur die Aussage: „Jahwefurcht lohnt sich, trägt Früchte, bringt Gutes, da sie selbst ein Gutes ist", und dieses typisch weisheitlich als Aussage, nicht als Imperativ. So können dann auch von Jahwefurcht wie Weisheit die gleichen Früchte kommen (vgl. x 27; xiv 26 f.; xv 16; xvi 6; xix 23 mit xiii 14, 18; xiv 1, 16; xv 10, 24; xxi 16). In diesem (!)) Sinne kann man dann die Jahwefurcht „Weisheit im Vollzug" nennen.[2] Sie ist ferner klar mit dem Tun-Ergehen-Zusammenhang gekoppelt und hat in ihm ihren Ort.[3] Jahwefurcht erkennt die von Jahwe gesetzte und erhaltene Ordnung, akzeptiert sie weise als Lebenshaltung,[4] um in ihr und durch sie ordnungsgemäß und damit gut zu leben. Jahwefurcht ist hier auch, da in den Aussageworten wie den Mahnworten mit Begründung[5] schon „verarbeitet", ein „Gegenstand der Reflexion"[6] geworden, damit aber auch auf diese Art der Weisheit eingegliedert, indem ihre Bedeutung für die Weisheit und damit für das ordnungsgemäße, gute und schöne Leben bestimmt wird. Jahwefurcht hat die Wirkung eines

---

[1] So A. STROBEL, *Die Weisheit Israels*, Aschaffenburg 1967, 38.

[2] CHR. BAUER-KAYATZ, *Einführung*, 33; vgl. auch Prov. xxxi 30 als Fazit in xxxi 10-31; zur grammatischen Form dort—nicht st.cstr.!—s. J. BECKER, o.c., 211, Anm. 6.

[3] Vgl. J. BECKER, o.c., 224: „Jahwefurcht und Retribution"; ähnlich DEROUSSEAUX, o.c., 307 und 321.

[4] SKLADNY, o.c., 15.

[5] Als Imperativ z.B. erst Prov. iii 7.

[6] PLATH, o.c., 56.

Lebens mit Zukunft und Erfolg. Frömmigkeit bietet Sicherheit, der Gerechte ist sicher in seinem Gottvertrauen (vgl. xviii 10, auch xxix 25).[1] Wenn man jahwefürchtig ist, werden positive Folgen eintreten. Jahwefurcht als gutes Verhalten setzt gutes Ergehen aus sich heraus.

Die wohl ältesten Sammlungen V (xxv-xxvii) und VI (xxviii-xxix) erwähnen nun die Furcht (Jahwes? xxviii 14) nur einmal; in den Sammlungen III und IV findet sie sich in Mahnsprüchen (xxiii 16 f.; xxiv 21 f.). In den von der Lehre des Amenemope beeinflußten Texten der Sammlung III (xxii 17-xxiii 14) wird von der Jahwefurcht ganz geschwiegen. Dagegen sprechen die israelitischen Prägungen der Sammlung II (x-xxii 16) schon häufiger von der Furcht Jahwes. Damit ist ein fortschreitendes Aufnehmen und Hineinwirken dieses Terminus nicht zu bestreiten, was sich dann in Prov. i- ix, Qohelet und Hiob weiter fortsetzt.[2] So ist zwar einerseits eine fortschreitende Aufnahme der „Jahwefurcht" in die Weisheitsliteratur des Alten Testaments (vgl. weiter dann noch Jes. Sir.) zu vermerken, andererseits aber nicht zu übersehen, daß sie zumindest in der hier zu untersuchenden älteren Weisheit erst einmal weisheitlich umgeprägt und vereinnahmt wurde.

Wurde bisher aber vielleicht zu vordergründig gefragt? Ist mit der Erwähnung der „Furcht Jahwes" nicht doch viel stärker die „Beziehung zum Jahweglauben" gegeben"[3], zumal sie z.B.—wie erwähnt—in der durch die Weisheitslehre des Amenemope bestimmten Sammlung xxii 17-xxiii 11(14) nicht auftaucht? Wurde im Gegensatz zu diesen Thesen hier schon einmal betont, daß „Jahwefurcht" jedenfalls in der älteren Weisheit vom weisheitlichen Denken geprägt und umschlossen wurde, so ist jetzt noch darauf zu verweisen, daß „Furcht Gottes" auch in der Weisheitsliteratur des Alten Orients sich findet [4] und dort in ähnlichem semantischem Feld steht. Wer Gott und damit Frömmigkeit mit in seine Weisheit hineinnimmt, ist auch dort ein rechter Weiser, der gemäß der Weltordnung zu leben versucht und

---

[1] Obwohl hier nicht nochmals auf die Frage der Prädikabilität weisheitlicher Texte eingegangen werden soll (vgl. *EvTh* 30, 1970, 393-417), sei doch auf dieses Ergebnis nachdrücklich verwiesen und gefragt, ob es hier mit dem Verstehen getan ist und nicht die Frage der Wertung und Geltung dieser Aussagen für uns sich mit Notwendigkeit stellen muß.

[2] Dazu DEROUSSEAUX, o.c., 315ff.

[3] So CHR. BAUER-KAYATZ, *Einführung*, 31; vgl. HERMISSON, *Studien*, 71: „...enge Verbindung der israelitischen Weisheit mit dem Jahweglauben" hier besonders deutlich; vgl. PLATH, o.c., 61.

[4] Siehe dazu jetzt ausführlich DEROUSSEAUX, o.c., 21-66, auf dessen Belege verwiesen sei.—Vgl. noch unten S. 140 Anm. 8.

daher auch durch sie gesegnet wird und Erfolg hat. „Wenn du umsichtig bist, steht Gott auf deiner Seite; wenn du unvorsichtig bist, steht Gott nicht auf deiner Seite." „Begehe kein Verbrechen, (dann) wird dich die Furcht vor Gott nicht plagen," [1]—wobei jedoch bezeichnend ist, daß gerade diese Füllung („Angst vor Gott") sich in der israelitischen Weisheitsliteratur nicht findet. Babylonische Proverbien sagen: „Wer die Götter fürchtet, den vernachlässigt (?) nicht [sein Gott], wer die Anunnaki fürchtet, verlängert [sein Leben]." [2] Im „Leidenden Gerechten" wird auch die „Gottesfurcht" erwähnt, die dort wohl kultisches Handeln meint.[3] DEROUSSEAUX verweist [4] auf nicht wenige Texte aus der ägyptischen Religion, die von der Furcht (snḏ)(vor) der Gottheit sprechen (bzw. auch vor dem König,—etwa in den Amarna-Briefen), beginnend mit den Pyramidentexten. Er kann aber keine Belege aus der Weisheitsliteratur Ägyptens beibringen, und Furcht vor der Gottheit war im alten Ägypten kein wesentlicher Bestandteil der Frömmigkeit,[5] eher schon Furcht vor dem König, dessen Macht aber göttliche Macht war. Im Pap. Insinger jedoch findet sich [6] eine zweifache Erwähnung des „Gottesfürchtigen", in dessen Lehre auch die Hand eines geringen Mannes taugen kann. Schon häufiger finden sich im mesopotamischen Bereich Aussagen über „Gott fürchten" (Verb palâḫu; Substantiv puluḫtu), jedoch ist auch hier meist der Vollzug kultischer Handlungen gemeint.[7] Der Begriff „Gottesfurcht" mag sich folglich in der Weisheitsliteratur des Alten Orients relativ selten finden.[8] So scheint „Jahwefurcht" in der Tat ein neues Element in der Weisheitsliteratur Israels zu sein, das in seinem Ursprung (!) sicher vom Jahweglauben her geprägt war. Nur ist dieser Ursprung schon in der älteren alttestamentlichen Weisheitsliteratur nicht mehr in seiner Eigenheit aufweisbar und faßbar. Er ist verloren gegangen, ist weisheitlich überdeckt worden. Folglich kann

---

[1] Aus sumerisch-akkadischen Proverbien, zitiert nach H. W. F. SAGGS, *Mesopotamien*, Zürich 1966, 645.

[2] Bab. Prov. 79f. (vgl. 76); *AOT²*, 293: *ANET²*, 427: LAMBERT, o.c., 105.— Weiter siehe FICHTNER, o.c., 51 (nach ihm zitiert); PLATH, o.c., 69 (dort 69f. weitere Belege); DEROUSSEAUX, o.c., 58.—Dann noch LAMBERT, o.c., 247, mit unsicherem Text bei ii 11-14; *AOT²*, 293; *ANET²*, 593 iii 11-14.

[3] DEROUSSEAUX, o.c., 57f.; dort 58f. auch zu weiteren sumerischen Texten.

[4] DEROUSSEAUX, o.c., 21ff.; dort 62ff. zu Texten aus Ugarit.

[5] H. BONNET, *Reallexikon...*, *197*; HORNUNG, *Der Eine und die Vielen*, 192.

[6] In der Übersetzung von VON BISSING, o.c., 103f.; vgl. außerdem ebenda, 114.

[7] DEROUSSEAUX, o.c., 42ff.; vgl. zu den Texten aus Ugarit o.c., 62ff.

[8] Vgl. DEROUSSEAUX, o.c., 357.—Zuversichtlicher H. CAZELLES: „La crainte de Dieu est aussi bien le puluḫ accadien que le snḏ égyptien"; so in: *Les sagesses...*, 36, dort Anm. 5 Beleghinweise.

nicht allein mit dem Vorhandensein der Wendung argumentiert werden, sondern man muß sich vergegenwärtigen, daß und wie „Furcht Jahwes" in der älteren israelitischen Weisheit von weisheitlichem Denken her geprägt ist, wie aufgezeigt wurde, ihm auch dienstbar gemacht ist, was ein Blick auf den jeweiligen Kontext der Verbindung deutlich macht. Ob in „Jahwefurcht" statt „Gottesfurcht" schon ein entscheidender „Faktor im Zuge der Nationalisierung der sonst internationalen Weisheit" zu sehen ist,[1] ist daher zumindest fraglich, vor allem, wenn man zusammen mit der Nationalisierung auch eine Jahwesierung postulieren möchte. Dem Jahwenamen wird in der älteren Weisheit (und nicht nur in der älteren!) viel von seinem sonstigen Gewicht genommen. Jahwefurcht und Sittlichkeit sind in der älteren israelitischen Weisheit eben gerade nicht so sehr wie etwa im Heiligkeitsgesetz [2] (Lev. xix 14, 32; xxv 17, 36, 43) eine Verbindung innerhalb von Mahnungen (!) eingegangen, sondern Jahwefurcht begegnet vorwiegend in der Aussage, und es wird nicht so sehr das sittliche Verhalten selber als Ziel angesprochen, sondern viel mehr das gute Leben, die hoffnungsvolle Zukunft als Folge. Furcht Jahwes ist einerseits daher Mittel, andererseits Ausdruck der Weisheit, ist Demut (Prov. xv 33) als rechte Weisheit innerhalb der Ordnung Gottes. Auch wer Jahwe fürchtet, ist weise, hat—„naiv-optimistisch" [3]—Einsicht in alles (xxviii 5).

Es ist daher unnötig und unberechtigt, wie Derousseaux [4] versucht, möglichst oft bei Texten mit „Jahwefurcht" eine sekundäre Ergänzung (abgesehen von x 27 und xxviii 4) aus meist nachexilischer Zeit anzunehmen bzw. Spätdatierung der Belege zu erweisen. Eine solche Argumentation erscheint als zu einfach, zumal die Jahwefurcht (wie die Weisheit allgemein) in Prov. i-ix andere Akzente zeigt als in Prov. x ff. Außerdem spricht in Prov. x ff. wohl auch die knappe, einzeilige Aussageform der Sprüche wie ihr semantisches Umfeld gegen ihre späte Ansetzung,—womit über die Frage der zeitlichen Ansetzung von Prov. i-ix nichts gesagt sein soll. So ordnet sich auch die „Jahwefurcht" dem spezifisch weisheitlichen Denken ein und kann in den älteren Texten nicht als umprägendes oder bestimmendes Element des Jahweglaubens angesehen werden.—

Weil Jahwe die Ordnung der Welt setzt, garantiert und erhält,

---

[1] Plath, o.c., 71.
[2] Andres Plath, o.c., 73.
[3] Fichtner, o.c., 120.
[4] o.c., 307ff.

ferner als der Schöpfer beider genannt wird, kann schließlich auch
vom Vertrauen auf Jahwe gesprochen werden [1] (Prov. xvi 20; xx 22;
xxii 19; xxviii 25; xxix 25; xxx 5; vgl. xvi 3 und xviii 10). Auch hier
zeigt sich erneut eine durchgehend optimistische Grundhaltung.[2]
Vertrauen auf Jahwe schafft Wohl und Glück (xvi 20); denn wer auf
Jahwe vertraut, wird wirklich gelabt (xxviii 25) und ist wohl geborgen
(xxix 25). Wer auf die von Jahwe geschaffene Ordnung traut, ver-
heimlicht auch nicht seine Sünde,—da er dann ja kein Glück hat
(xxviii 13), sondern er bekennt sie und findet Erbarmen.

Weil xxii 19 am Anfang der Sammlung steht, welche Abhängigkeit
von der Lehre des Amenemope zeigt, dort die Aussage über das
Vertrauen auf Gott (Jahwe) sich gerade nicht findet, hat man oft auf
diesen Beleg verwiesen und gemeint, daß das „Vertrauen auf Jahwe"
ein Proprium israelitischer Weisheit und eine Einwirkung des Jahweglaubens sei („Damit du auf Jahwe dein Vertrauen setzt, tue ich dir
seinen Weg—vgl. dazu *BH*[3]—kund"), zumal der Vers einen deutlich
„hineingesetzten" Charakter hat.[3] Die auch hier noch einmal auftauchende Frage, ob die Weisheitsliteratur der Umwelt Israels ähnliche
Aussagen kennt, muß wiederum mit dem Hinweis auf Texte mit analogen Zeugnissen beantwortet werden. Gott segnet für Vertrauen mit
Schutz.[4] Zu dem oben genannten Vers Prov. xxviii 13 kann auf Amenemope verwiesen werden, wo auch über den Nutzen eines Sündenbe-
kenntnisses nachgedacht wird [5] oder dazu aufgefordert wird, sich in
die Arme Gottes zu setzen.

Allgemein sei noch vermerkt, daß sich die hier zitierten Texte aus
der Umwelt Israels leicht vermehren lassen, was jedoch aus Gründen
des Raumes unterbleiben mußte. Wichtig ist jedoch noch ein kurzes
Fazit.

VII

Wenn auch von einer fortschreitenden Aufnahme des Terminus
„Furcht Jahwes" in der altisraelitischen Weisheit gesprochen werden
kann und muß, die sich schon innerhalb der relativen Chronologie der
Sammlungen des Proverbienbuchs aufzeigen läßt, kann doch—wie

---

[1] Dazu SKLADNY, o.c., 65; RICHTER, *Recht und Ethos*, 181: Texte nicht vor
Jesaja!

[2] Vgl. allgemein dazu W. ZIMMERLI, *ZAW* 51, 1933, 177f.

[3] Mit W. RICHTER, o.c., 30: „...bringt unmotiviert Religiöses", aber als „ge-
wichtiger Zusatz".

[4] VON BISSING, o.c., 101 (Pap. Ins.); dort 101f. mehrfach betr. „Vertrauen".

[5] Siehe bei SCHMID, *Weisheit*, 219 und 220.

gezeigt wurde—nicht gesagt werden, daß der Jahweglaube Israels
auch die durch Israel aufgenommene oder selbst gestaltete Weisheitsliteratur entscheidend geprägt oder gar umgeprägt habe. Zumindest ist dies innerhalb der älteren Weisheitsliteratur nicht der
Fall. Es ist auch nicht so, daß der Jahwename mit seinem Gehalt und
Gewicht [1] sich auch hier als durchschlagend erwiesen hätte.[2] Der
Blick auf die Texte zeigt vielmehr, daß Jahwe hier völlig weisheitlichem
Denken integriert wurde. Es werden ihm keine anderen Tätigkeiten
und Wesenszüge zugeschrieben, als dieses in der Weisheitsliteratur der
altorientalischen Umwelt Israels bei den dortigen Gottheiten geschieht, wobei auch dort nicht bestimmte Wesenszüge konkreter
Einzelgottheiten im Vordergrund stehen, sondern es um das Göttliche
schlechthin und allgemein geht. Man kann somit auch nicht von der
„Freiheit des Weltverständnisses" sprechen, zu der die Weisheit Israels gerade durch den Glauben an Jahwe autorisiert wurde,[3] da sich
in der Weisheitsliteratur Israels dieses besondere Weltverständnis und
dieser Jahweglaube zunächst kaum zeigt (anders erst in den Gottesre-
den des Hiobbuchs, bei Jesus Sirach und in der Sapientia Salomonis).
In der älteren Weisheit ist Jahwe vor allem der „Bürge der sittlichen
Ordnung und gerechten Vergeltung" [4], und diese Charakterisierung
stellt ihn—wie manches andere, was hier zur Sprache kam—für die
Weisheitsliteratur nicht über, sondern neben die Götter der Umwelt
und verzichtet auf eine differenzierende Abhebung. Sicherlich sieht
und erkennt die israelitische Weisheit eine von Jahwe durchwaltete
Wirklichkeit,[5] aber sie sieht eben diese Wirklichkeit vorwiegend als
Ordnung, und dieses Schwergewicht gilt für das übrige Alte Testament
nicht. Anders gefragt: Wenn gesagt wird, daß dieses Wissen von
Ordnungen „vom Jahweglauben umschlossen" war,[6] muß zurückge-
fragt werden: „Von welchem Jahweglauben?" Man wird sich daran
gewöhnen müssen, daß genauso wenig wie jede Nennung „Gottes"
denselben Gott meint oder „Gott" mit analogem Gehalt füllt, auch

---

[1] Vom Gewicht des Jahwenamens in der Weisheitsliteratur spricht A. ROBERT,
o.c., 174; vgl. zur Rede von „Gott" die auf S. 123 in Anm. 5 genannte Literatur.
[2] So A. STROBEL, o.c., 37: „Dieser Gottesname allein ist schon Ausdruck für die
ganze Bundestheologie". Dieser Satz bleibt reines Postulat!—Vgl. auch G. VON
RAD, *Weisheit in Israel*, 214: „...ein äußerst traditionsschwerer Name"; siehe auch
GEMSER, *HAT* 16², 67.
[3] So G. VON RAD, o.c., 88.
[4] GEMSER, o.c., 65 (vgl. Prov. x 3, 27, 29; xi 31; xii 2; xv 25, 29; xvi 3, 5, 20;
xviii 10; xix 17; xx 22; xxi 12; xxii 4, 12).
[5] G. VON RAD, *Weisheit in Israel*, 89.
[6] ebenda, 188.

Jahwe innerhalb des Alten Testaments nicht gleich Jahwe ist. Die
Differenzierung alttestamentlicher Bücher, Schriften, Traditionen
usw., die es uns heute oft schwer machen, von "dem" Alten Testament
zu reden, wird wohl auch durch eine Differenzierung innerhalb Jahwes
einen neuen verstärkenden Schwierigkeitsschub erhalten und die
Frage nach der Mitte des Alten Testaments auch von hier neu bele-
ben (Man vergleiche nochmals etwa Prov. xxviii 26 mit xxix 25; xiii 14
mit xiv 27; dazu xvi 20a neben xvi 20b; zu xv 8—mit xxi 3, 27—dann
Merikare in *AOT*[2] 35, Zeile 129). Griechische Mythologie kann sehr
unterschiedlich von Zeus reden, und der Zeus z.B. des Hesiod, auf den
hier gerade wegen mancher Nähen zur Weisheitsliteratur verwiesen
sei, ist nicht der Zeus mancher Mythen. Man wird in Zukunft sehr
genau nachfragen müssen, ob z.B. der Jahwe der Propheten oder auch
der des göttlichen Rechts auch der der alten Weisheit ist. Was in den
Proverbien der älteren Weisheit über Jahwe gesagt wird, geht—abgesehen von der selbstverständlich „monotheistischen" Eingrenzung,
die jedoch ohne wirklich grundlegend verändernde Folgen bleibt—
nicht über das hinaus, was die Weisheitsliteraturen des Alten Orients
jeweils über Gott sagen.[1] Prov. x ff. von Kap. i-ix her zu interpretie-
ren [2] soll zwar durch die Voranstellung dieser Kapitel nahegelegt werden und wird auch oft vertreten. Es bleibt aber zu fragen, ob dieses
Verfahren wirklich weiterhilft und angesichts der Spannungen sowie
der Aussagen in Kap. x ff. vertretbar ist.

In der Weisheitsliteratur wird vielmehr Theologie zwar nicht als
Anthropologie, wohl aber als Phänomenologie versucht.[3] Daher gehören die Texte mit theologischen Themen auch kaum den Volks-
sprichworten an, sondern sie sind eher Kunstsprüche.[4] Käme die alte
Weisheit Israels wirklich [5] vom Glauben an Jahwe, vom Kultus und
vom Wissen um die Gebote her und hätte sie aus diesem Grund ihre
begrenzte Thematik, müßte dieses von den ähnlichen Texten der
Umwelt des alten Israel auch gelten, was betr. Jahwe unmöglich ist

---

[1] Vgl. SCHMID, *Weisheit*, 147f.; RANKIN, o.c., 39; SCOTT, *Interpretation* 24, 1970,
29.

[2] So z.B. R. E. MURPHY, „The Kerygma of the Book of Proverbs", *Interpretation* 20, 1966, 3-14.

[3] Man kann nicht sagen, daß die Weisheit Phänomenologie betreibe, nicht aber
Theologie (so R. KNIERIM, *Hauptbegriffe für Sünde...*, *84*); vgl. auch ZIMMERLI,
ZAW 51, 1933, 204 über die „eigentümlich rationale Vergewaltigung der gesam-
ten Wirklichkeit".

[4] Vgl. dazu schon oben und G. VON RAD, *Weisheit in Israel*, 39ff.; HERMISSON,
Studien, 68ff.

[5] So G. VON RAD, *KuD* 2, 1956, 66f.; ders., *Weisheit in Israel*, 96.

und wofür es auch in analoger Fragestellung keinen Anhalt gibt. Der Jahweglaube wird zwar insofern (ohne daß irgendeine Heilstat zitiert wird usw.!) auch vorausgesetzt, als er verwendet (!) wird, als er Motiv menschlichen Handelns werden kann, jedoch eines sehr eigenständig geprägten Handelns, das mit der weisheitlichen Weltsicht des Alten Orients eng verbunden ist.

Natürlich gab es auch in Israel Entscheidungen und Alltagsfragen die nicht stets vom Zentrum des Jahweglaubens her beantwortet und betrachtet wurden. Darüber besteht kein Streit und darum geht es nicht. Wohl aber geht es umgekehrt darum, nun den Jahwe, der hier in der alten Weisheit anders als sonst im Alten Testament gesehen wurde, auch „anders" sein zu lassen. War die ältere Weisheit Israels schon „eine Antwort des mit bestimmten Welterfahrungen konfrontierten Jahweglaubens"?[1] War aber die Welterfassung von Prov. x-xxix erst *ein* Arbeitsgang, bei dem Jahwe vornehmlich als die dem Menschen gesetzte Grenze ins Blickfeld kam,[2] der in Prov. i-ix ein zweiter folgte und folgen mußte, stellt sich die Frage nach Hiob und Qohelet mit ihren kritischen Anfragen an die Weisheit[3]—und damit das Problem des „Scheiterns" zwar nicht des Alten Testaments insgesamt, wohl aber weisheitlicher Theologie schon innerhalb des Alten Testaments und ihrer Rettungsversuche in Jes. Sir und Sap. Sal.

Im Alten Testament selber wird somit die Frage nicht nur nach dem Verstehen sondern auch die nach der Wertung und Geltung dieser Texte angesichts dieses Traditionsweges laut. Versuche der Aufnahme weisheitlicher Texte und „Theologie" in heutige Verkündigung müssen sich den hier aufgezeigten Problemen stellen.

---

[1] G. VON RAD, *Weisheit in Israel*, 390.

[2] ebenda, 380 (trifft diese Charakterisierung zu?).

[3] Zu ihrem Ort bei G. VON RAD kritisch schon W. ZIMMERLI, „Die Weisheit Israels", *EvTh* 31, 1971, 680-695, dort 691ff.—Vgl. etwas schon G. VON RAD selbst (o.c., 171, Anm. 19) über die Josephsgeschichte und das dort durchbrochene Tatsphäredenken.

WISE AND FOOLISH, RIGHTEOUS AND WICKED

R. B. Y. SCOTT
Toronto

Our understanding of the history, literature and theology of ancient Hebrew Wisdom is hampered by certain unanswered and possibly unanswerable questions. Was wisdom at first primarily an intellectual and cultural phenomenon which gradually changed until it could be made the vehicle of religious teaching? Was its original objective moral training or intellectual development, or both? Was it directed primarily to the preservation of an established system of values in family and community life? If so, whence and in what degrees were these values derived? From common social experience? From the wisdom tradition of older neighboring civilizations? From the special beliefs of Mosaic Yahwism? And finally, was the "old wisdom" of the early monarchy an unitary affair, or did differing kinds and understandings of wisdom co-exist in some degree of tension?

Such questions cannot be fully answered because the surviving literary evidence in the Old Testament is insufficient and much of it is ambiguous. References to wisdom and wise men in the narrative books, in certain of the prophets and psalms are useful indicators, but in most cases are only incidental to other concerns of the writers. Esther, Daniel, Tobit and Baruch make relatively minor contributions. Our principal sources remain the five major "wisdom works"—Proverbs, Job, Qoheleth, Sirach and Wisdom of Solomon. Of the last three of these, the thought and general tenor, the literary structure, the *Sitz im Leben* and the approximate period of composition are fairly clear. There is more room for disagreement with respect to Job, and still more so with respect to Proverbs. The last-named work gathers together wisdom materials that are widely divergent in literary form, viewpoint and thought content, and—especially in the two sections entitled "Proverbs of Solomon"—in an almost haphazard arrangement. Proverbs is an accumulation of variegated materials old and new, apparently assembled for use as a source-book in a school for youth,[1] and edited by the principal author of the discourses and poems

---

[1] Cf. Prov. i 2-6; xxii 17-21.

in chapters i-ix. Its content ranges from popular adages lacking any moral or religious content—such as "To a hungry man everything bitter tastes sweet"—to a profound theological exploration of the relation of wisdom to the divine work of creation.[1] The rhetorical discourses in chapters i-ix differ in literary form from the "Thirty Sayings of the Sages" in xxii 17 ff., with its Egyptian background. The distinction of both from the intervening body of discreet and heterogeneous couplets is striking, even with the recognition that here and there occur couplets which echo the teaching of the opening chapters. Equally remarkable is the great variety among the couplets themselves, in the topics treated and in the presence or absence of ethical emphasis and religious language.

It is therefore clear that the Book of Proverbs in its present form is the end result of a long process of compilation. The common denominator of the highly various materials of many origins and periods is that all could be used in one way or another for the purpose of instruction in wisdom. The problem arises as to how such variegated materials without contextual connections can help our understanding the history and nature of Israelite wisdom. In particular—to what extent and in what ways was this wisdom "religious," and in what respects and to what degree was it "secular"?

These are question-begging terms. Religious beliefs and resulting attitudes in one form or another were so all-encompassing in the ancient world that no aspect of human life and thought lay outside its concern. Yet Von Rad can speak of "the sphere of the rational and empirical... (where) Jahweh could only be comprehended as limitation." [2] This sphere may be called "secular" without prejudice to the larger question of a writer's or speaker's comprehension of and attitude to his total spiritual environment. The plain fact is that many of the "proverbs of Solomon" are secular in the sense that in themselves they neither express nor necessarily imply religious belief. This corresponds to the fact that the terms ḥokmah and ḥakam connote not only ethical and religious wisdom but technical and artistic skills and even the reasoning faculty.[3] They may be used pejoratively of the craftiness of the wicked.[4]

---

[1] xxvii 7b; viii. This adage appears also in *The Words of Ahiqar*, xii 188; see ANET, p. 430.

[2] G. von Rad, *Old Testament Theology*, vol. i, (1962), p. 440.

[3] Ex. xxxv 31-33; Is. xxviii 24-26; Jer. ix 16; Job xxxviii 36; xxxix 17.

[4] Job v 12-13; xxxvii 24; cf. Prov. xii 2, 5; 2 Sam. xiii 3.

Nevertheless, in VON RAD's view, even in the sayings of "old wisdom" that seem most secular the Israelite was struggling to understand
and relate himself to a meaningful order of existence which he sensed
behind the multifarious experiences of daily life. This order was trust-
worthy and good. It tended toward life. Failure to relate oneself to it
was evil and turned a man toward trouble and death. This unseen
order was not identified with Yahweh, though Yahweh might act
through it and it was he who set limits to what man could do. Hence,
even in sayings which have no overt religious content a religious
attitude toward the whole experience of life is to be presupposed.[1]
VON RAD grants that the theological exploration and evaluation of
wisdom belongs to post-exilic Judaism.[2]

A very different picture of "old wisdom" has been drawn by Mc-
KANE, who envisages it as "primarily a disciplined empiricism engaged
with the problems of government and administration." [3] This was the
self-confident wisdom of the royal counselors attacked by the prophets
because it took no account of Yahweh's sovereignty over events in
history. More recently McKANE has analysed the wisdom sentences
of Proverbs x 1-xxii 16; xxv-xxix according to language and content,
distinguishing from sayings which express religious belief or a pious
moralism, others which "are set in the framework of old wisdom and
are concerned with the education of the individual for a successful and
harmonious life." [4] The latter envisage a wider group than young men
aspiring to careers at the royal court, but there is the same suggestion
that old wisdom had no *necessary* religious ingredient or foundation.
The sayings marked by religious language or by a "moralism which
derives from Yahwistic piety" are thought by McKANE to represent
a later re-interpretation of the "old wisdom" material; he argues that
terms having a positive meaning in the older educational framework
are used pejoratively in the framework of later piety.[5]

It would appear that VON RAD and McKANE differ so radically in
their interpretation of the "Solomonic" sayings in Proverbs because
they have reached their conclusions about the nature of old wisdom
in Israel on other grounds, and then have read the sayings in the light
of these conclusions. The former declares that "empirical and gnomic

---

[1] *O.T. Theol.*, i, pp. 419-41; *Weisheit in Israel* (1970), pp. 80 ff., 106 ff., 123 ff.,
165 ff.

[2] *O.T. Theol.*, i, pp. 441-53.

[3] W. McKANE, *Prophets and Wise Men*, (1965), p. 53, *passim*.

[4] W. McKANE, *Proverbs*, (1971), pp. 11, 415.

[5] *Op. cit.*, pp. 17-18.

wisdom starts from the unyielding presupposition that there is a hidden order in things and events... and this order is kindly and righteous." Israel's " 'world' was a sustaining activity of Jahweh," and "the insights attained into the world surrounding her were in the last analysis (of) orders apprehended by faith." Teachers and pupils were members of the same cultic community, and hence "the starting point of this education is knowledge of God, and of his revelation and commandments." "This wisdom teaching... passes over into theology where the subject-matter contains some kind of pointer or reference to Jahweh, his activity, or what pleases or displeases him," [1]—(this McKANE refers to as "God-language").

McKANE takes his cue from the story of the court counselors Abishai and Ahithophel in 2 Sam. xvi 15-xvii 23, and from the profane and calculating self-assurance of their successors in Isaiah's and Jeremiah's times that brought them into conflict with these prophets.[2] Many of the proverbial sayings, he finds, give no indication of the underlying religious assumptions which VON RAD discerns, but seem to be concerned rather with preparing youth "for a successful and harmonious life." Only toward the end of the monarchy did the sages begin to come to terms with the affirmations of Yahwist faith.[3]

Before deciding which of these two divergent readings of the evidence is on the right track we must revert to the fact that the materials incorporated in the Book of Proverbs have a wide range both chronologically and in the nature of their contents. The issue of the religious constituents or presuppositions of pre-exilic Israelite wisdom cannot be settled simply by quoting the famous maxim in i 7: "The fear of Yahweh is the beginning of wisdom," if for no other reason than that this represents only one of several different views of the matter to be found in the book. Nor is the issue to be settled by analysing the contents of the several "collections" of wisdom sentences, as SKLADNY has done in his in many ways valuable study of x-xv, xvi-xxii 16, xxv-xxvii and xxviii-xxix.[4] These bodies of material are not homogeneous, and there is overlapping between them in subject matter, phraseology and literary forms. The differences among them are mainly differences in proportion of the several elements of their contents.

---

[1] *O.T. Theol.*, i, pp. 421, 427, 433, 437.

[2] *Prophets and Wise Men, passim.*

[3] *Proverbs*, pp. 11, 19.

[4] U. SKLADNY, *Die ältesten Spruchsammlungen in Israel*, (1962). For convenience, these divisions of the text are designated A, B, C, and D, following SKLADNY.

To call these divisions of the text "collections" is again to beg the question. It is a methodological error to take for granted that the divisions marked off by titles (as in x 1, xxii 17, xxiv 23, xxv 1) represent neat parcels of sayings of distinct character and independent origin which can be arranged in chronological sequence and dated approximately, as SKLADNY has attempted to do. The present Book of Proverbs is better seen as the end result of a centuries-long process of composition, supplementing, editing and scribal transmission, a process which has blurred some lines of demarcation between its component parts.

The evidence for this statement is threefold:

a) The titles are not reliable indicators of the beginnings and contents of the following sections. The same title, *mišle šelômô*, is used in i 1 as a general title of the present book, in x 1 at a point where there is a marked change in form and substance from what has preceded, and at xxv 1 where the opening verses 2-10 are more appropriately to be associated with the preceding "further words of the sages" than with the adages that follow in xxv-xxix.[1] If, on the other hand, those scholars are correct who take xvi-xxii 16 (B) and xxviii-xxix (D) to be distinct collections, these are without titles, (as are also the distinct sections beginning at xxx 7 and xxxi 11). Indeed, all the titles in the present form of Proverbs appear to be editorial with the exception of those in xxx 1 and xxxi 1. The fact that some sections have titles while others do not leaves unsettled the question as to how much of what follows each title was intended by the editor to be included under it. In any case the titles provide no proof that the sections they introduce have not subsequently been added to, or otherwise altered.

b) Apparent displacements of the Hebrew text, whether due to scribal error or to the insertion of additional material, are more apparent in the introductory nine chapters [2] than in the "Solomonic collections,"

---

[1] It is not clear where the section ends which begins at xxii 17 and shows literary dependence on Amen-em-ope. The declaratory sayings in xxiv 2-9 appear intrusive in their context. Further, the short supplementary section in xxiv 23-34 with its separate title contains only three verses of "instruction" like that found in xxii 17 ff.; this second title would more suitably apply to xxiv 27-29 together with xxv 2-10. The title in xxv 1 may originally have preceded xxv 11.

[2] Note the insertion of the first poem of the personified Wisdom between the first and second of the hortatory discourses (i 8-ii 22); the negative precepts with motive clauses in iii 11-18, 25-26, 31-32 which resemble the form of the Thirty Precepts of xxii 22 ff. more than anything else in chapters i-ix; the interruption at vi 1 of the series of discourses, by short poetic essays on topics common to the Solomonic sentences but unmentioned elsewhere in chaps. i-ix; the intrusion of the miscellaneous verses ix 7-12 between two parts of the same poem.

where the succession of heterogeneous sayings would make them hard to identify. Nevertheless there are a few oddities that blur the distinctions between the different divisions of the present text, and affect—even if slightly—the characterization of their contents. For example, xiv 1 stands out from its surroundings like an erratic boulder: Wisdom and Folly are here metaphorically personified as in i 20 ff., viii 1 ff., ix 1 ff. and 6 ff. but nowhere else in the book; the archaising spelling *ḥokmot* is found only here and in i 20, ix 1 and xxiv 7; and Wisdom's building of her house recalls ix 1. Again, the pedagogical address "my son" appears inexplicably in xix 27 (B) and xxvii 11 (C); this is characteristic, rather, of the preceptorial discourses in chapters i-vii and of the "Thirty Sayings." In the admonition inserted at xx 13 (B), the word *šenah* is elsewhere confined to chapters iii-vi and to xxiv 33 (= vi 10). Conversely, a few declaratory adages are found among the "Thirty Sayings" at xxiii 24 and xxiv 3-9.

c) The occurrence of *duplicate and variant couplets and single lines* has customarily been explained as pointing to their origin in distinct collections, on the analogy of similar phenomena in the Pentateuch and the Psalms. The argument loses its force when it is observed that the duplicates and variants are found not only between but also within the supposedly distinct collections, and even within a single chapter (xxviii 12b, 28a). Three types of duplicates and variants can be distinguished:

   i) Identical or virtually identical couplets: xiv 12 (A) = xvi 25 (B); xviii 8 (B) = xxvi 22 (C); xix 24 = xxvi 15; xx 16 (B) = xxvii 13 (C); . xxi 9 (B) = xxv 24 (C); xxii 3 (B) = xxvii 12 (C).

   ii) Couplets in which very similar thoughts are differently expressed: x 1 (A) & xv 20 (A); cf. xiii 1a (A), xvii 21, 25 (B), xix 13a, 26b (B), xxix 3a (D).
x 15 (A) & xvii 18 (B); cf. xx 16 (B) = xxvii 13 (C).
xiii 14 (A) & xiv 27 (A); cf. x 11a (A); xvi 22a (B).
xiv 20 (A) & xix 4 (B); cf. xix 6 (B).
xvi 2 (B) & xxi 2 (B); cf. xvii 3 (B), xxvii 21 (C).
xix 1 (B) & xxviii 6 (D); cf. x 9a (A), xix 22 (B).
xxi 19 (B) & xxi 9 (B) = xxv 24 (C); cf. xix 13b (B).
xxviii 12 (D) & xxix 2 (D); cf. xxviii 28 (D), xxix 16 (D).

   iii) Identical single lines attached to different second lines: x 2b (A) = xi 4b (A); x 6b (A) = x 11b (A); x 15a (A) = xviii 11a (B); xi 13a (A) = xx 19a (B); xii 14a (A) = xiii 2a (A) = xviii 20a (B); xv 33b (A) = xviii 12b (B); xvii 3a (B) = xxvii 21a (C); xix 1a (B) =

xxviii 6a (D); xxvi 12b (C) = xxix 20b (D); xxviii 12b (D) = xxviii 28a (D).

Note also that xi 14b (A) and xxviii 21a (D) are found also outside the A, B, C, D divisions at xxiv 6b and xxiv 23b respectively, and that vi 10-11 re-appears in xxiv 33-34.

This plethora of repetitions cannot wholly be explained on the analogy of a theory of "collections." For one thing, too many of them are found within the same divisions and in some cases quite close together. For another, the variants do not show peculiarities of view-point and vocabulary which link them to their present contexts and distinguish them from their counterparts elsewhere. What is striking is that in some cases a variant has been produced by introducing specifically *religious* terminology;

xiii 14a	"The teaching of the wise is a fountain of life (*m^eqor ḥayyim*)"
xvi 22a	"Good sense is a fountain of life to its possessors (*m^eqor ḥayyim*)"
x 11a	"The speech of a righteous man is a fountain of life (*m^eqor ḥayyim*)"
xiv 27a	"The fear of Yahweh is a fountain of life (*m^eqor ḥayyim*)"
xv 17	"Better is a dinner of herbs where love is than a fatted ox and hatred with it" [cf. xvii 1 (B)]
(B) xvi 8	"Better is a little with righteousness than great revenues with injustice"
(A) xv 16	"Better is a little with the fear of Yahweh than great treasure and trouble with it"
(D) xxviii 21	"To show partiality (in judgment) is not good; a man may be at fault over a morsel of food" (cf. xxiv 23-25)
(B) xviii 5	"To be partial to a wicked (guilty) man is not good, or to deprive a righteous (innocent) man of justice"
(B) xvii 15	"He who pronounces a guilty man innocent and he who pronounces an innocent man guilty are both abominable to Yahweh"

(A) x 15a = xviii 11a (B)   "A rich man's wealth is his strong city"

(B) xviii 10   "The name of Yahweh is a strong tower"

(C) xxvii 21   "As a melting-pot is for silver and a smelter for gold, so praise tests a man"

(B) xvii 3   "As a melting-pot is for silver and a smelter for gold, so Yahweh is an assayer of (men's) hearts" [1]

These examples suggest that couplets using "religious" or "wisdom" terms sometimes were composed on the basis of traditional sayings in which these notes were lacking. The old and the new are immediately adjacent in xv 16-17 and xviii 10-11. It is noteworthy that these parallel "religious" and "secular" sayings are widely distributed among the four divisions A, B, C and D. Furthermore, they are to be compared with the many other sayings which characterize the righteous and unrighteous, speak of the active concern of Yahweh with men's lives or use the phrase "the fear of Yahweh" with the meaning "piety." McKane is surely correct in segregating those sayings which utilize "religious" terminology as a distinct type of material in x 1-xxii 16 and xxv-xxix, rather than as evidence for a religious element in four "collections" of different origin. For example, although the greatest concentration of sayings mentioning Yahweh is found in chapters xv (A) and xvi (B) and only one is found in xxv-xxvii, they are otherwise broadly distributed and speak everywhere with the same voice.[2]

Another suggestive fact is that in the antitheses of "wise man" and "fool," "righteous" and "wicked" the contrasted terms, their synonyms and equivalent phrases, are not interchangeable. Each pair, broadly speaking, is associated with its own vocabulary and set of ideas. Of approximately 145 antitheses in chapters x-xv, only in one or two instances (x 31; xi 9) is the righteous associated with wisdom, and only once is contrasted with the fool (x 21). In no case is the wise man contrasted with the wicked. Both sets of antitheses present alternative ways of life and divide men into two classes accordingly, each with its appropriate destiny. But these contrasted groups remain distinct.[3] As has often been noted, these antithetical sayings are found

---

[1] Cf. also xv 18 (A), xxix 22 (D) and xxviii 25 (D); xviii 18 (B) and xvi 33 (B).

[2] See below, p. 164

[3] Contra SKLADNY, *op. cit.*, p. 12. Cf. x 9, 17; xii 15; xiii 3, 4, 18, 20, etc.; xi 5, 19; xii 26, 28; xiii 6, 22, etc.

chiefly in chapters x-xv, the "righteous-wicked" type predominating
in x and xi, and the "wise-foolish" type more frequently in xiv and xv.
Both appear sporadically in sections B, C and D.

The present writer's analysis supports McKANE's conclusion that a
line of demarcation marking a real difference is to be drawn between
the sayings marked by the presence or absence of religious terms and
ideas.[1] It seems questionable, however, if his further distinction between Class "A" sentences (concerned with the education of the
individual) and Class "B" sentences (concerned with the harmful effects
on the community of the individuals' anti-social behavior) is equally
justified. Both presuppose the Israelite community and, to a degree,
its special quality of life. At the same time McKANE lumps together
in each of his principal categories A-B and C[2] sayings which really
differ in character and *Sitz im Leben*. There appear to be four types of
"secular" sayings, i.e., those which *do not* affirm or suggest religious
beliefs[3]:

1) Folk sayings (or literary couplets based on folk sayings) which
are more suitable to exchanges between adults meeting "in the gate"
than to authoritarian instruction of youth in home or school.

2) Folk sayings or their derivatives which seek to impress on the
hearers the moral standards and values of home and community, but
without any indication that these are grounded in an unseen order of
reality.

3) Teaching proverbs in literary couplet form in which wise men
and fools are characterized and their opposite fortunes are emphasized.
The apparent setting is that of schools for youth who aspire to a
"higher education" than was received in the home or tribal community.

4) Teaching proverbs more specifically directed to the professional
training of scribes and public officials.

Before discussing these different types of sayings, something must
be said about the distinction between folk sayings and the balanced,
rhythmic couplets that predominate in x 1-xxii 16 and xxv-xxix.[4] Folk

---

[1] I am indebted to Professor McKANE for the stimulation of his commentary
on *Proverbs* which has led me to re-examine the evidence for and to abandon the
theory of the four "collections."

[2] I.e., those which do not, and those which do, utilize the language of piety.

[3] It must be emphasized that this omission does not mean that their authors
were not religious men but only that religious belief is not expressed or implied
in these particular sayings.

[4] It may be that "Proverb of Solomon" was the special designation of this
literary form, with reference to that king's legendary reputation as a literary genius.

sayings are quoted occasionally in Old Testament narratives and by the prophets, e.g.

1 Sam. x 11-12   *hᵃgam šaʾûl bannᵉbîʾîm*

1 Ki. xx 11   *yithallel ḥoger kimᵉpatteᵃḥ*

Jer. xxxi 29   *ʾabôt ʾakᵉlû boser wᵉsinne banîm tiqhênah*

Ez. xviii 1   *ʾabôt yoʾkᵉlû boser wᵉsinne banîm tiqhênah*

Hos. iv 9   *kaʿam kakkohen* [1]

These and similar examples in Proverbs display marks of the traditional adage: they are terse and pointed and make use of picturesque imagery; they are taunting, sardonic or pathetic in tone, and their form often displays alliteration or assonance. They are truisms unmarked by the special interests of the wisdom teachers, except where their original non-poetic form has been expanded into rhythmic couplets for pedagogical purposes.

Four sayings in Proverbs preserve the older prosaic form:

xxvii 10c	*ṭôb šaken qarôb meʾaḥ raḥôq*
xxvii 5	*ṭôbah tôkaḥat mᵉgullah meʾaḥᵃbah mᵉsuttáret*
xxiv 26	*šᵉpatayim yiššaq mešîb dᵉbarîm nᵉkohîm*
xxiv 23	*hakker panîm bᵉmišpaṭ bal ṭôb*

The last of these re-appears in abbreviated form in xxviii 21a, where it is utilized as the first line of a couplet. Other couplets which seem to have been formed on the basis of colloquial sayings or maxims are:

xi 2a	*baʾ zadôn wayyaboʾ qalôn*
xxv 27a	*ʾakol dᵉbaš harbôt (hᵃrbeh) loʾ ṭôb*
xvi 26a	*nepeš ʿamel ʿamᵉlah lô*
xvii 14a	*pôṭer mayim reʾsît madôn*
xx 14a	*raʿ raʿ yoʾmᵃr haqqôneh* [2]
xxii 7b	*ʿebed loweh lᵉʾîš malweh*

Other possible examples are xvii 15a, xviii 5a (both legal maxims), xviii 22a, xix 4a, 13b, xxv 25, xxvii 18a.

Couplets that are variants of the same saying and have some of the characteristics of colloquial sayings may well have been derived from this source. A good example is:

---

[1] Cf. Gen. xvi 12ab; xxii 14b; 2 Sam. xx 18; Jer. xiii 23a; xvii 11ab.

[2] Note how the second line spells out what is implied in the taunting first line.

xx 9	*ṭôb (la)šebet ('al pinnat gag) me'eset midyanîm (ûbêt ḥáber)*
xxv 24	*ṭôb šebet ('al pinnat gag) me'eset midyanîm (ûbêt ḥáber)*
xxi 19	*ṭôb šebet (be'eres midbar) me'eset midyanîm (waka'as)*

The original saying with five-accents would include one of the two first variants but neither of the final ones, which have been added to create a couplet. Other apparent examples of folk proverbs which have been expanded similarly are xviii 22a, xix 4a and 13b, xxv 25.

At this point the remark must be made that not all these non-literary sayings are necessarily the product of remote antiquity in Israel like "the proverb of the ancients" in 1 Sam. xxiv 13. Similar sayings might emerge among the common people at any time. Alternatively, some may have been coined by the teachers themselves to illustrate and enforce their instruction in wisdom. The distinction here being made is of four types of non-religious sayings is according to their content, form and apparent *Sitz im Leben*, leaving open the question of their date of origin.

The differences among the four types can best be illustrated by quotation:

1) *Folk sayings* (or derivatives) *representing not moral instruction but adult comments* on persons and social situations, expressing scorn, sarcasm, resentment of the rich and powerful, pleasant or sad experiences:

xi 16	A gracious lady clings to honor as ruthless men cling to wealth
xi 22	Like a gold ring in a pig's snout is a pretty woman who lacks good taste
xvi 26a	A worker's appetite works for him
xviii 23	A poor man entreats, a rich man answers harshly
xix 7a	All a poor man's brothers hate him
xix 4a	Wealth brings many new friends
xxii 13	The sluggard says, "There is a lion outside! I shall be slain in the streets!"
xix 13b	A quarrelsome wife is like a ceaseless dripping (cf. xxvii 15)
xv 30b	Good news refreshes the body [1]

2) *Folk sayings* (or derivatives) *which embody moral instruction* of the home or community but *not in terms of formal instruction in wisdom* and warnings against of folly. Examples are:

---

[1] Other sayings which may belong to this category are: x 15a; xiii 8, 23; xiv 4a, 20; xv 15; xviii 22a; xix 6b; xx 25; xxi 9 and parallels; xxv 20; xxvii 10c; xxviii 19; xxix 5, 24.

xi 2a	First comes presumption, then disgrace
xiii 24a	(A father) who withholds punishment hates his son
xvii 1	Better a dry crust with concord than a house filled with feasting and strife
xvii 13	If one returns evil for good, evil will not leave his house
xvii 14a	The beginning of a quarrel is like starting a flow of water
xx 29	Young men are honored for their strength, old men for their gray hairs
xxvii 5	Open rebuke is better than concealed approval [1]

3) *Teaching proverbs* in couplet form comprise a major elment in x-xxii 16 and xxv-xxix, so much so that they give their tone to the whole body of material. Nevertheless, this group of sayings with its clear objectives of distinguishing wisdom from folly and of training youth in the former and teaching them to despise the latter, has its own features of thought, literary form and vocabulary. These features in general sufficiently differentiate the Wisdom-Folly sayings from the other categories, although there is some overlapping and conflation which blurs the lines of the distinction.

The special terminology of this group of sayings is most evident in the antitheses which predominate in x-xv, in comparison with the "Righteous-Wicked" antitheses in the same chapters. The *ḥakam* or *ḥᵃkam leb* is called also *nabôn*, *'îš* (and) *rab tᵉbûnah*, *maskîl*, *'îš mᵉzimmot*. His characteristic qualities are that he is *'arûm*, *ḥarûs*, *ṣanuᵃ'*, *'erek 'appayim*, *šômer mûsar*. Contrasted with him is the *kᵉsîl*, *'ᵉwîl* or *ḥᵃsar-leb*, with the sub-types *pᵉtî*, *leṣ*, *bôged* and *'aṣel*. Among his typical characteristics are *kap rᵉmiyyah*, *sin'ah*, *ka'as*, *mirmah*, *ḥemmah*, *qin'ah*. He is *ḥôreš ra'*, *'ôzeb tôkaḥat*, *mᵉraddep reqîm*, *rob dᵉbarîm*. The wise man accepts, the fool rejects the discipline of instruction in wisdom—*miṣwah*, *tôrah*, *dabar*, *mûsar*, *gᵉ'arah*, *tôkaḥat*.

The same or related ideas and vocabulary are continued in the less frequent "wisdom-folly" antitheses in xvi-xxii 16 and xxviii-xxix,[2] and are found also in the other categories of parallelistic couplets.[3] In the later chapters three forms of wisdom instruction other than the simple declarative sentence are more frequent than in x-xv: (i) Proverbs of comparative value like xv 17 [4]; (ii) Precepts in the imperative mood like xiv 7 [5]; (iii) Similes in which the different kinds of fool are stereo-

---

[1] Other possible examples are: xvi 18; xvii 6; xviii 3a, 9, 19, 24; xx 11a, 17, 19a, 20; xxv 27a.

[2] xxvii 12 is a duplicate of xxii 3.

[3] E.g. xi 25, 29; xvi 21; xvii 21; xxvi 24-26; xxvii 17; xxviii 22; xxix 20.

[4] xvi 16; xvii 10, 26; xix 1, 22; xxi 9, 19; xxvii 10c; xxviii 6.

[5] xix 20, 27; xxv 17, 21-23; xxvi 4-5; xxvii 1, 2, 11 etc.

typed, as in x 26; xv 12.[1] Double or triple similes like x 26 are specially
frequent in xxv-xxvii. Favorite words are *kabôd*, *ʿaṭeret*, *marpeh*. Other
words—*ʾûṣ*, *ṣîr* (messenger), *ʾatam*, *mahᵃlumôt*, *nirgan*, *tûšiyyah*—are
peculiar to this group among the sayings.

What it means to be a wise man or a fool is brought out less by the
use of attributive adjectives than by descriptions of their behavior and
its effects on others and on themselves. The one brings pride to his
parents, the other, shame. The one takes pleasure in good behavior,
the other finds his fun in recklessness, slander, deceit and quarreling.
The fool is passionate, the wise man self-controlled, especially in
speech. The one is violent, the other cautious and patient. The one
makes trouble, the other strives for harmony. The one shows intel-
ligence and foresight, the other is self-satisfied in his stupidity and
refuses to learn.[2]

The behavior described is accompanied by certain effects which are
of a piece with it rather being rewards or punishments, social or divine.
The deed or attitude correspond with these effects in an orderly structure of experience.[3] A father always is glad when his son displays
wisdom, and conversely. A fool is familiar with beatings because of
his wild talk. A gentle answer deflates anger as surely as a harsh word
arouses it. A tranquil mind or a passionate nature have contrary effects
on bodily health.[4] But there are other instances where consequences
become sanctions supporting the teacher's incitement to wise conduct
"Poverty and disgrace come to him who refuses correction, but he
who accepts reproof will be honored." "A man who remains obstinate
after much reproof will suddenly be broken beyond repair." [5] It is in
the nature of things that folly brings ruin, but there is no intimation
that this is a judgment of God.

A group of subjective reflections, somewhat philosophical in tone,
may or may not belong with the instructional sentences considered
above. "Even with laughter the heart may be grieving, and joy may
turn to sorrow in the end." "A man's spirit may sustain him in illness,
but if his spirit is cast down who can raise it (by himself)?" [6]

4) The fourth group of sayings appertains to *training for professional
service in government*—as counselors at the royal court and in diplomacy,

---

[1] xvii 2, 12; xviii 2, 6, 7; xix 10, 19, 24; xxvi 1 ff.; xxvii 3; xxix 11.

[2] x 1; xv 21; xii 18; xi 12; xxvi 17-21; xii 16, 23; xiv 16-17; xvi 32; xxii 3, etc.

[3] See H. GESE, *Lehre und Wirklichkeit in der alten Weisheit*, 1958, pp. 33 ff.

[4] x 1; xiv 3; xv 1; xiv 30. Cf. xvi 24; xvii 9; xxv 23; xxix 8, 21.

[5] xiii 18; xxix 1. Cf. x 8b; xiii 13; xv 10; xxi 21; xxviii 20.

[6] xiv 13; xviii 14. Cf. xii 25; xiii 12; xiv 10; xv 13; xxvii 19, 20.

in the administration of justice and in the bureaucracy. Here the emphasis is no longer on the distinction between two ways of life and two kinds of people, but

(i) on accommodation to the king's absolute power, as in xvi 14: "A king's wrath is an intimation of death, and a wise man will appease it";

(ii) on the best ways to deal successfully with the powerful, as in xxv 15: "With patience a chief man may be persuaded, and a soft tongue will break a bone";

(iii) on true justice as essential to stability of the kingdom, as in xvi 12: "Wrongdoing is hateful to kings, for right is the firm base of a throne." [1]

The references to the operation of courts of justice seem to belong with this group, together with some at least of the sayings about false witnesses.[2] The same is true of the infrequent references to the national community in xi 14; xxviii 15; xxix 18, which stand out the mass of sayings dealing with individuals. One curious point is that the trainess are warned that they may be confronted by powerful men intent on feathering their own nests.[3] In xxix 4 the meaning seems to be that the king's justice may be undermined by the venality of a judge.

The vocabulary of these passages favors their distinction from the teaching sentences discussed under 3) above. The word *ḥakam* occurs only twice, and the words *maskîl* and *tᵉbûnah* once each; *nabal* is found once here and once in section 3), and the words *kᵉsîl* and *'ᵉwîl* not at all. Even more striking is the disproportionate occurrence here of words unique or rare in Proverbs: *'ôpan, 'êmah, gerem, dob, hagah* (remove), *hadar* (Hit.), *hᵃdarah, ẓakah* (Pi.), *ẓa'ap, ẓarah* (Pi.), *ṭahar, ṭal, yadah* (Hi.), *lᵉ'om, kᵉpîr, malqôš, mᵉšaret, mattan, naham* (vb.), *naham* (n.), *sîg, sa'ad, 'ab, ṣalaḥ* (Hi.), *qabab, qesem, qaṣin, raḥab* (Hi.), *raḥam* (Pu.), *šaqaq*.

In considering these four types and groups of sayings it can be said with confidence that no positive religious note is struck in them. At the same time only the first and fourth can be regarded as secular in content, since the others affirm moral values which were affirmed also by Yahwist religion.

Three further types and groups of sayings must now be examined

---

[1] Further examples of (i) are xvi 10, 15; xix 12; xx 2, 8, 26; xxi 1; of (ii), xiv 35; xvi 13; xviii 16; xxi 14; xxv 6-7; of (iii) xx 28; xxv 4-5; xxix 4a, 14.

[2] xvii 23, 26; xviii 5, 17; xxi 7; xxv 26; xxviii 1, 21. In distinction from the Righteous-Wicked antitheses the same words carry here their older meanings "innocent" and "guilty."

[3] xxii 16; xxviii 2, 15-16; xxix 12.

which quite specifically relate the teachings of wisdom to those of religion and make use of religious language. These are:

5) Sayings which exhibit the contrast between the *ṣaddîq* and the *rašaʿ* as in the third group the *ḥakam* is contrasted with the *kesîl/ʾewîl;*

6) Sayings which portray Yahweh as a present, active and determining factor in the life experience of individual persons;

7) Sayings which introduce the phrase "fear of Yahweh" with the meaning "piety, religious belief."

Each of these groups of "religious" sayings has recognizable characteristics:

(5) As has often been noted, the "righteous-wicked" antithesis is particularly prominent in chapters x-xv, alongside the "wise-foolish" antithesis. This at once suggests that the two are analagous, as indeed they are. But that does not mean that they are equivalent and interchangeable. In what sense, then, are the former paired terms used?

The words *ṣaddîq-rašaʿ* clearly do not have here the forensic meaning "innocent-guilty," that they have in subsequent sayings about proceedings in courts of justice, such as xvii 15, 26 and xviii 5.[1] In two verses only—xi 10-11—the contrast is drawn apparently between parties or political factions in the community, as later in xxviii 12, 28; xxix 2, 16. The labels are applied from he standpoint of cultic orthodoxy.[2] With this exception the antitheses in chapters x-xv (and a few comparable ones in later chapters [3]) either (i) pronounce the opposite consequences for the *ṣaddîq* and the *rašaʿ*[4], or (ii) indicate the moral and religious differences between them, largely through the substitution for these terms of synonymous words or phrases.

The commonest equivalents of *ṣaddîq* are *yašar* and *ṭôb*.[5] Others are *tamîm, ṭahôr, zak, meraddep ṣedaqah, šôḥer ṭôb, hôlek betummô, hôlek beyašrô, tam derek, nôṣer darkô*. The synonyms of *rašaʿ* are *raʿ, bôged, ḥôṭeʾ, ḥaṭṭaʾ, ʿiqqeš leb, meʿaqqeš darkô, neʿqaš derek, sûg leb, ḥanep, nelôz derakaw, ʾîš ʿawel, poʿel ʾawen*.

In the vast majority of the contrasting statements about the *ṣaddîq* and the *rašaʿ* in Proverbs the reference undoubtedly is to religious

---

[1] Cf. xx 26; xxi 15; xxv 26; xxviii 1.

[2] Cf. Pss. xxxii 10-11; xxxiii 1-3; xcii 13-14; cxviii 15, 20.

[3] xxi 12, 18, 26, 29; xxviii 5, 10, 18; xxix 6, 7, 27.

[4] E.g., x 2, 3, 6, 7, 16, 21, 24, 25, 28, 30.

[5] xi 3, 6, 11; xxi 18; xxix 27, etc.; xiii 22; xiv 19; xv 3.

belief and non-belief and corresponding character and behavior, —as repeatedly in the Psalms and elsewhere in the Old Testament.[1] The criterion for the division is acceptance or rejection of obedience to Yahweh's commandments, both cultic and ethical. This is an extension of the meanings "innocent" and "guilty" according to the laws of the community as determined in a court of law.

The distinction, however, is not the same as that between the wise man and the fool, even though in practice the two groupings might broadly coincide, especially with regard to moral rectitude. Wisdom was an accomplishment to be acquired in varying degrees through the discipline of learning, even though it might also be seen as a divine reward for this discipline. Righteousness was different. It was a status before Yahweh resulting from what VON RAD calls "an act of avowal," a pledge to serve and obey him. "A man was either *ṣaddîq* in the eyes of Jahweh or he was not." [2] Hence there is a distinction between the *ḥakam-kᵉsîl* sayings and the *ṣaddîq-raša'* sayings in Proverbs that goes beyond the differences in vocabulary. In the former a teacher seeks to persuade youth to seek wisdom, by emphasizing its values for the experience of living and the unhappy consequences of folly. The wise man finds a richer and longer life, material prosperity and social approval; the fool suffers corresponding penalties.[3] These and similar results come also to the *ṣaddîq* and the *raša'*, but with a difference. The latter's fate often is simply the negation of what the former can expect.[4] Their respective destinies are stated in the abstract generalities of dogma rather than with the particularities of concrete and familiar experience.[5] Whereas the wise and the foolish are recognizable human beings in imaginable situations, the qualities and behavior of the righteous and the wicked are described in a curiously colorless fashion, e.g., xi 5:

The righteousness of the blameless keeps his way straight, but the wicked falls by his own wickedness.[6]

(6) The recurrent sayings in chapters x-xxii 16 and xxviii-xxix [7]

---

[1] Cf. Pss. i, xi, xxxvii, cxxv, and note 2, p. 160. Cf. Ezek. iii 18 ff., xviii 19 ff.

[2] *O.T. Theol.*, i, pp. 380-82.

[3] x 14, 17; xi 2, 15, 29; xiii 20; xv 7; xvii 2; xix 29; xxi 17, 21, etc.

[4] x 3, 9, 16, 28, 31; xi 6, 7, 8, 18; xii 3, etc.

[5] xi 28, 31; xii 3, 7, 12, 21, 28; xiii 6, 21; xiv 9, 11; xxi 12, 18 etc.

[6] x 2, 6, 20, 28, 32; xi 3, 9, 28, 30; xii 5, 6, 13, 20, 26, etc. A partial exception is xii 10.

[7] In xxv-xxvii Yahweh is named only in xxv 22. In xxv 2 "God" and "the king" are correlated, as are "Yahweh" and "the king" in xxiv 21.

which speak of Yahweh's free and determining participation in the life experience of individuals provide the strongest possible evidence for a religious dimension in Israelite wisdom, and have been made to bear the chief weight of proof by scholars who lay stress on this element. If the whole body of teaching wisdom couplets were a single entity representing views held in common by the wisdom teachers, the question being discussed in this paper would not arise. But if, on the other hand, the sentence literature of Proverbs is an anthology from various sources accumulated over a considerable period of time—as seems evident to the present writer—one cannot assume that the religious factor was equally accepted by all its contributors, yet articulated only by some.

Four pieces of evidence suggest that those sayings which specifically affirm Yahweh's active presence represent an annotation or editing of an already existing collection of wisdom couplets of the various types already discussed.

i) These may be identified by their characteristic ideas and vocabulary: *ḥakam-kᵉsîl* sayings—"A man's mind plans his way but Yahweh orders his steps," xvi. 9. Other examples are—xvi 1, 3, 20; xix 14, 21; xx 12, 24, 27; xxi 30; xxviii 25. Possibly xvii 3, cf. xxvii 21; xix 3.

"professional school" sayings—"The horse may be arrayed for the day of battle, but the victory is Yahweh's," xxi 31. Another example is xvi 33.

ṣaddîq-rašaʿ sayings—"Yahweh does not let a righteous man go hungry, but he rebuffs the craving of the wicked," x 3. Other examples are x 29; xi 20; xv 8, 9, 26, 29; xviii 10; xxviii 5.

ii) The fact that many of these sayings seem designed *either* to correct views expressed in other proverbs, *or* to put them in a new light by adding a religious dimension. Often the "Yahweh sayings" are found in the immediate context of the saying they correct or supplement. For example—"The name of Yahweh is a strong tower into which the righteous man may run and be inaccessible," xviii 10. "A rich man's wealth is his strong city, like an inaccessible wall so he supposes," xviii 11. Other examples are x 3, cf. x 4, 22; xi 20, 21; xv 9, 10; xvi 1, cf. xv 23; xvi 3 and xix 21, cf. xv 22, xx 18, xxi 5; xvi 9 and xx 24, cf. xvi 30; xvi 33, cf. xviii 18; xxii 2, cf. xxii 7.

iii) The introduction of topics and thoughts not found in chapters x-xxii 16 and xxv-xxix except in the "Yahweh sayings". Most of these follow naturally from the introduction of the deity by name—Yahweh as the creator of all (xvi 4; xx 12; xxii 2; xxix 13); the divine watchfulness (xv 3, 11); Yahweh's concern with men's inner thoughts and motives (xvi 2b; xvii 3b; xx 27; xxi 2b). The offering of sacrifice is mentioned only here (xxi 3, 27 [1]), and also the offering of prayer (xv 8, 29; xxviii 9). More surprising is it that the obligation to use honest scales, weights and measures is mentioned nowhere else than in connection with Yahweh's concern (xi 1; xvi 11; xx 10, 13).

iv) There is some vocabulary peculiar to these sentences in the "Solomonic" sections of Proverbs, although in some cases appearing also in chapters i-ix, xxii 17-xxiv, or xxx-xxxi: *'almanah; 'ebyôn* (ct. *dal,* x 15, etc.; *mahsor,* xxi 17; *'ani, 'anaw,* xv 15, xvi 19, etc.; *raš,* xiii 8, etc.); *'ôyeb* (ct. *śaneb,* xxv 21, etc.); *ẓarah; kuppar* Pu.; *migdal; nešamah; ṣa'ad, miṣ'ad; šûḥah 'amûqah; takan.*

Yahweh is named in 61 of the approximately 500 couplets or larger units of x-xxii 16, xxv-xxix (plus two references to him as "the Maker"), so that this supplement of "Yahweh sayings" is extensive as well as distinctive. Together with the introductory chapters i-ix it amounts to a working over and recasting of the traditional gnomic materials to bring them within the compass of religious literature.

(7) The last and least significant of the three groups of sayings marked by religious terminology is that in which *yir'at YHWH* is used as a conventional term for piety and *yere' YHWH* for the pious individual. The distinction from Group vi is that here the reference is to a quality or attitude of man rather than to Yahweh's presence and activity.

That *yir'at YHWH* had become a conventional name for piety is evident from the thrice-repeated description of Job as

tam weyašar yere' 'elohîm wesar mera' (Job i 1, 8; ii 3; cf. xxviii 28). Both parts of this stock phrase are found in Proverbs xvi 6b (cf. iii 7; viii 13), in an extended form in xiv 27, and, defectively, in xiv 16. Elsewhere in the body of sayings *yir'at YHWH* appears in x 27; xiv 2, 27; xv 16, 33; xix 23; xxii 4; and *yere' YHWH* in xiv 2, 26.[2] The second half of the conventional phrase appears by itself in xvi 17.

The supposition that these sayings belong in Group v, with *yir'at YHWH* as a synonym of *ṣedaqah* and *yere' YHWH* as a synonym of *ṣaddîq* seems to be ruled out by the fact that these terms appear to be deliberate substitutes in variants of couplets in both Groups iii) and v):

---

[1] Reading *tepillat YHWH* with LXX in xxi 27. The same is implied in xxviii 9.
[2] In xiv 26 as emended to *biyre' YHWH* to provide an antecedent for *lebanaw.* In xiv 16 "YHWH" is omitted and *yare'* here seems to mean simply "cautious"; cf xiv 15; xxii 3; xxviii 14.

xiii 14   *tôrat ḥakam mᵉqôr ḥayyim lasûr mimmoqᵉše mawet*
xiv 27   *yir'at YHWH mᵉqôr ḥayyim lasûr mimmoqᵉše mawet*
xvi 8   *ṭôb mᵉʿaṭ biṣdaqah merob tᵉbû'ot...*
xv 16   *ṭôb mᵉʿaṭ bᵉyir'at YHWH me'ôṣar rab...* [1]

The possibility that these sayings were introduced in a late editorial
annotation of Proverbs i-xxii 16, (i.e., after chapters i-ix had been
prefixed to chapters x ff.), is raised by the obvious gloss in viii 13,
coupled with the fact that in several instances where *yir'at YHWH*
appears the Hebrew text is uncertain or awkward. In xv 33, for
example, the reading in the first half-couplet is dubious and the second
half-couplet has been transferred from its original setting in xviii 12.
Other instances of awkwardness in the Hebrew text (some minor
only) are found in xiv 26; xvi 6; xix 23 and xxii 4—a total of five of
the nine occurrences of *yir'at* or *yᵉre' YHWH* in chapters x-xxii.

CONCLUSIONS

1. There is no firm evidence that the sentence proverbs in chapters
x-xxii 16 (or, x-xv, xvi-xxii 16), xxv-xxvii, xxviii-xxix once existed as
independent "collections" corresponding to these divisions of the
text. The titles in i 1; x 1 and xxv 1 are editorial only and have no
evidential value. The contents of the divisions are not homogeneous
in subject matter, literary forms or vocabulary; on the contrary, there
is a high degree of homogeneity in several types of sayings distributed
in two, three or four of the generally accepted divisions. Evidence of
duplicate or variant couplets and half-couplets and of real differences
between types of sayings points to the origins of the corpus of wisdom
sayings through a process of accumulation, supplementing and
editorial modification over a long period of time.

2. McKANE's distinction between sayings with or without religious
content and terminology is justified,[2] but can be carried farther. Seven
types of sayings have been isolated in the foregoing analysis; only the
last three of these display a positive religious content. This is without
prejudice to the question whether and to what extent the authors of
the four types of "secular" sayings were themselves religious believers.
The point at issue is not the presuppositions of the speaker—which
can only be guessed at—but the content of what he actually says.
Examples of the seven types of sayings are to be found distributed as

---

[1] Cf. also xix 23 with x 16 and xi 19; x 27 with xxviii 16b.

[2] See above, p. 148.

follows among the four customary divisions of the text (A = x-xv;
B = xvi-xxii 16; C = xxv-xxvii; D = xxviii-xxix);

Group 1—A, B, C, D
Group 2—A, B, C
Group 3—A, B, C, D
Group 4—B, C, D
Group 5—A, B, D
Group 6—A, B, C, D
Group 7—A, B.

It must be emphasized that what is here proposed is not a "documentary theory" of composition from seven written sources. The
process envisaged, rather, is that of the gradual and piecemeal growth
of a nucleus of written material through additions and modifications
representing the views and language of different wisdom teachers.

3. The use of sentence sayings from Proverbs in discussions of the
nature of "old wisdom" in Israel and of its religious content and
premises cannot be indiscriminate, but must take into account the
differences in viewpoint and objectives among the various contributors to the corpus of wisdom sayings. Questions remaining to be
determined are the possible interrelationships of the different elements,
their external literary connections and chronological order, the contributions of scribal editors and glossators and the bearing of this and
other investigations on the history of Wisdom in ancient Israel.

THE TEMPLE VESSELS—A CONTINUITY THEME

BY

P. R. ACKROYD
London

The concern of this discussion is not with the nature of the vessels or with any aspect of their description such as may be found in biblical dictionaries or *Realenzyklopädien;* nor is it intended to attempt a survey of the development of such vessels with an examination of the uses to which they were put in such a way as to draw out—if that be possible—the changing beliefs and attitudes of the worshippers and officiants. This latter, assisted as it might be by archaeological evidence, would, if the task proved to be a possible one to undertake, perhaps point towards the relationship between practice and belief in a way which might illuminate some of the many problems in the history of Israel's religious life and thought.

These two aspects of the subject, with which we shall not be concerned, offer the one an important part of the reconstruction of actual life and practice, and the other a potentially valuable contribution to wider questions of thought and belief. For their full study it is unlikely that there is anything like sufficient evidence in the Old Testament and in the archaeological finds. But there is a third aspect of the subject which is capable of some investigation. This is the more general question concerning the relationship which is believed to subsist between the actual existence of the objects themselves and the continuing religious life of the community. It is for this reason that the subtitle of this discussion is "A Continuity Theme," for I believe we may see in some of the statements which are made about the temple vessels indications of certain aspects of the concern, which belongs to any religious community, that there shall be no break within its life which will irremediably cut it off from the source of life and blessing which is believed to rest in the deity. The idea that at a certain point in time all links with the past may be cut and that we may begin as if we had no predecessors whether in knowledge or in faith, is quite devoid of any reality. We may, of course, resolutely set out faces against the past, and attempt to produce a pattern of belief and practice which entirely denies what has previously been said and done; but in this case, we are inevitably formulating a new position on the basis of the old, even in the process of repudiation. The more natural and more common method of reform is a subtle combination of rejection and acceptance. We are more prone in the contemporary situation to suppose that we can cut ourselves off from the past; the inhabitants of the ancient world were certainly not. And more than this, they were conscious of a need, which has its parallels too in contemporary thinking, that, whatever breaches with the past might occur, there should be a demonstrable link between the later and the earlier stages of a community's life. It is clear that they could consider the past as indicating failure and misunderstanding which must be denied if the life of present and future was to be stable.[1] But the failure and misunderstanding of the past were themselves seen as reactions against a known standard, an already existing pattern. In rejecting the reactions, they were endeavouring the restore continuity with a true past, and by this to maintain their own religious life and practice in the consciousness that it must cohere with what was already known and experienced.

Some aspects of this question of continuity were raised in my inaugural lecture in London on that subject.[2] Recently, in an endeavour to clarify the nature of the diversity within the Old Testament tradition, while still seeing the nature of continuity, I have concerned myself with the evidence for discontinuity.[3] And it is from this point that the present discussion may be said to take off, since it will have as a central theme the consideration of how the temple vessels are connected with the problem of maintaining continuity between the moment which lies before a disaster with that which comes after.

But there is also a more positive aspect of this. The description of the vessels themselves, the cataloguing of them as they actually existed at a given moment or as they were believed to have existed at some particular point of importance, provides an indication not simply of

---

[1] On this theme, cf. J. VOLLMER, *Geschichtliche Rückblicke und Motive in der Prophetie des Amos, Hosea und Jesaja* (BZAW 119, 1971). This study rather overstresses the forward-looking aspect of prophetic thought, but it provides a useful critique of that exaggerated view which sees the prophets too onesidedly in terms of "the tradition."

[2] *Continuity: A Contribution to the Study of the Old Testament Religious Tradition* (Blackwell, Oxford, 1962).

[3] "The Theology of Tradition—an approach to Old Testament theological problems," *Bangalore Theological Forum* 3 (1971). pp. 49-64.

practice but also of order, the continuing order which is traced back into the past and which provides authentication for the present. Hence the first part of the discussion will be devoted to considering some aspects of this more descriptive material; in the second part we shall consider how the temple vessels appear as a theme concerned with the establishment of continuity across a break in the tradition; and as a third part we shall briefly note some of the indications which are to be found in still later writings of the persistence of this same theme, to bridge other moments of discontinuity or to establish authority for the beliefs and practices of later generations.

I

There is a remarkable fact to be observed concerning the long descriptive passages in the Old Testament which deal with the temple vessels. It is that when these passages were incorporated into the works in which they now stand, the objects described can no longer have existed; the descriptions are quite evidently of past conditions. Although at the time of compilation there probably were in use comparable objects to those described, yet all this loving attention to detail is devoted to the past. This is true whether we consider the description of the temple of Solomon in 1 Kings, incorporated in the Deuteronomic History which took more or less its present shape in the mid-sixth century B.C., after the destruction of the temple in 587; or whether we consider that of the Chronicler in 2 Chronicles which is incorporated into a work whose final shaping can hardly be earlier than the fourth century B.C. The same may be said of the description of the tabernacle and its contents in Exodus. Here the problem is complicated by our uncertainty as to what kind of tent-shrine may have existed in the pre-settlement period, how far the descriptions bear a relationship to such a tent-shrine as may have existed, and how long such a shrine continued to exist into the settlement period—and indeed how far the tabernacle theme is to be seen as a projection back of the temple theme. The tabernacle theme is itself a continuity theme, and might appropriately be examined alongside that of the vessels it is supposed to have contained. This is particularly clear for the Chronicler. In his account, the tabernacle existed at Gibeon in the time of David and Solomon and was only then subsumed into the temple. But whatever the precise interpretation of this particular theme may be, it remains the case that the eventual compilation of the

Tetrateuch, the Priestly Work, took place when all this lay in the distant past.

Two points of reservation must be entered here. On the one hand we may quite properly argue that, however much these descriptions are of objects belonging to the past, they have their counterpart in contemporary practice. This is in fact an important pointer to the significance of the descriptions being preserved. On the other hand we may observe that both in this respect and in many others the later compilations preserve a great deal of material which belongs to the past, describing conditions which no longer exist—as an occasional scribal note indicates (cf. 1 Sam. ix 9)—and that it has always been necessary to emphasise that the older material acquired a degree of what will eventually be called "canonicity," an authoritative status, which made it impossible (or at the very least rather difficult) for the later editors to excise what was in fact no longer relevant. But on this we might comment that an examination of the two forms of the same material which we have in Samuel-Kings and in Chronicles shows that one compiler at least could show both a remarkable degree of respect for his sources and a very considerable degree of freedom in handling them. If at times he quotes verbatim or virtually so—though perhaps a few such passages are due to later insertion by a scribe who added what was missing from the earlier text—at other times, and this most evidently in the whole survey of the period of the monarchy from Rehoboam to Zedekiah, he could so rewrite and re-present that we have difficulty at times in recognizing that he is dealing with the same rulers. (Think of Manasseh!) He did in fact substantially modify the material concerning the temple vessels in 1 Kings, except for one passage which is of this verbatim kind and which is for various reasons suspect.[1] But the inclusion of this passage, whether due to the Chronicler or to his commentators, still has its significance within the matter with which we are concerned.

For it is not simply the fact that these descriptions are preserved which is important. It is the extent and the detail of them. It is a very substantial part of Exodus which is devoted to the tabernacle, and not only that, but virtually the entire material appears twice, once as command to do and once as description of what is done. It is a substantial part of the descriptions in 1 Kings which is devoted to the equipment of the temple, even though this is a relatively small part

---

[1] 2 Chron. iv 11-v 1; cf. 1 Kings vii 40-51.

of the whole work in which it belongs; the same is true for 2 Chronicles, though to this we should really add the large preparatory sections in 1 Chronicles.

The very setting out of the lists and descriptions of the vessels does much more than provide points of comparison or contrast with contemporary usage; or at a lower level indications of the way in which lost or damaged vessels might be replaced. It provides an overall picture of what belongs essentially to the true cultus, to the existence of a proper relationship with the deity; and we may note that some emphasis is laid on the enumeration of vessels, a concern with the completeness of their provision. In this respect, this kind of description must be placed alongside the delineation of buildings. Here again we may see that such plans and measurements could possibly provide a basis for reconstruction. But in the case of the Old Testament the details are never quite sufficient and the older reconstructions which lacked any correlation with the evidence of archaeology were inevitably in danger of being fancy rather than fact, and even with archaeological evidence there remain substantial differences of view among the experts. But blue prints for building is hardly what they are really intended to be; they are directed rather towards exemplifying, in the process of description, that belief in the pattern to which temple buildings are supposed to conform, the pattern which, in the case of the tabernacle (e.g. Exod. xxv 9), of Ezekiel's temple (chs. xl ff.) and of the Chronicler's temple (e.g. 1 Chron. xxviii 19), is believed to have been divinely given. For such divinely given temple plans we have examples from other ancient cultures.[1] The temple vessels as essential component parts of the temple itself would then have the same function, that of depicting the order to which practice must conform, the order which is itself linked to what the deity himself ordains. So, as in the tabernacle sections, and as by implication in the temple descriptions—and more explicitly in the Chronicler's form of these—what is being provided is not simply the necessary objects for religious use, but what corresponds to the divine command.

The temple vessels, seen in this way, take their place within that larger area of thought in which attempts are being made at defining the relationship between the divine and human spheres in terms of temples which have a correspondence to the divine dwelling or to the cosmos seen as expressive of the divine dwelling. The larger aspects

---

[1] Cf. e.g. the statue of Gudea of Lagash with its building plan. *ANEP* No. 749.

of this need not concern us here; they have been the subject of numerous studies, among which we may note particularly that of R. E. CLEMENTS.[1]

The theme of making such vessels, or the emphasis on their provision, or on their purification (cf. 2 Chron. xxix 18) and guarding (cf. 1 Chron. ix 28 f.), equally provide points at which we may detect the concern with the continuing in proper form of the religious observances which are seen as necessary to the well-being of the community.

These more positive aspects of the materials concerning the temple vessels may well conceal something of the more negative side. Just as we may reasonably see in the enactment of a law against a particular offence some evidence that the offence is liable to be committed, so in this care and concern we may see an anxiety lest the vessels be neglected, lest their proper care be not undertaken, lest there be some disaster occasioned by a break in the proper procedures. And what belongs to preserving continuity may also be seen as the most appropriate mechanism for re-establishing that continuity once it has been broken.[2]

II

With this, we reach the second part of this discussion and here the element of discontinuity comes to the fore. We may preface this by the general comment that discontinuity is something which may be the result of some quite minor lapse, some accident, some unforeseen incident which disrupts normal procedures. Some aspects of this less drastic interruption—though serious enough for the community when it is observed in such an example as the narrative of 1 Sam. xiv—have been discussed in the article already mentioned on "The Theology of Tradition." [3] The great breaks, such as that of the exile, deserve fuller attention, and they receive it in the Old Testament in regard to the larger questions of political existence, of restoration to community life, of temple rebuilding and the like. In this context there belong also those many themes which are connected with showing the relationship between the older and the subsequently established mechanisms of political and religious life. But such concern with rehabilitation and its nature shows itself also in regard to what we might consider the smaller details, and it is here that we may place the concern with the temple vessels.

---

[1] *God and Temple* (Blackwell, Oxford, 1965).
[2] A particular example of this may be seen in Neh. xiii 4-9.
[3] Cf. above p. 167 n. 3.

When we examine the evidence, however, we observe that this theme is given considerably more attention than we might expect it to receive. This points to its importance. It will therefore be our next task to examine some aspects of the material which sheds light on this concern.

There are three main sections of material to be considered: 2 Kings xxiv-xxv with Jer. lii as a parallel to part of the text, together with the related material in Jer. xxxvii-xliv; Jer. xxvii-xxviii; 2 Chron. xxxvi and Ezra i-vi and vii-viii.

(a) 2 Kings xxiv 13 is quite categorical. All the gold vessels of the temple of Yahweh which Solomon had made were broken up by the king of Babylon "as Yahweh had spoken." This destruction is associated with the first capture of Jerusalem in 597. The last phrase "as Yahweh had spoken" links this aspect of the disaster with a particular divine word, though it is a divine word which we cannot satisfactorily identify. The evidence which we shall see that these and other verses concerning the temple vessels are probably not part of the original narrative may well point to the inclusion of such a precise authentication of the destruction as a result of later correlating of various tradition elements. But to say, as J. GRAY does, for example,[1] that it has been drawn from Jer. xxvii 22 is to overlook the fact that the divine word here purports to refer to a foretold destruction of vessels, whereas the word ascribed to Jeremiah is concerned with their being carried to Babylon and there preserved (on the questions of the text of Jer. xxvii 22, see below). It may be that there is a loose link to the Jeremiah message, and we may observe that the Chronicler uses Jeremiah with greater precision in his very different account of the fall of Judah; but it is more likely that we have an extension to this particular part of the temple furniture of the prophecies of destruction of the temple which are to be found not only in Jeremiah and Ezekiel but also in Micah iii 12. The prophecy and fulfilment pattern forms one of the important bases for the Deuteronomic account of the fall of the two kingdoms.[2]

2 Kings xxv 13-17 associates a further destructive action with the period of the second capture of Jerusalem in 587. V. 13 relates that the bronze pillars, the stands, the bronze sea were broken up and their

---

[1] *I and II Kings* (S.C.M. London,[2] 1970), p. 760.

[2] On this theme, cf. G. VON RAD, *Deuteronomische Studien* (1947) esp. pp. 55 ff.; E.T., *Studies in Deuteronomy* (1953), pp. 78 ff., and P. R. ACKROYD, "The Vitality of the Word of God in the Old Testament," *ASTI* Vol. 1, (1962), pp. 7-23.

material carried to Babylon. V. 14 adds a further list of vessels which were taken; it is not stated that these were broken up. V. 15 adds yet another detail; a further series of vessels, both of gold and silver, was also carried away. The meaning here is not absolutely clear, but it is most probable that it means that the metal of which these objects were made was carried away.[1] The implication of this would seem to be that the same is really intended also for the vessels of v. 14.[2] The point is further suggested by the emphasis in v. 16 on the incalculable amount of bronze contained in the larger pieces.

The parallel text in Jer. lii 17 ff. provides the same information; its account is in some respects more detailed, suggesting a greater emphasis on the totality of the disaster. Here is added too a reference to the twelve bronze bulls under the sea (v. 20); that these bulls had been removed by Ahaz and replaced by a stone base—and the bronze presumably used for other purposes as is indicated by the reference to the breaking up of some other vessels (2 Kings xvi 17)—is either overlooked by the writer of this form of the text,[3] or the sea is deliberately included in the interests of completeness.[4]

The difference in detail between these two texts need not here be examined; what we observe is that the emphasis on even greater destruction and an even more final disaster in Jer. lii fits well with its more negative attitude towards the situation in Judah,[5] which may also be seen in the absence of any reference here to the governorship of Gedaliah.[6]

---

[1] The Hebrew text is so rendered in R.S.V. and N.E.B. So too J. GRAY, op. cit., p. 767.

[2] J. A. MONTGOMERY, *The Books of Kings* (I.C.C. 1951), p. 563 offers no comment on the meaning of v. 15; he seems to imply that the gold and silver vessels were kept whole, though since he offers no translation of the text, it is impossible to be sure. He offers a harmonising comment that "these must have been small articles left over from the earlier looting." But this is an unwarranted assumption. It would be more natural to think that new vessels had been introduced under Zedekiah. It is in the Jeremiah text (cf. below) that the theme of two stages of removal appears, not in Kings. MONTGOMERY also assumes that v. 13 indicates the breaking up of the large pieces, and v. 14 the carrying away intact of the small ones. This may be so, but the whole context hardly warrants so confident an affirmation.

[3] J. GRAY, op. cit., p. 767.

[4] We may note that the Ahaz narrative provides an example of the obverse: Ahaz is the disrupter of continuity by his destruction of vessels.

[5] Cf. my comments in "Historians and Prophets," *SEÅ*, 33 (1968), p. 18-54, cf. pp. 42 f. and "Aspects of the Jeremiah Tradition," *Indian Journal of Theology* 20 (1971), pp. 1-12.

[6] We may arrange the traditions in a logical (though not necessarily chronological) order. Jer. xl-xlii has a positive appraisal of Gedaliah and advice to those

We may note in regard to these two passages in 2 Kings xxiv and xxv (Jer. lii) that they interrupt the course of the narrative. Significantly, no mention of the temple vessels appears in the closely parallel text of Jer. xxxix. It is probable that one or both of them are later insertions in the text.[1] But for our present purpose, we may observe the longer and shorter forms, and consider the value of each. At whatever stage the narrative took on its present form and by whatever processes its various elements were woven together, as we have them in 2 Kings, the final effect it to stress that temple and vessels were brought to an end. There is no room for restoration.[2]

It is in the light of this that we may see the significance of the emphasis on the vessels and their description in 1 Kings. As is well known, the Deuteronomic History holds out no easy hope of restoration, though it contains a number of passages—and not only its last verses—which point beyond disaster. But in the contrast between this picture of total loss and the description of vessels in detail we may see a discreet way of suggesting that there can be restoration; it must be by way of recovery of the past, by way of a repetition, in some sense, of the events of the past. The writers, tracing through the history from the wilderness (in Deuteronomy) to the building of the temple under Solomon (before the first moment of disaster) are inviting their readers, to whom the loss of the land is a part of their experience, to set what hope for the future they can have in the reality of the divine action which led them into the land in the first instance and through to the moment when, in rest from their enemies (cf. Deut. xii 10; 2 Sam. vii 1), they were able to establish the central shrine. To a community transported as it were again to the wilderness beyond Jordan, the descriptions of past experience are both a warning against

---

who set out for Egypt to stay in Judah; 2 Kings xxv 22-26 contains only a brief reference to Gedaliah and his assassination; Jer. lii has no reference to Gedaliah; 2 Chron. xxxvi equally has no reference to Gedaliah, and its attitude to Judah is even more strongly negative.

[1] Cf. J. GRAY, *op. cit.*, pp. 760 f. for xxiv 13 f.; he treats xxv 13-17 as an integral part of the narrative. Cf. J. A. MONTGOMERY, *op. cit.*, pp. 554 ff. on xxiv 13 ff. and p. 563 on xxv 13-17: "an intruded antiquarian but historical note."

[2] The subject of the parallel text of Jerusalem's fall and its aftermath in Jer. xxxvii-xliv is discussed in my articles noted on p. 173, n. 5. This Jer. text in ch. xxxix provides an important witness to a variant text. We may observe that the whole section provides examples of being both a shorter version than that in 2 Kings (so the "temple vessels" theme) and a longer version (so Jeremiah's actions and the Gedaliah narrative). The relationship between the two texts is not to be viewed as a simple one.

the repetition of failure and a promise of the possibility of restoration.[1]

(b) Jer. xxvii-xxviii contains two passages which dwell on the theme of the temple vessels, viz. xxvii 16-22 and xxviii 1-9. The latter passage may conveniently be taken first, since it relates a specific incident in which this theme is a detail on which some emphasis is laid, whereas the former passage is entirely devoted to the temple vessels as a theme.

The message of the prophet Hananiah in xxviii 2-4 makes three points.[2] First, that God has broken the yoke of Babylon, a statement which provides the verbal commentary on the symbolic action performed by this prophet (xxviii 10) by way of controverting the action of Jeremiah in wearing the yoke. Second, that the temple vessels carried to Babylon will be returned within two years. Third, that Jeconiah (Jehoiachin) will be restored to the throne of Judah and the exiles brought back. The latter two points provide the positive counterpart to the negative of the overthrow of Babylon; they envisage a twofold restoration, that of temple and worship and that of the Davidic king still regarded, as witness Ezekiel and the Weidner tablets, as the legitimate ruler, together with a rehabilitation of the community. It has, of course, been pointed out that the statement about the bringing back of the temple vessels is a direct contradiction of 2 Kings xxiv 13 in which the only statement concerning the vessels in the first capture of Jerusalem relates their breaking up.[3] But such a comment misses the real point. We are dealing with a variety of traditions which do not necessarily all coincide. To attempt harmonisation is unsatisfactory; more important is to see what particular point is being made by the presentation with which we are concerned.[4] Clearly restoration of the vessels implies re-establishment of that continuity of the cultus which was in some measure interrupted by the disaster of 597. The vessels are a symbol of this. The comment on this oracular pronouncement attributed to Jeremiah (xxviii 6-9) repeats the main part of Hananiah's prophecy, with emphasis on the restoring of temple vessels and of exiles; but it further indicates by implication that there is room for doubt concerning the validity of the pronouncement which has been made. The sequel in vv. 10-17 elaborates this in the complete word of rejection of Hananiah.

---

[1] For this theme, cf. also Hosea ii.

[2] The shorter LXX text contains essentially the same material.

[3] So e.g. GRAY, op. cit., p. 760 with reference to Jer. xxvii 19 ff. which makes the same point.

[4] Cf. on this the article "Historians and Prophets" mentioned on p. 173 n. 5.

The other passage (xxvii 16-22) takes its start from the same basic theme, but develops it differently. It makes a general utterance concerning "prophets" (in the plural) who proclaim restoration of worship, the re-establishment of continuity, in terms of the bringing back of the vessels taken in 597. This contains the same point as we find in xxviii 3, and clearly it depends on the same type of tradition. It should probably be regarded as a doublet of the specific Hananiah incident. The same theme is then continued in a mocking word concerning these supposed prophets, who if they really exercised the function should intercede with Yahweh so that he would not permit the remaining vessels in the temple to be transported. We may see here another line of thought, not precisely the same as that of ch. xxviii. The taking of the vessels is regarded as happening in two stages—first in 597, second in 587. But there is to be no withdrawing of the divine word of judgement. Instead, there is a pronouncement "concerning the pillars and the sea... and all the other vessels" (v. 19).[1] They are to be taken to Babylon. But to this the passage adds a significant point, namely that these vessels are to remain in Babylon until they are brought back by Yahweh himself and restored to the holy shrine. It is to be observed that this form of the text is considerably longer than that of the Septuagint [2]; there the phrases which speak of the return of the vessels are absent, and we read simply: "They shall be brought to Babylon, says the Lord." According to RUDOLPH [3] the restoration words have been added on the basis of Ezra i 7 ff. But the dissimilarity of the texts—except in the reference to Nebuchadrezzar as the king who took the vessels away (an obvious point)—is such as to suggest that the expansion of the Jeremiah text is due rather to a certain kind of understanding of the temple vessel theme, an understanding expressed also in the Chronicler's narrative but not in identical form.

Thus we have two types of statement here. If we follow the LXX, we have a doom oracle in terms of the carrying away of the temple vessels; the first disaster is to be followed by the second. This may be seen to take further the theme of the narrative of ch. 28, to which it provides a more generalised parallel. If we follow the MT—and for our present purpose the important point is the existence of a certain kind of interpretation, not the unravelling of the textual history—then

---

[1] Again here the LXX is shorter, but the main point is not affected.

[2] There are other "omissions" in the LXX text in this section, but they do not affect the overall interpretation.

[3] *Jeremia* (H.A.T.[3] 1968), p. 177.

we have a theme of restoration built into a theme of exile; the idea of continuity with the previous temple is maintained by the promise of the restoration of the temple vessels. This may be seen to build in effect on a reversal of the Jeremianic word of ch. xxviii and to accept in a modified form the rejected oracle of Hananiah. An examination of the whole section Jer. xxvi-xxxvi reveals that such restoration themes are commonly to be found there. It is true that at a number of points the restoration element is not in the LXX where it appears in the MT, and we can therefore argue that a more uncompromising form of this Jeremiah corpus also existed alongside the more hopeful one. Yet the existence of the more hopeful form is attested by the MT, and is to be seen as an important witness to the transformation of the prophetic word, even to the extent of a direct reversal of earlier and more obviously Jeremianic sayings.[1]

(c) The most consistent continuity theme connected with the temple vessels is found in the writings of the Chronicler. We have already noted the presence there of both the preparatory work for the temple under David and the description of the carrying through of the work under Solomon. This in itself provides a basis for the subsequent emphasis upon the vessels in the exilic age and after. There are also some intervening passages which have the effect of emphasising continuity in a slightly different form, namely as expressed in the votive gifts of rulers who thereby preserve continuity: Asa in 2 Chron. xv 18, which speaks of his father's and his own votive gifts in the form of temple vessels; the provision of vessels after the restoration of the true Davidic line under Joash in 2 Chron. xxiv 14; and the purification of the vessels under Hezekiah in 2 Chron. xxix 26 f. The obverse to these is to be found in the loss of the vessels to Samaria under Amaziah in 2 Chron. xxviii 24. In 2 Chron. xxxvi 7, we are told that some of the temple vessels were removed when, as this narrative relates, Jehoiakim was taken captive to Babylon. (As in other cases, the Chronicler's account differs sharply from that of Kings). We may perhaps see here a link between the Chronicler's account and the Jeremiah material which defines the removal of the vessels in two

---

[1] Cf. the reversals in xxxii 36 ff. and xxxiii 10 ff. E. W. NICHOLSON, *Preaching to the Exiles* (1970), p. 12, criticizes the suggestion, made by J. BRIGHT, "that there has been some misunderstanding of the prophet's teaching by those responsible for the sermons." He speaks instead (p. 13) of "a conscious and deliberate development of the prophet's teaching." But in a number of cases, such as those here mentioned, there appears in the long run to be a much more radical handling of the material, than could be naturally covered by "development."

stages, as indeed we observe that the Chronicler makes precise reference to Jeremiah and his prophecies three times in this chapter. In 2 Chron. xxxvi 10 the removal of Jehoiachin to Babylon is accompanied by the taking of the choicest temple vessels. In xxxvi 18, the removal of all the temple vessels is associated with the final disaster to Jerusalem; the emphasis on the total removal, "vessels great and small"—surely a formula of completeness—is in line with the Chronicler's view, made clear in this passage as elsewhere, that nothing was left in Judah which could permit a true worship; everything had gone to Babylon so that the land was left empty.

In Ezra i, the full reversal of this is indicated. Vv. 7-11 [1] do not merely state that Cyrus produced the temple vessels and committed them to Mithredath and hence to Sheshbazzar; we are also informed that an inventory was made and that what was restored represented the totality of the vessels.[2] Thus the restoration of the temple includes the bringing back of the vessels, and with them the guarantee that there is a direct link with the earlier worship of the community. The point is further developed in Ezra v 14 f.; vi 5, where it is also said that Nebuchadrezzar had placed the vessels in the temple in Babylon. Of this passage, GALLING writes: "In regard to the temple it is not *de jure* a matter of a new building—(we may note that GALLING there neatly sidesteps the unanswerable question as to how far it was a new building *de facto;* it would be nice to know, but theologically speaking this is relatively unimportant [3])—but of a continuation, and for this reference is made for evidence to the building edict of Cyrus and to

---

[1] For the full discussion of this passage, cf. K. GALLING, "Das Protokoll über die Rückgabe der Tempelgeräte" in *Studien sur Geschichte Israels im persischen Zeitalter* (1964), pp. 78-88, updated from its original publication in *ZDPV* 60 (1937), pp. 177-83.

[2] The list here, whatever its origin, is clearly designed to stress completeness and also to underline that care for the vessels which is elsewhere a concern of the Chronicler (cf. 1 Chron. ix 28 ff.).

GALLING (cf. especially his conclusion, *op. cit.*, p. 88) argues that the terminology, the numbers, and the comments on the state of the vessels all point to these verses (Ezra i 8-11a) depending on the original (Aramaic) document of the year 538 B.C. This view does not sufficiently deal with the problem of what actually happened to the vessels (cf. below, for a further comment). If the main arguments are accepted, then they point to the use of a document, but it is more probable that, as in other instances, the Chronicler has applied a document belonging to one situation (an inventory of actually existing vessels) to a quite different moment. An immediately adjacent example may be seen in Ezra ii = Neh. vii; but there are many such cases of reapplication in the Chronicler's work.

[3] Cf. P. R. ACKROYD, *Exile and Restoration* (1968), pp. 25 ff. and references there.

the handing back of the cult objects to Sheshbazzar the commissary." [1]
We may note also in this form of the material, where the reference to
the placing of the vessels in a temple in Babylon appears, that a further
motif has been introduced, which finds its counterpart in the adven-
tures of the Ark in 1 Sam. iv-vi. What may be seen as a perfectly
normal procedure—for where else would such objects be placed but
in the shrine of the deity who has shown himself superior in power? [2]—
is in fact a witness to the continuing efficacy of the temple vessels as
associated symbols of the divine power and presence. For the power
of Babylon has fallen, and as the Second Isaiah so vividly expressed
it, the gods of Babylon have bowed in submission (Isa. xlvi 1). The
breach of the exilic age is healed.

The point is carried a stage further, as in the similar passages in
2 Chron., by the inclusion of a reference to yet further temple vessels
for the renewal of religious life under Ezra—vii 19 in the royal
commission, viii 26-28, with an emphasis on the care given to their
preservation on the journey, and viii 33 f. at their handing over and
the checking and recording of the whole supply of vessels. Here
various themes associated with the temple vessels are drawn together.
Ezra (and behind him the Persian king) are furthering the worship of
the temple; they are also engaging in a restoration of true worship
which stands in a line with that established at the very outset under
David.[3] The same point is underlined in Neh. x 40 (EVV 39) at the
end of the covenant document which is probably also to be associated
with Ezra. The Nehemiah story, which at so many points runs parallel
with that of Ezra [4] has a comparable emphasis in Neh. xiii 5, 9, where
Nehemiah acts to restore the vessels to their proper place of safe keeping.

Now it is clear that these various passages in which the temple
vessels are discussed cannot simply be harmonised into a neat and
coherent pattern. We need to consider the purpose and emphasis of
each. We have seen 1) that the theme can be used to underline total
destruction and loss, as it is in 2 Kings-Jer. lii, and in one form of the
texts of Jer. xxvii-xxviii; the continuity element in the theme is here
provided not by any suggestion that somehow the vessels were
preserved and restored, thus re-establishing an earlier form, but by

---

[1] *ATD*, p. 200.

[2] Cf. GALLING, *Studien*, p. 79.

[3] Again here we may see a continuing of piety, of care and guardianship, and
of emphasis on the total number of the vessels.

[4] Cf. P. R. ACKROYD, *The Age of the Chronicler*, Supplement to *Colloquium—The
Australian and New Zealand Theological Review* (1970), pp. 24-27.

the emphasis laid upon the original provision of the vessels in the temple description; 2) that the theme can be used to underline continuity, by preservation through the period of exile, as this is done by the MT in Jer. xxvii and by the Chronicler with a much greater logic. The Chronicler indeed utilises the temple vessels theme as one of those by which, alongside other kinds of institutional description, he endeavours to establish the reality of the link between his contemporaries and the original establishment; and by implication and sometimes by statement right back before that to the Exodus period.[1] Thus across the disaster of the exile, in which the loss of the temple might seem to mark an irreparable breach, there is a continuity established which enables the later worshipper to know, through the actual vessels in use, that he stands with his ancestors in the faith. This theme makes its contribution to the wider one of continuity in priesthood and in worship as ordered by the levitical officials of various kinds.[2]

III

This is not the end of the story, and some references to the subsequent use of the theme may be briefly noted. Daniel i 2 describes the carrying away of the remainder of the temple vessels at a siege of Jerusalem in the third year of Jehoiakim (a siege not otherwise attested and hardly historical); and Dan. v picks up the story of the vessels by showing how their use for improper purposes by Belshazzar provides the moment for the word of judgement against Babylon. 1 Esdras, in addition to repeating the material found in the book of Ezra, adds a theme of restoring the vessels to the story of Darius who is reminded by Zerubbabel of the vow that he made to restore the vessels set aside by Cyrus (iv 43-46), and its fulfilment is related in iv 57. 2 Esdras x 21 f. gives a description of the disaster in terms which underline the loss of the temple and its worship—the lamp is out, the ark has gone as spoil, the holy vessels are defiled. Loss and restoration are expressed in 1 Macc. in the same terms: i 23, the vessels are taken as booty by Antiochus; iv 49, they are renewed, and so too xiv 15.

---

[1] Cf. on the levitical orders and their link to the tabernacle in 1 Chron. ix 17 ff., in which the guardianship of the temple vessels is particularly stressed (so vv. 28 f.).

[2] We may also note that the Second Isaiah in lii 11 makes use of a similar theme in which the bearers of the sacred vessels are enjoined to make the return to Zion. The suggestion has been made to me by A. GELSTON that the theme of the temple vessels could be regarded as an appropriate Old Testament counterpart of the "restoring of the gods" claimed by the Cyrus Cylinder. Certainly we may see a parallel, since such a restoration is in either case connected with the re-establishing of religious and cultic continuity.

2 Macc. i-ii uses not this theme but its near counterpart, in that it purports to tell how continuity was preserved by recovery of the sacred fire hidden by pious priests and brought back by Nehemiah; and also by the hiding of tent, ark and incense-altar by Jeremiah which are to remain hidden so that at the final moment of the gathering of the scattered people there will be a true restoration of the shrine, as it was in the time of Moses and in the time of Solomon. The theme of the vessels is also used in Baruch i 8 f. The relevance of such material to later disasters will be evident, not least to that of 70 A.D.

IV

The problem of the temple vessels is often posed in the form of a discussion about what happened to them; were they destroyed or preserved in captivity? Were they lost to sight entirely or kept and produced again at the moment of restoration? It may be doubted if a satisfactory historical answer is to be found, though we may certainly observe that the earliest of our sources most naturally suggests the breaking up of the vessels for the sake of the valuable metal they comprised.[1] Furthermore, in so far as such vessels are seen to be intimately related with the worship and hence with the life of the people, their removal from use can be seen as one part of the action of the conqueror against the conquered.

But the historical answer, whether it can be given or not, is of relatively little significance. What is important is to see the way in which this apparently minor theme is given a prominence which suggests that it was anything but unimportant to the later community. The community which sought to re-establish itself after the exile, deeply conscious of its ancestry in faith, but also aware of the problem of continuity with that faith, made use of the theme of the vessels, as it made use of other themes, to make good its claim to be the true successor (perhaps thereby to invalidate the claims of others), to be directly linked with those who stood on the other side of the exilic gulf. What they could see to be validated in spite of the historical break, their successors could see to be true also in later situations of distress. It is the same people of God which lives on in consciousness of its ancestry of faith.

---

[1] Cf. the earlier part of this discussion, where the degree of uncertainty about the interpretation of 2 Kings xxv 13-17 is indicated. But whatever we may say of this passage it remains clear that 2 Kings xxiv 13 is contradicted by Jer. xxvii-xxviii; 2 Kings xxv still cannot accord with Ezra i.